C000104458

PUBLIC

EastEnders and its Audience

David Buckingham

To h/id
love B
xrdgs 8₮

BFI Publishing

First published in 1987 by the
British Film Institute
21 Stephen Street
London W1P 1PL

Copyright © David Buckingham 1987
EastEnders is a trademark of the British Broadcasting Corporation

Set in Linotron Sabon by
Fakenham Photosetting Limited
Fakenham, Norfolk
Printed and bound in Great Britain by
Anchor Brendon Ltd, Tiptree, Essex

British Library Cataloguing in Publication Data

Buckingham, David Dennis
   Public secrets: EastEnders and its audience
   1. EastEnders and its audience.
   1. EastEnders (Television program)
   I. Title
   791.45'72   PN1992.77.E/

ISBN 0–85170–210–4

PUBLIC SECRETS

CONTENTS

ACKNOWLEDGMENTS

A great many people have helped in preparing this book. I would particularly like to thank the following:

At the BBC: Michael Grade, Jonathan Powell, Julia Smith, Tony Holland, Vivien Marles, Judy Niner, Keith Samuel, Cheryl Ann Wilson and Helen Martin.

In London schools and youth centres: Melanie Ancliff, Ruth Gibbons, Jenny Grahame, David Guile, Anne Hennessey, Peter Sanders, Martin Sohn-Rethel, Gloria Stott and their students, whose responses to *EastEnders* are recorded in Chapter Four.

Also Mary Whitehouse, Richard Paterson, Robert Allen, Vivienne Adams, Mike Primavesi and Mike Todd; and my colleagues Phillip Drummond, Bob Ferguson and Susan Gibbons.

I am particularly grateful to William Cannell, Netia Mayman and Celia Greenwood for their valuable comments on the manuscript, and to Roma Gibson and Geoffrey Nowell-Smith for their editorial work.

This book is dedicated to Celia and Nathan, for their tolerance and good jokes.

INTRODUCTION

1985. Britain is suffering its worst economic recession since the 1930s. Official unemployment figures at the start of the year are a record 3.3 million, and show few signs of decreasing. Even within the context of world recession, Britain's level of economic growth has deteriorated faster than that of its overseas competitors. The rate of profit of British industry has been steadily eroded: business liquidations have doubled over the previous five years, and investment is at an all-time low.

In response to this long-term economic decline, the Conservative government is shifting resources from the public to the private sector, by selling off nationalised industries, and by privatising sectors of the welfare state. Both through legislation and through the use of para-military policing, it has attacked organised labour, gaining its most spectacular victory with the collapse of the National Union of Mine-workers strike in March. Meanwhile, it is encouraging a resurgence of traditional moral values, based on respect for authority and the sanctity of the nuclear family.

The combined effects of economic recession and government policy are most severe in the inner cities. Unemployment and cuts in social services have fallen with disproportionate weight on the working class of the older urban areas. The average incomes of poorer families are declining relative to those of more prosperous households, leading to an increasing divide between the 'rough' and 'respectable' working class. The breakdown of traditional working-class communities is leading to an increase in social isolation and the growth of a marginalised population of the unemployed and disaffected.

The impending crisis in the social order erupts in the late summer, just as it did four years earlier, with violence on the streets of many of Britain's major cities. Most notably in Handsworth in Birmingham and in Brixton and Tottenham in London, young people, provoked by increasingly repressive policing of their neighbourhoods, fight pitched battles with police armed with riot shields and cs gas. Arson and

1

looting are widespread: two people die in Handsworth, and a police officer is killed on the streets of Tottenham. In the aftermath of the disturbances, the Home Secretary lends support to police chiefs arguing for the use of plastic bullets and other riot control equipment which have not hitherto been used on mainland Britain.

In February, amid considerable publicity, the BBC launches its new twice-weekly serial *EastEnders*. It is the BBC's first attempt to produce a continuing serial which will run for fifty-two weeks a year since the ending of *The Newcomers* in 1969. Devised by its producer, Julia Smith, and its script editor, Tony Holland, who have earlier worked together on such series as *Z-Cars*, *District Nurse* and *Angels*, it will be recorded at the BBC's newly-purchased studios at Elstree.

After a slightly uneasy start, *EastEnders* becomes the most popular programme on British television within the first year of its life. The ratings begin to rise in August and September, and peak at around 23 million in the early months of 1986. Although the figures themselves are disputed by its rivals, there is little doubting the scale of the programme's popularity. The tabloid press, engaged in its own bitter circulation war, becomes almost obsessed with the details of the stars' private lives, and runs regular exclusives predicting (often inaccurately) future events in the serial. Meanwhile, Mary Whitehouse, television's own moral watchdog, condemns the programme as a cynical violation of family viewing time. Yet the drama of Michelle Fowler's baby, the evil deeds of Nick Cotton and the marital turmoil of Den and Angie Watts appear to have gripped the imagination of the British public.

EastEnders had been almost a year and a half in the making, and arrived at a particularly critical point in the BBC's history. Ever since the start of Channel Four, the second ITV channel, the BBC's audience share had been steadily declining, to the point where it was now running at little over 40 per cent. The Conservative government's commitment to a free-market economy, and its distrust of BBC bureaucracy – not to mention some ministers' criticisms of its 'left-wing bias' – had led to an increasing uneasiness in its traditionally cosy relationship with the Corporation. These factors, combined with the BBC's uncertainty about the impending advent of new broadcasting technologies, and a widely-felt 'lack of inspiration' in its programming compared with the innovative work of the sixties, led many critics to perceive a sense of crisis in public service broadcasting.

The extensive public debate which followed the BBC's screening of *The Thorn Birds* in January 1984 epitomised the contradictions in its role. This glossy, highly popular mini-series had the misfortune to coincide with Granada's adaptation of Paul Scott's novels about the decline of the British Raj, *The Jewel in the Crown*. While the latter was widely praised as an example of 'quality' television in the British public service tradition, the former was derided, not merely in the press but also in parliament itself, as imported commercial trash. Critics of the Corporation enthusiastically described the contrast between them as symptomatic of the BBC's abandonment of its public service responsibilities. Yet here was clear evidence of the double-bind from which the BBC had somehow to extricate itself. If it failed to reach a sizeable proportion of the mass audience, it would be condemned as elitist; yet if it attempted to do so – as it had done successfully with *The Thorn Birds* – it would be criticised for 'catering to the lowest common denominator'.

The appointment of Michael Grade as Controller of BBC1 in September 1984 was, in BBC terms, an unconventional one: a scion of a major show-business family, he was wooed away from a lucrative job as president of Embassy Television in Hollywood. Regarded by some critics as a last, desperate measure to save the Corporation, Grade's appointment was part of a broader attempt to redefine public service broadcasting in a manner which would be compatible with mass popular appeal. Although Grade himself was not responsible for commissioning *EastEnders*, he was certainly responsible for the high profile – both in terms of publicity and in terms of scheduling – which it received. Broadcast at 7 p.m. – and subsequently at 7.30 – on Tuesday and Thursday nights, it formed part of an early evening package with the new chat show *Wogan*, scheduled on the remaining weekdays. Between them, the two programmes were responsible for a dramatic rise in the BBC's ratings.

How do we account for the immense popularity of *EastEnders*? As a soap opera, it is an example of the most consistently popular genre on British television – a genre which in recent years has enjoyed a remarkable resurgence. Between them, *EastEnders*, *Coronation Street*, *Crossroads* and imported soaps like *Dallas* and *Dynasty* regularly account for nearly all the top twenty positions in the monthly ratings charts.

EastEnders has a good deal in common with many of its rivals – not merely with *Coronation Street*, with which it has repeatedly been compared, but also with the US soaps. Set in a largely working-class neighbourhood in the fictional borough of Walford in London's East End, it focuses on the relationships of a fairly enclosed community of characters. At the centre of the serial is the large extended family headed by the matriarchal figure of Lou Beale, a family which now extends across four generations. While the serial clearly draws on nostalgic definitions of working-class life, it also has a significantly comtemporary feel, both in terms of form and content. Thus, while its approach is predominantly naturalistic, it incorporates elements of comedy and melodrama, and generates a narrative pace which is often little short of frantic. Unlike its more established British competitors, it has a significant number of younger characters, and features a broad range of different ethnic groups. Its 'gritty' treatment of controversial moral and social issues has attracted widespread praise and condemnation.

In several respects, then, *EastEnders* draws upon the familiar qualities and staple concerns of soap opera. Its storylines are largely based on the problems of personal relationships and family life. It allows its viewers privileged access to the intimate secrets of its characters, and invites them to pass moral judgment on their behaviour. It develops a number of different narrative strands simultaneously, and encourages viewers to speculate about future developments. Yet although these characteristic features of soap operas clearly must account for a significant part of their appeal for audiences, they are not in themselves sufficient to guarantee their success.

In the case of *EastEnders*, its popularity was far from pre-ordained, and appears to have taken many critics and the producers themselves by surprise. The programme could easily have proven an embarrassing and costly disaster. *Albion Market*, a soap opera launched by Granada shortly after the start of *EastEnders*, and one which was in many respects similar, in fact died a ratings death after little more than a year. The demise of *Albion Market* was perhaps partly a function of scheduling: its Friday/Sunday slot was not best suited to attracting a regular audience, and has never worked well for soap opera. Nevertheless, the reasons why a programme succeeds or fails in reaching an audience are not simply to do with scheduling, nor are they merely a matter of genre. Audiences are not the passive victims of scheduling decisions, and they do discriminate, often in very discerning ways, between different examples of the same genre.

Popular television is often accused by its critics of 'catering to the lowest common denominator', which implies that success is comparatively easy to achieve. In fact, as television producers know only too well, the whole process is highly unpredictable, not least because broadcasting institutions are very isolated from their audiences: broadcasters have few reliable and systematic ways of discovering 'what the public wants' and – perhaps more crucially – why it wants it. For this reason, they are often unwilling or unable to explain the success of their own programmes, relying instead on what amounts to 'professional intuition'.

Yet the broadcasters' definitions of their audience are not the only ones in play: viewers themselves also have a considerable degree of power to define their relationship with television, and may often do so in quite different ways from those envisaged by its producers.

In analysing the popularity of *EastEnders*, I shall be centrally concerned with investigating the relationship between the programme and its audience. It is a relationship which, I shall argue, is more complex and ambiguous than has often been assumed.

Academic research into soap opera has a history which stretches back over forty years, to the beginning of radio soaps in the United States, yet it has largely sought to explain its popularity in terms of the pathological inadequacies of its audience.[1]

Early accounts of radio soap opera characterised their listeners as educationally backward, and as emotionally and socially deprived. The typical listener was identified as a lower-class housewife who used the soaps as a means of escape from her isolation in the home and as a source of advice on her emotional problems. Her lack of understanding of the complexities of adult life led her to mistake the fantasy world of the soap operas for reality. Listeners with more discriminating perspectives and with a wider range of experience were, it was argued, less likely to be satisfied with the stereotyped characters and situations which soaps provided.[2]

This view of soap opera as a form of escapist fantasy for the intellectually inadequate has continued to set the agenda for academic research, and remains one of the commonsense 'truths' about television which permeate public debate. As Dorothy Hobson has illustrated, television critics' characteristic ridiculing of the genre is matched by their barely concealed contempt for the idiots who enjoy it.[3] The 'typical' soap opera viewer is often seen as the person who writes in for a job at the Crossroads motel, or sends Michelle Fowler a wedding present – in other words, someone who is incapable of distinguishing between fiction and reality.

Yet this identikit picture of the soap opera viewer is inaccurate in several respects. While the audience for soap opera is certainly weighted towards women and towards the working class, it is in fact far more socially extensive than is often suggested. Even in the case of radio soaps in the early 1940s, a significant proportion of the audience was middle-class, and in more recent times, it has become increasingly representative of the population as a whole, including larger numbers of men and young people in particular.[4] In many ways it is dangerous to generalise about the demographic composition of soap opera audiences, without at least making distinctions between different types of soap opera.

More crucially, the view of the audience as inherently immature and unsophisticated, and therefore more vulnerable to influence, is also highly questionable. Certainly, more recent research suggests that viewers rarely watch soap operas in order to get advice about how to solve their own personal problems[5], and that even very young children are able to distinguish between television fiction and reality[6]. The assumption that critics are able to 'see through' television, while ordinary viewers cannot, is both arrogant and patronising.

More recent attempts to defend soap opera and its audience, while in many respects providing a salutary antidote to this approach, have similarly assumed that the typical viewer is a 'fan', whose relationship with their favourite programme is one of intense emotional identification.[7] The possibility that viewers might also watch soap opera in a relatively distanced and critical manner, and find pleasure in doing so, has largely been discounted.

The danger of defining soap opera exclusively in terms of 'pleasure' is that pleasure itself comes to be seen as a phenomenon which is beyond criticism or analysis. Yet if pleasure cannot be regarded as merely a form of escapism or delusion, it would seem equally inadequate just to celebrate it. If we are to understand the pleasures of soap opera, they cannot be seen as unitary or somehow timeless: on the contrary, they must be situated within their social and historical context.

Nevertheless, it would be naive simply to compare *EastEnders* with the reality it purports to represent. If the serial is to appear plausible to its viewers, it must take into account broader social and political forces of the kind identified at the start of this introduction – not least because viewers themselves are likely to experience their effects in the texture of their own daily lives. However, it would be misleading to suggest that it is merely a form of social documentary, and should therefore be judged exclusively in these terms. Inevitably, its representation of the world is partial; but to suggest that viewers are unable to recognise this, or that they somehow fail to realise that it is fictional, would be to ignore the complex processes whereby audiences make sense of television.

The relationship between *EastEnders* and its audience cannot be regarded either as a dangerous process of 'mass deception' or as a matter of 'catering to the lowest common denominator'. On the contrary, as this book will show, it is a relationship which is characterised by a considerable degree of diversity and contradiction.

1
CREATING THE AUDIENCE

Television production involves the creation, not merely of programmes, but also of audiences. One of the BBC's primary aims in producing *EastEnders* was to build a large audience at a crucial point in the evening's viewing – even if the eventual size of that audience appears to have exceeded expectations. Yet it would be false to suggest that the programme was merely a calculated or even cynical attempt to grab the ratings, as some critics have argued; while the ratings are certainly a major consideration, a number of other factors also enter into the equation.

Not the least of these is the BBC's own public service ethos. In the context of the general crisis in public service broadcasting, *EastEnders'* unprecedented success was bound to raise a number of awkward questions, not merely for critics, but also for the programme-makers themselves. To what extent is mass popularity compatible with 'quality' in broadcasting? How can the drive for ratings be reconciled with the notion of 'responsibility' which is central to public service? In what ways can we regard a programme like *EastEnders* as being of benefit to the public at all?

If the BBC's public service tradition represents one set of constraints, the financial risk involved in the undertaking made for other, more logistical considerations. Decisions about the location of the serial, the balance of characters, and the kinds of storylines which could be developed had clear economic implications. The BBC's long-term commitment to the programme meant devising a format with considerable, even indefinite, room for future development – a factor which had to be balanced with the need for an early success in the ratings.

Finally, the autonomy which is traditionally granted to producers within the BBC means that particular individuals have a key role in determining the nature of programmes. Of course, it would be naive to regard *EastEnders* as the expression of a 'personal vision': the individuals concerned – in this instance, Julia Smith and Tony Holland –

are television professionals with a considerable track record, who could be relied upon to come up with the goods as required. Nevertheless, they do possess a considerable degree of control over the programme, and many of its characteristic concerns derive from their own personal commitments.

In this chapter, I shall identify some of the ideas and assumptions about the audience which have informed the planning and production of *EastEnders*. How do those responsible for the programme conceive of their audience, and their relationship with it? How far do they use the specific information derived from audience research? To what extent do these ideas influence production decisions? And how do they relate to the public service tradition in broadcasting?

Grabbing the ratings?

The BBC's decision to produce a new bi-weekly continuing serial dates back to 1981, well before the concern about declining viewing figures became a matter of urgency. The initial 'in principle' decision was made by Bill Cotton, then Controller of BBC1, and the early planning was commissioned by his successor, Alan Hart.

Michael Grade, who subsequently inherited *EastEnders*, certainly perceived its value in terms of the competition for ratings, and in particular as a means of increasing the BBC's early evening share, which had slumped to little more than half that of ITV:

> I think it was clear to the BBC that one of the reasons for the discrepancy in the share between ITV's audience and the BBC's audience was down to *Coronation Street*, *Emmerdale Farm* and *Crossroads*. The BBC did not have anything of that kind in its locker. ITV certainly didn't invent the soap opera. The BBC were doing *The Groves* and *Mrs Dale's Diary* and *The Archers* years before. So it was nothing new for the BBC to be in the soap business. But it had somehow gotten out of the soap business over the years, and it seemed the right time to get back into it, as a means also to boost the early evening schedule, which had been languishing for some time.[1]

The choice of a continuing serial as a means of building ratings would therefore appear at first sight to be an obvious one. Yet there were clearly significant risks. A new serial would involve a far greater financial outlay than any of the likely alternatives, such as game shows. While the running costs of a regular soap opera are comparatively small, it takes many years to recoup the substantial initial investment, and an early exit from the schedules would mean financial disaster as well as public embarrassment.

Furthermore, the number of soaps already being screened led many to doubt whether the public would be willing to accept yet another: indeed, the B B C's first audience research report on the subject in early 1984 concluded that enthusiasm for a new bi-weekly serial was 'at best moderate'.[2] The B B C's own past experience with continuing television serials could hardly be said to inspire confidence either: although 1970s serials like *The Brothers* and *Angels* had done fairly well in terms of ratings, and had lasted for several years, they had not been screened continuously for the full 52 weeks. The B B C's only experience in producing continuing serials on television was as long ago as the 1960s, with *Compact* (1962–65), *United* (1965–67) and *The New-comers* (1965–69), of which only the first had achieved any substantial success in the ratings.

The initial projections of *EastEnders*' potential audience were therefore relatively modest by soap opera standards. Julia Smith and Tony Holland emphasised the continuity between *EastEnders* and their own previous work on *Angels* in this respect:

> TONY HOLLAND We didn't set out to succeed. We weren't asked to succeed. We weren't asked to be one and two [in the ratings] and get twenty-three million viewers. We were asked to produce a show of sixty minutes duration split into two sections of thirty minutes, with the same budget as *Angels* and hopefully to have the same sort of audience rating....
>
> JULIA SMITH *Angels* at its height had an audience of about thirteen million. And everybody thought if we got up there by our third year, that would be quite nice. You see, this is other people imposing things on the B B C. The B B C doesn't work like that. Michael Grade may have tried to hype it up since he came. But basically that is not how the B B C works.... We don't see this as being any different from any other programme we've worked on. Our attitudes towards it are exactly the same.[3]

The decision to opt for a continuing serial was thus not merely informed by the desire to reach a large audience. Soap operas possess a symbolic importance for television institutions, above and beyond their function in terms of ratings. By building a loyal audience, often over decades, they can become a highly significant element in the way viewers perceive the institutions themselves. *Coronation Street*, for example, can be seen as providing a specific regional identity for Granada Television, despite the fact that the majority of its productions have no such regional flavour. If, as recent research has suggested, popular perceptions of the B B C remain to some extent tied to the rather staid and middle-class 'Auntie' image, a successful soap opera could clearly do much to alter these.[4]

Jonathan Powell, who became Head of Series & Serials in November

1983, and played a key role in the development of *EastEnders*, felt that a continuing serial could also serve as an important training ground for new talent, just as *Coronation Street* has done at Granada. Using new writers and directors alongside more experienced ones would provide his own department, and the industry in general, with 'a substantial injection of talent'.

While Powell acknowledged *EastEnders*' considerable strategic value in terms of ratings, he also saw it as filling a gap in the overall spread of drama programming:

> It was clearly an area of popular drama in which the BBC wasn't offering something to the public.... I think that the point of any department in the BBC as a matter of fact – although it's not my business to say so – is to offer the correct balance of material across the whole spectrum of taste. And I think that a drama department of this size without a bi-weekly is a drama department without a very important linchpin in the panoply of ground that it's covering.[5]

At the same time, Jonathan Powell and Michael Grade refuted the suggestion that *EastEnders* was merely a means of keeping the mass audience happy, and thereby enabling the BBC to get on with its real business of producing 'serious' television: both were keen to emphasise its dramatic 'quality' and the 'responsibility' with which it dealt with controversial issues. *EastEnders* was regarded as tangible proof that popularity did not necessarily mean 'catering to the lowest common denominator'.

If the drive for ratings was therefore not the only motivation behind the decision to produce *EastEnders*, it certainly assumed a central significance in the period immediately before and subsequent to its launch in February 1985. The Peacock Committee, the latest in a series of government enquiries into the running of the BBC, appeared set to recommend a degree of privatisation, which many advocates of public service broadcasting saw as the thin end of a very thick wedge which would eventually destroy the Corporation. More was clearly at stake in the 'Soap Wars' so enthusiastically reported by the tabloid press than the success or failure of individual programmes. If the supremacy of *Coronation Street* was in some sense symbolic of ITV's overall dominance of the ratings, the failure of *EastEnders* would doubtless have been seized upon with relish by the BBC's enemies.

Early stages

Julia Smith was initially approached with a view to producing a new continuing serial in the Autumn of 1983. A veteran drama producer, she had started her BBC career as an assistant floor manager, and later moved on to directing such popular successes as *Dr Finlay's Casebook*,

The Newcomers and *Z-Cars*, as well as classic serials like *The Railway Children*. Her work as director, and subsequently producer, of *Angels*, a bi-weekly serial set in a hospital, had been widely acclaimed for its realistic and sometimes controversial treatment of contemporary social issues. To assist in the planning, Smith was later able to enlist the help of her long-time collaborator, script editor Tony Holland. Their close working partnership had begun on *Z-Cars* in the sixties and had contined through *Angels* and, most recently, *District Nurse*.

A number of potential themes for the new serial had already been identified, and pilot scripts commissioned. Smith's original brief was to investigate their implications in terms of production teams, studio locations and budgets. The success of *Angels*, and the public protests which repeatedly arose when it reached the end of its thirteen-week run, had led to the suggestion that it should be continued for the full fifty-two weeks. Yet this was eventually ruled out: it would have required too much research and rehearsal time in order to ensure the accuracy of the medical setting. Meanwhile, the other two leading contenders, set in a shopping arcade and a mobile trailer park, also posed significant logistical problems.

In the event, the initial proposal for *EastEnders* was devised in considerable haste. At 6.15 one evening in January 1984, Jonathan Powell contacted Julia Smith by telephone. He was due to meet BBC1 Controller, Alan Hart, the following morning at twelve o'clock and wanted to take a definite idea for the new bi-weekly. Could he please have a draft on his desk in forty-five minutes? Across the road in the local wine bar, Smith and Holland rapidly drew up their proposal: it was completed in half an hour. By one o'clock the following day, they were given the go-ahead.

The proposal which Smith and Holland produced was in many respects more conventional than some of the other ideas which they had been considering: set in an enclosed working-class inner-city community, it bore more than a passing resemblance to *Coronation Street*. Yet if the BBC was aiming to produce a soap opera for the 1980s, there were considerable risks involved: to depart too far from the tried and tested would be to court disaster.

Locating the serial

In re-entering the highly competitive 'soap business', the BBC inevitably had to exercise a considerable degree of caution. Key decisions in planning the serial had to be made with extreme care and forethought, as they would for the most part be impossible to reverse once the programme was on the air. The price of failure, in terms of both money and reputation, was very high indeed.

The choice of a location for the serial was clearly crucial, and required a number of considerations to be held in the balance. Julia

11

Smith and Tony Holland were strongly committed to the East End location, for a variety of reasons. Both are Londoners, and felt that the capital city was 'entitled' to have its own soap opera. They also felt that an East End community would possess considerable dramatic potential for a long-running serial:

> TONY HOLLAND   If your brief is to provide a show which can be on twice a week every week of the year, and may go on for more than a year, may go on for two, may go on for twenty-two, you need an incredible amount of mileage. You need a mobile society. You need a lot of story mileage. I don't believe you can do this in a Wimpey home, and I would knock down *Brookside* because of that, because it has no history.... You need a society that has a background, a history and a culture.

As an area which has historically been populated by waves of different immigrant groups, and which has recently begun to be 'gentrified', the East End would provide a setting which could plausibly contain a broad mixture of characters. Furthermore, it would allow a greater potential for turnover of new characters, thus enabling the serial to remain contemporary – a distinct advantage over the relatively static community of *Coronation Street*, which they felt had become stuck in a 'timewarp' of the early 1960s, when it had been originated.

Like Julia Smith and Tony Holland, Jonathan Powell felt that the East End location would provide 'roots' and 'identity', 'an attractive folklore and a sense of history', which was essential for the genre. He also argued that a 'flagship' programme like a continuing serial should provide a regional identity for the BBC, even though the Corporation as a whole has a national role. If the independent television companies had soap operas set in their own regions, then the BBC's should, he felt, be set in London.

Logistical factors were also significant here. In 1983 the BBC had purchased Elstree Studios, just outside London, from the independent company Central Television. Although the location of the new serial had not yet been decided at this stage, Elstree was clearly earmarked for it. While it would theoretically have been possible to make the programme at Elstree and set it in Manchester, Julia Smith was strongly opposed to the idea. In order to achieve the degree of authenticity she felt was essential, actors would have to be moved from Manchester down to London, and the cost of this operation would certainly have been prohibitive.

Nevertheless, the choice of London as a location for the new soap opera was regarded with scepticism in certain quarters; none of the long-running soaps prior to *EastEnders* had been set in the south, and there was some concern that the BBC already appeared to be too London-centred.

JONATHAN POWELL When I first went to talk to Alan Hart and people, they were very supportive and generally excellent about the whole thing, but the one question they did ask was 'Are you right to set it in the south?' It seemed to me to be a very sensible question. I wanted to be able to say more than 'Well, I think so because my instinct tells me'. I also rather wanted to be able to say that to myself. As one journalist said, for a producer and a new baby executive, it was a kind of mega banana skin to walk on. So I thought, let's get audience research in, and see what this all means....

Accordingly, in January 1984, the BBC's Broadcasting Research Department commissioned the market research agency Marplan to conduct a national telephone survey to assess the demand for a new serial, and the relative appeal of different locations and settings.° On the first point, the findings were relatively gloomy. Only 13 per cent of the sample of 450 people claimed to be 'very interested' in the idea, while 36 per cent expressed moderate interest; a further 50 per cent were either 'not very' or 'not at all interested'. In terms of location, Manchester was selected as the most popular overall, with London a close second and Birmingham a poor third. However, Manchester tended to be unpopular with Southerners; Birmingham was unpopular with people in the Midlands; while London was not particularly unpopular in any one region, and thus appeared to have the most widespread appeal. A serial set in a working-class neighbourhood had greater appeal than one set in a middle-class neighbourhood, while a mixed neighbourhood was least popular.

Such research clearly has its limitations: it is essentially asking for reactions to a hypothetical concept, rather than to an existing programme, and thus respondents may tend to opt for ideas which are similar to what they already know. Nevertheless, the lack of consumer interest was quite notable, and was unlikely to stimulate confidence in the project. In another situation – for example, North American network television – it might never have seen the light of day. The BBC's decision to stand by its commitment in spite of the findings is perhaps symptomatic of its historical refusal merely to 'pander to market forces' – although ironically in this instance it was a decision which had a remarkable payoff.

In terms of location and setting of the serial, however, the research largely confirmed the producers' feelings. Jonathan Powell interpreted it in this way:

The crucial bit they came back with really was that the north/south divide seemed to be based around money and class rather than actual geography, and that placing it in an area like the East End, which was inner city, effectively working-class, cut under the barriers enough to support our instinct that it was right, or that it was a supportable thing to do.

Audience research appears to have been used largely as a means of confirming beliefs which were already held, and as valuable ammunition in arguing the case with senior management. Indeed, where research came up with information which contradicted those beliefs – for example when it showed very little consumer demand for a new serial – it was to all intents and purposes ignored.

Developing the concept
With the location agreed, the major logistical problem was the outside shooting. The projected budget of the serial – which had by now acquired the working title *East Eight* – would allow for fifty minutes of studio recording and ten minutes of insert material each week. In the spring of 1984, work began at Elstree on constructing the set which was to become Albert Square. It was the biggest outdoor set the BBC had ever built. What was remarkable to observers even at this stage was the meticulous attention to detail. Although the houses were built of plywood and fibreglass, there were real roads and telephone kiosks, and even real weeds in the gardens. Considerable care was taken to ensure that the shop fronts and houses looked authentically scruffy and dilapidated.

Meanwhile, Julia Smith and Tony Holland had begun devising the characters. After a period of 'research' which reputedly involved touring the East End boroughs of Dalston and Hackney, 'just talking to the people', they eventually found it necessary, as they had earlier done with *Angels*, to escape from London in order to get the job done.

JULIA SMITH   In a normal office environment, my script editor and myself were making no headway at all; in the end, therefore, we packed typewriters and paper and, at our own expense, flew to Lanzarote. In the space of two weeks we invented twenty-five characters, made families, created a community. We wrote the biographies of the characters up to the time the audience would meet them, starting with what their childhood was like – their whole background prior to the moment we first went on air. Some members of the community we had invented knew each other since childhood; some were very new arrivals and were therefore treated with suspicion. There was the publican, his wife, and their adopted daughter. We had a Bengali shop, a Jewish doctor, a Caribbean father and son, a Turkish Cypriot cafe-owner married to an English girl. There were some older people who remembered the Blitz and found today's world more frightening in some ways. Our youngest character was minus six months old, our oldest seventy years.[7]

The forty-seven pages of biographies produced in Lanzarote formed the 'bible' for the team of writers, directors, set designers, wardrobe people and others who were engaged to work on the serial as its projected starting date in late 1984 loomed closer.

In developing their characters, and subsequently devising the major storylines for the first two years, Smith and Holland inevitably had to make a number of key decisions about the kind of serial *EastEnders* would turn out to be, and the type of audience it would attract. The possibility of a glamorous British version of *Dallas* or *Dynasty* clearly had to be ruled out, if only on the grounds of cost. Yet while *Coronation Street* certainly provided an influential model of a successful home-grown soap opera, both Holland and Smith felt that it offered a rather outdated and nostalgic view of working-class life. Until recently, the Street has rarely featured unemployed or black characters, for example, and it has had difficulty in replacing 'big' characters such as Len Fairclough and Elsie Tanner, or in finding characters with whom younger viewers can identify. In a sense, *Coronation Street* had grown old with its audience, and if *EastEnders* was to achieve similar success it would clearly have to attract a younger, more socially extensive audience, and ensure that it had the mileage to retain it for a good many years to come.

Brookside, British television's newest home-grown soap, provided a further model: as Channel Four's highest-rated programme, with a regular audience of around six million viewers, it had attracted critical acclaim for the quality of its acting and for its treatment of contemporary social issues. Yet here again, Smith and Holland were aware of some of the problems which *Brookside* faced. While the setting, in a real housing estate on the outskirts of Liverpool, made for a considerable degree of naturalism, the space restrictions in the houses meant that it was confined to a single-camera approach, which made for a rather laborious visual style. Furthermore, the lack of any central meeting point for the characters made it difficult for the writers to weave the different storylines together. Smith and Holland also felt that *Brookside*'s coverage of 'social issues' was at times rather self-conscious and didactic.

If *EastEnders* was to stand any chance of long-term survival, it would have to begin, as *Coronation Street* had done in 1960, with a commitment to reflect the realities of contemporary inner-city life – realities which Smith and Holland defined at least partly in terms of 'social problems'. In interviews, they have repeatedly argued that the serial is 'a slice of life' which is based in 'documentary realism', and which therefore inevitably confronts 'controversial social issues':

> JULIA SMITH   We decided to go for a realistic, fairly outspoken type of drama which could encompass stories about homosexuals, rape, unemployment, racial prejudice, etc. in a believable context.[8] Above all, we wanted realism. Unemployment, exams, racism, birth, death, dogs, babies, unmarried mums – we didn't want to fudge any issue except politics and swearing.[9]

Smith and Holland have very definite ideas about *how* such 'issues' should be dealt with in a dramatic context, and refute the idea that the programme is 'issue-based'. Nevertheless, as with their work on *Angels*, *EastEnders* was clearly intended from the start to be a programme which would acknowledge 'social problems' rather than sweep them under the carpet.

The initial balance of characters chosen thus meant that certain issues were bound to be raised, given the commitment to a degree of realism. The decision to include a range of ethnic minority characters, for example, meant that racism was inevitably on the programme's agenda. Likewise, the presence of a number of teenage characters meant that 'teenage problems' – pregnancy, unemployment, family strife – would inevitably be dealt with in some way.

The balance of characters also had clear implications in terms of the kind of audience *EastEnders* was attempting to build. Prior to the launch of the BBC's new early evening package, its audience at this time of day tended to be predominantly middle-aged and middle-class. In order to broaden that audience, *EastEnders* would have to appeal both to younger and older viewers, and also to the working-class audience which traditionally watched ITV. The choice of a working-class setting, and the broad age range of the characters thus also made a good deal of sense in terms of ratings.

In addition, *EastEnders* sought to extend the traditional audience for British soaps, which is weighted towards women and towards the elderly. Having a number of strong younger characters, it was argued, meant that the programme would have a greater appeal for young viewers than other British soaps, as well as providing a means of re-generating the narrative in the longer term. Strong male characters would also serve to bring in male viewers who were traditionally suspicious of the genre. Julia Smith had a definite idea of her potential audience profile:

> I'm not going for the stereotypical middle-class, BBC audience. The professional classes won't get home early enough to see the programme. I expect the audience to consist of working people who

watch television around tea-time before going to bingo or the pub. Soap operas traditionally appeal to women, but we have to remember that men watch them too – even if they don't admit to it. And with at least five teenagers in the cast I expect to pick up a lot of young viewers.[10]

Audience research was involved at this stage. The B B C Broadcasting Research Department reduced the biographies which Smith and Holland had produced in Lanzarote to brief thumb-nail sketches which were tested in six small discussion groups held in London and Manchester in February and March of 1984. Participants were asked for their opinions of soap opera in general, before being introduced to the concept of the new bi-weekly; they were then asked to discuss the outlines of the characters, and to anticipate some of the stories in which they might become involved.[11]

The research largely confirmed commonsense wisdom about the appeal of soap opera. 'Credibility', in the form of 'true to life characters' and 'realistic plots and story lines' was found to be an essential ingredient. Viewers enjoyed being able to eavesdrop on the characters' lives, and gossip about them, without having to suffer any of the consequences or difficulties of being involved in 'real' relationships. 'Familiarity' with the characters and with the location was also found to be vital. Viewers liked to feel that they knew the characters well and could predict the ways in which they would react to situations, although there was also a danger of characters becoming too predictable. Significantly, it was noted that viewers' opinions of the home-grown soaps had been influenced by their viewing of U S imports such as *Dallas* and *Dynasty*. The glamour of the U S soaps had highlighted the mundaneness of serials like *Crossroads* and *Coronation Street*, which many criticised as 'old fashioned'.

Responses to the idea of the new bi-weekly and to the thumb-nail sketches suggested that they connected with a number of familiar stereotypes in viewers' minds. Viewers predicted that the serial would feature large, matriarchal extended families living in run-down and overcrowded accommodation; that it would be based in a small, enclosed community, thereby providing considerable potential for conflict, intrigue and gossip; and that it would make great play of 'Cockney humour'.

The character sketches themselves were very brief, giving only the character's name, age and occupation, yet they provided considerable fodder for discussion. Many of the comments were highly stereotyped, but they were in some cases remarkably acute in their predictions. Lou Beale was described as a 'tyrant' who would rule her family with an iron fist; Pauline would have a heart of gold; her daughter Tracey (who subsequently became Michelle) would get pregnant, probably by one of the married characters; Jack Parker, the publican (Den Watts), would be a 'Jack the lad', involved in shady deals, while his daughter Sharon would be spoilt; Ethel would be an Irene Handl-style Cockney and an incorrigible gossip.

In general, respondents expected the new serial to succeed, given the BBC's reputation for high production standards, although some expressed concern that the BBC was 'a bit highbrow', and argued that the script writers should know the locality well if they were to avoid giving an idealised image of East End life. They felt that it should be 'humorous, amusing and lively' and contain at least some 'larger than life' characters. The influence of US soaps led to considerable discussion of the importance of high production values – an area in which existing home-grown soaps were found to be lacking. Finally, the respondents felt that the new serial should address current social issues, such as unemployment, crime and racism, but that these should 'grow' out of the characters, rather than being tackled in a more didactic manner.

The potential viewers' ideas corresponded closely to the biographies which Julia Smith and Tony Holland had produced, and it is therefore difficult to assess how far this information influenced their decisions. Vivien Marles, the researcher most closely involved in the project, felt that it did have some influence:

> Because what people had said largely co-incided with their own ideas, they warmed to it, and were very keen, and took a lot of it on board. In fact they changed at that point a number of characters, dropped some and added a few more in.[12]

Nevertheless, she felt that in general the programme-makers used this information very selectively, and largely as a means of confirming their own instincts:

> I am very sensitive to the fact that this programme was not a product of audience research. The producer was very clear right from the beginning about what sort of programme she wanted to make. Although they've been extremely receptive, I could never say that changes were made as a result of audience research. I think it's much more of a working together. Where audience research findings have coincided with the producer's gut feelings, then changes have been made. I actually believe that if all of this research had said something completely different, *EastEnders* would probably be the same as it is today. But it is hypothetical. You can't tell.

This impression was confirmed by Jonathan Powell and Michael Grade: both argued that the research had not been undertaken in order to formulate the programme (as is sometimes the case in US network television), but in order to test out the producers' instincts and to pinpoint any potential problems. While the information might be used in a case where the producers were already uncertain about a particular aspect of the programme, it could equally be ignored if it flatly contradicted their ideas.

Julia Smith and Tony Holland were certainly concerned to refute the idea that they had used audience research in formulating *EastEnders*. Holland was extremely scathing about such research, and asserted that he completely ignored it. Smith argued that audience research was more for the benefit of management than for the programme-makers themselves:

> They used it because they haven't got the confidence, if you like. Or they had to prove to somebody that it was possible to do it.... It made it slightly easier for me, that my instincts had been correct. They weren't going to fight me any longer. But I would have gone on fighting if it had turned out the other way.

The launch

After almost a year of frenetic activity, *EastEnders* was launched at 7 p.m. on 19 February 1985. Julia Smith's original target date of September 1984 had been postponed twice: firstly at the instigation of the new Controller of BBC1, Michael Grade, who had preferred a January start; and secondly when *EastEnders*' companion in the BBC's new early evening package, the chat show *Wogan*, had not been ready in time. Julia Smith was certainly uneasy about the late start: *East-Enders* no longer had the long winter months in which to build up a loyal following before the summer downturn in the ratings.

If the initial projections of *EastEnders*' audience size had been relatively modest, the publicity which surrounded its launch was rather less so. In an unprecedented move, the BBC had appointed a publicity officer specifically to promote the new serial. The programme had been trailed in *Radio Times* and on screen for many weeks beforehand, leading many newspaper critics to accuse the BBC of 'hype'. An ostentatious press launch, complete with lavish press pack and 'showbiz walkpast' of the cast, only fuelled their scepticism. The high profile certainly succeeded in giving the programme public visibility – and encouraged as many as 13 million viewers to tune in to the first episode – but it also increased the risks attached to failure. If *EastEnders* was going to make mistakes, it would do so in the public eye, without the opportunity to ease itself in gently.

Michael Grade, fresh from the competitive world of the American networks, was unrepentant:

I believe in getting as much publicity for programmes as possible. If you say something is wonderful and it isn't, then you pay the price. But in terms of *EastEnders* there is nothing we did in promoting it that I wouldn't do again. The fact that the show is so good justifies the hype. It was a hype, of course. You're launching a £4–5 million project – do you let it creep onto the air?

In retrospect, Grade professed that he had always been confident that the programme would succeed:

I knew it was going to be a monster hit. All my experience told me so, my professional instincts honed over the years in the heat of battle. I knew from the first three or four minutes it was going to be a monster.

Yet, as Jonathan Powell pointed out, the BBC's investment in the programme meant that it had no option but to be committed to its success:

It was psychologically very important, the fact that we built that lot. It cost a fair amount of money. The fact that we were committed to it, I think some of the success of the programme was due to that, because it was so completely inescapable. It had to succeed. It was important to the programme, to the people who made it, to the organisation.... We were right to allow ourselves no options. We didn't even allow ourselves the option of failing.

If the confidence of Grade and Powell resembled that of gamblers playing with very high stakes, Julia Smith herself was considerably more cautious. She expected the programme to take as long as two or three years to establish itself with the audience, and anticipated that its strong start would be followed by a significant dip in the ratings over the summer months.

The ratings war
EastEnders' success in the ratings was far from instant, although its eventual rise to prominence in the autumn of 1985 certainly exceeded even the most optimistic expectations. The figures were carefully monitored by the BBC's Broadcasting Research Department, and further qualitative research was undertaken in order to gauge more detailed reactions.

The continuous monitoring showed an interesting pattern of response. As Julia Smith had predicted, the audience size began to fall after the initial burst of interest: after three weeks on air, BBC1's early evening share had returned to the pre-*EastEnders* norm of 7 million, compared with ITV's 13 million. Nevertheless, the show's appreciation indices – which measure the audience's interest and enjoyment of programmes – steadily increased, rising from 58 in February, through 70 in April and 75 in May to reach 80 by the end of August, a figure which was nearly ten points higher than the average for British soap opera. Although *EastEnders* appeared to be losing the ratings battle, the dramatic rise in its appreciation indices suggested that it was building a loyal following which would provide a firm basis for future growth.

Qualitative research on two early episodes, again using small group discussions, revealed that viewers were able to follow the storylines, and felt that the characters had potential, but found the programme rather dreary and depressing. In particular, they found the conflicts within families rather 'too close to home' and therefore upsetting to watch. This criticism was also reflected in press reviews and in a series of letters published in *Radio Times* in April. Here again, it is difficult to assess the extent to which this information influenced the programme's producers, although it certainly co-incided with Michael Grade's own views:

> The only criticism I had of the show in the early days was that it was too strident in tone. There was not enough humour in the show, it was all a bit *Sturm* and *Drang* in the first weeks. And Jonathan Powell agreed, and we made that adjustment as quickly as we could. We lightened it up a bit here and there and that also helped.

Nevertheless, one major reason for *EastEnders*' eventual success in the ratings was its careful scheduling. Michael Grade had arrived at the BBC with a reputation derived from his work at London Weekend Television of being a scheduling wizard. One of the problems he had identified very early on was the lack of fixed points in the BBC schedule – and in particular in the early evening. *EastEnders* and *Wogan*, in addition to pulling ratings, would also provide a much-needed stability at the start of the evening's viewing. The sheer longevity of a soap opera was also a significant point in its favour: as Grade observed, the BBC's past attempts to dent the ratings for *Coronation Street*, for example by scheduling a popular situation comedy against it, had only proved successful in the short term.

At the same time, Grade did not subscribe to the view that 'inheritance' was all-important – the idea that if you caught an audience at the start of the evening, it would stay with you until close down. Particularly in an era of remote control keypads, this approach was largely outdated. Nevertheless, if *EastEnders* were to be followed by a sequence of popular programmes, it would certainly go a long way to increase the BBC's overall audience share:

If you've got good programmes that are following it, the audience look at it as a package. They say, 'Right, I'll watch BBC from 7.00 to 9.00 and then I'll switch to ITV because I want to watch their drama.' They'll watch a package of programmes, with a gem like that in the middle which attracts. So there is a package idea, but the pieces around it have to be the right pieces.

Nevertheless, the initial decision to schedule *EastEnders* at 7 p.m. represented something of a gamble since it meant competing with ITV's *Emmerdale Farm*, a rural soap opera with a steady and respectable share of the ratings. Michael Grade described this first phase of the 'Soap Wars' with considerable relish:

I put *EastEnders* at 7.00 because *Emmerdale Farm* was not networked. As a response to it going at 7.00, ITV for once got its act together and networked *Emmerdale Farm*. That was a blow, but I knew – from my knowledge of ITV – that *Emmerdale Farm* went off the air in the summer for a number of weeks, and I only had to wait for that window, and then I would be away. What they did was that they somehow squeezed extra episodes and repeats, so there was no break in the clouds. So I thought, this is crazy, this is silly now, I'm going to have to move it. And because of the sort of press we have in this country, I didn't want them rubbishing the show – 'panic move' – they'd have written that as a failure story. I had to dress up the presentation of that move in such a way as to protect the show, so I gave all kinds of reasons for the move, trying to disguise the fact that I was having to move it because it had reached a plateau and wasn't moving off.

It was at about this point – in September 1985 – that Mary Whitehouse began her public attacks on the programme, and this provided Grade with a further explanation for the shift from 7.00 to 7.30. His claim that the move was made in order to protect 'family viewing time' was, not surprisingly, received with some scepticism by the press.

In addition to the two weekday episodes, Grade also decided to schedule an omnibus repeat edition at 2 p.m. on Sundays, a move which was primarily intended as a means of keeping the programme in the BBC's top ten. Adding the omnibus figures to those for the weekday broadcasts – which had long been standard practice on the part of BARB, the Broadcasting Audience Research Bureau – would, he felt, keep the ratings up for the first year and thus stave off press criticism. His original intention had been to drop the omnibus edition once the programme had established itself in its weekday slots, but it too eventually acquired a large constituency, not least because it was cleverly scheduled opposite ITV's statutory half-hour of religion.

Following the shift to 7.30 in September 1985, *EastEnders'* ratings began a meteoric rise which eventually peaked at around 23 million in February and March of 1986. This rise co-incided with the regular seasonal upturn in the ratings, and also with the ending of the latest series of *Dallas*, but *EastEnders'* climb to the top of the ratings charts was both faster and earlier than even its most enthusiastic advocates could have expected. The appreciation indices also continued to rise, averaging a phenomenal 85 in the early months of the new year. Studies of the demographic profile of the audience showed that the programme was successfully reaching a genuine cross-section of the population in a way that no British soap opera had previously managed to do, and that it was particularly popular with teenagers, traditionally the least captive section of the television audience. Ironically, qualitative research suggested that it was precisely those features which had initially been found alienating – and in particular its abrasive treatment of 'social issues' – which viewers were now ready to praise.

The broadcasters and their audience

Ideas about the audience thus entered into every stage of the devising of *EastEnders.* The programme ultimately owes its existence to the BBC's need to reach a new early evening audience; many of the specific production decisions – about the location and setting of the serial, about the balance of characters, about publicity and scheduling, and about the themes and storylines – were to a certain extent informed by ideas about the type of audience the programme was aiming to reach, and by assumptions about what would interest and entertain it, and thereby keep it watching. Yet what is most remarkable is that these ideas and assumptions were based on comparatively little direct evidence about the audience itself.

In a paper delivered to the Market Research Society in 1986, Vivien Marles and Nadine Nohr, of the BBC's Broadcasting Research Department, described the launch of *EastEnders* as 'the launch of a new brand into a difficult market'.[13] The marketing metaphor is in many respects appropriate, yet what distinguishes the launch of *EastEnders* from, say, the launch of a new chocolate bar, is how little market research was actually undertaken. Compared, for example, with US television, where the findings of audience research can effectively seal the fate, not merely of particular series, but also of individual characters within them, audience research in British television remains a relatively small-scale, marginal operation. In the case of fictional programmes, it is unusual to undertake research prior to going on air, as was the case with *EastEnders*, although the limited scope of even this research remains surprising when one considers the substantial investment which was at stake.

Furthermore, at least according to the programme-makers, the evidence which was available was largely ignored. Julia Smith and Tony Holland were certainly adamant that they had not deviated from their initial conception, despite the considerable pressures upon them:

TONY HOLLAND   All the time we're saying, 'Think of the number you first thought of.' That's what we're doing. 'What did you set out to do in the first place?' ... Apart from one story, we've done everything we intended to do two years ago, and we're still on course. We've stuck to what our original intention was.

Of course, this is not to suggest that they remain indifferent to audience response, although their ways of assessing that response appear rather impressionistic. They regard ratings as an unhelpful indicator, not least because the production of new programmes takes place several weeks ahead of the figures appearing. Instead, they prefer to rely on more personal and subjective methods:

TONY HOLLAND   To be quite honest, we're terribly thrilled by the ratings. It is very thrilling to think that for one episode, half the population was watching ... It's terrifying, but it thrills you. Although we're thrilled, and rush for the figures each week to see what they are – at least I do – it's a straw poll, a feeling in the air that we pick up on. I buy the tabloids every day because my punters read them. I want to know what they're reading about. I want to know what they're calling Sarah Ferguson. I need that information so it sounds as though it's off the street. But I'm more inclined to do my own audience research, and Julia does the same in her world. What I pick up off the street reaction is my judge of the ratings.... It's better for me to hear somebody in a bar saying 'When's Angie going to get her revenge, Tone?' I can pick it up from the tea ladies, I pick it up from somebody in the corridor, whatever.

This lack of information made it extremely difficult for them to explain the reasons for *EastEnders*' success. Indeed, in the case of Smith and Holland, this was a question which they were steadfastly unwilling to address, arguing that to analyse their success would interfere with their creative work.

JULIA SMITH   There's nothing to say about it. What is there to say? It's a humble little twice-weekly serial churned out with a lot of hard work. An hour's worth of television, to entertain the public, that's all it is.... What is there for scholars to write about? In our minds, it's totally simple. We follow our noses, we don't do anything else. We had an instinct, we followed it. We follow our noses, we work on instinct, and that's that. There's no intellectualism.

While Tony Holland acknowledged that there was 'a certain built-in craft' to scriptwriting and production, it was this spontaneous creative intuition which was all-important:

We just go by our noses. That's why we try to do the show hand-to-mouth, with as little planning as possible.

Analysing television, they argued, would destroy the 'magic and illusion and thrill of entertainment'. It was at least partly for this reason that they claimed not to watch other soap operas – with the notable exception of *Brookside*: not only would this influence them, or give them 'second hand' ideas, it might also make them self-conscious about their own programme.

Others were more forthcoming, however. Michael Grade felt that the story of Den and Angie Watts was 'the spark that set off the fire': characters with weaknesses, or with 'a hint of villainy about them' were a perpetual source of fascination for audiences. Jonathan Powell, on the other hand, argued that the story of Michelle's baby had been the winning factor: it was a 'human story' which had 'touched a public nerve'. Yet he, too, argued that the ratings did not tell the whole story:

It was a question of *response*. Once it *responded* then you began to be able to play the tune, you began to be able to sense what your programme was. It was the response that was important, I think, the sense of response rather than the sense of audience....

Discussing the controversy following Mary Whitehouse's public criticisms of the programme, he described this phenomenon at greater length, and in almost mystical terms:

It was a good reminder of what you're playing with when you have something that's at that fever pitch, which the programme was – where somehow you're not just dealing with an audience any more. It's like a family row, and you're right in the middle of it: the programme is right in the middle of the culture and has almost gone beyond the screen. It's almost living out there. I don't claim anything special about the programme, except to note that at times the programme, as others do, went beyond the screen and almost lived – did live, actually – in the street. Somehow the barriers between the television screen and people's hearts and emotions were broken down.

25

For Smith and Holland, however, 'response' was more of a distraction, even a source of irritation. The public interest reflected – and, admittedly, stirred up – in the tabloid press made it more difficult, they argued, for them to get on with the job of producing the programme itself. Tony Holland even reported that there was a strict rule in his local pub that nobody was allowed to discuss *EastEnders*. They were particularly exasperated by the volume of letters from 'pressure groups' arguing for their pet 'issues' to be covered. They felt that the programme had become 'public property', and that others were attempting to take control of it away from them:

> JULIA SMITH It does seem that now almost the one thing we're not being given time for is to make the programme or to care about the programme, because we're being pulled more and more by various people who think it is their right to have access to us. It's taking a lot of time and effort to cling on. We're there to make a programme, we're not there for all these other reasons.

Both Smith and Holland claimed to be strongly anti-elitist, and committed to popular drama: in this sense, they argued, *EastEnders* was merely an extension of their previous work on *Z Cars* and *Angels*. They were not interested in making 'serious' or 'esoteric' drama for small audiences, and did not want to be seen to be 'effete' about their own work. Holland contrasted their approach with that of writers in 'Fringe' theatre, who, he claimed 'have absolutely no experience of life whatsoever':

> They haven't gone through all the struggles we went through. . . . We actually know what's going on out there in the street. That's why we've got an instinct for it. . . . If you're in the business of communication, which is what television is all about, where you want people to relate to what you're doing, you actually want someone to watch the damned thing, you're devoted to that loyal and in our case huge audience. I don't want to do the programme for me. Julia doesn't want to do it for her. We're doing it for them.

Yet at the same time, it is significant that they did not regard themselves as part of their own potential audience:

> JULIA SMITH I wouldn't watch the programme if I wasn't making it. I've never watched a soap opera in my life, I wouldn't start now. I don't watch television. I'm a professional. I make it. I'm like a manufacturer. . . . If I watch television, I'll watch the news. I watch

the odd opera. I enjoyed Huw Wheldon last night. I'm a horribly middle-class esoteric viewer.

As these quotations suggest, the programme-makers' conception of their relationship with their audience was confused and even contradictory. On the one hand, they felt able to claim privileged knowledge of 'what's going on out there in the street', and to value 'street reaction'. Yet on the other hand, the tangible manifestations of this reaction in audience research, in the popular press and in viewers' letters were ignored or regarded with suspicion. In each of these cases, there are certainly good reasons to doubt whether the data is in fact representative; yet to rely instead on 'intuition', or on even more impressionistic evidence, can scarcely be regarded as any more adequate.

As Philip Elliott has observed, one of the key skills in producing popular television is the ability to empathise with audience groups of which one is not oneself a member.[14] In the absence of any sustained, direct contact with their potential viewers, broadcasters typically put themselves and their colleagues into the role of audience. Producers may have favoured target audience groups, and may use their imagined reactions as a means of judging their own work. Yet these assumptions about the audience are fundamentally based on speculation, since there is very little hard evidence which broadcasters are prepared to trust – apart, of course, from the ratings, which are ultimately the crudest possible form of data.

This is not to suggest that broadcasters' attitudes towards their audience are merely arrogant or indifferent. The existing structures of broadcasting institutions place an extraordinary pressure on programme-makers: producing a programme as expensive and as popular as *EastEnders* requires a very high degree of 'nerve', because there is very little margin for error. Even when the ratings are high, there remains a perpetual fear that they might start to fall away and that one will be unable to discover the reasons why. Keeping one's nerve thus inevitably means insulating oneself from the variety of demands on one's attention – of which the audience is merely one among many.[15]

At the same time, it is clear that this arrangement leaves broadcasters with a considerable degree of freedom to determine the kinds of programmes they feel should be made, and this is – perhaps paradoxically – even more true in 'public service' broadcasting than in the commercial companies. As Julia Smith argued:

> I'm absolutely convinced that this programme could not have been made anywhere but the BBC. Because only in the BBC could two programme-makers be allowed to do their own thing, and fail if they were going to fail.... Nobody but the BBC could be as immune, could have sheltered us in that way.

Serving the public

EastEnders' extraordinary popularity nevertheless means that it enjoys a rather ambiguous relationship with the 'official' Reithian definition of 'public service broadcasting'. The charge of 'catering to the lowest common denominator' could be made not only by the BBC's enemies, but also by those within the Corporation who believe in broadcasting as a means of uplifting public taste. While Tony Holland agreed that the BBC had allowed Julia Smith and himself a considerable degree of autonomy, he also acknowledged that their work was 'very commercial', and in some respects had more in common with the ethos of independent television than with that of the BBC. For example, part of the 'craft of script-making', as he defined it, lay in knowing the correct time of year to 'blow the big story': getting in a good story at Christmas meant that you might stand some chance of keeping your audience until Easter, despite the seasonal drop in the ratings.

> We are, in that sense, not typical of the BBC. It has been considered for some years, although I think it's changing, that to actually promote a product – and we're the only people in the BBC that I know of who call our show a product – a lot of people in the corridors of power think it's terribly vulgar. But we like the packaging, we like the promotion, we like the hype.

As Holland indicated, this Reithian view of public service broadcasting is gradually changing, although it remains influential. Michael Grade and Jonathan Powell both contested the view that popularity was incompatible with the principle of public service – a view which they described as both outdated and condescending:

> MICHAEL GRADE   That's a patronising argument by people who believe that the BBC should be an elitist ghetto of cultural high ground, inaccessible to the working classes, or inaccessible to people who aren't highly educated, appreciative of the finer things of life.

At the same time, they refuted the suggestion that *EastEnders* was primarily about 'grabbing the ratings', or about popularity at any price. The idea that it was 'a lowest common denominator show' was incorrect, both on the basis of its broad demographic appeal, and on the grounds of its 'quality':

> JONATHAN POWELL   If we really wanted to grab the ratings, we wouldn't make *EastEnders* like we make *EastEnders*. I think *East-Enders* has attracted a large audience because it's good, it's mature, it's grown up and it talks to people on their level. It talks to them on a mature level. It's an entertainment programme, fine: but entertain-

ment is not a dirty word. It addresses, within a quite wide interpretation of an entertainment format, quite significant and human problems. There are good episodes and there are bad episodes, sure, but there are 104 a year, so there are bound to be. But there are episodes of *EastEnders* which I would frankly be very happy to put up as a one-off play.

Significantly, although popularity is clearly valued, 'quality' is still defined here by standards which derive from the 'cultural high ground' of the single play.

While Grade and Powell were therefore keen to argue the case for *EastEnders* as 'quality' television, they were also aware of its strategic role within the broader range of BBC programming, and within the context of public criticism of the Corporation. There was a sense in which the popularity of *EastEnders* enabled other, less popular, programmes to exist:

> JONATHAN POWELL I'm sure it helps our image to have programmes like this. I'm sure it helps to attract people to other programmes. And it creates space, too.... You have to create your space, allow yourself the space for specialised programming. It works when the balance is right. I don't think this department works with just *EastEnders* and *Bergerac*, but equally I don't think it just works with *Bleak House* and *Edge of Darkness*. They all complement each other.

Michael Grade argued that the BBC had always been in the business of producing popular programmes, although in the current context a major success like *EastEnders* could perform a particularly important function for the Corporation as a whole:

> It's a problem for our enemies, because they don't want us to be popular. If we weren't popular, then there is a case for breaking up the BBC and selling it off to private enterprise. We do stand in the way of a lot of people making a lot of money. My belief is that we need to be popular, but we don't need to be popular all the time, every day, every week of the year. We need to *prove* that we can be as popular as the other side with quality programmes when we want to be.

In many ways these comments reflect the broader dilemma which has faced public service broadcasting in this country since the introduction of commercial television, and which was brought to a head in the period immediately preceding the launch of *EastEnders*. On the one hand, the BBC is obliged to justify its monopoly over the licence fee by producing programmes of artistic 'quality' and 'responsibility'. Yet on the other hand, that monopoly can only be sustained if the BBC is seen to speak to the nation as a whole, rather than to a privileged minority, and it is therefore obliged to compete with ITV for a reasonable share of the mass audience. As Michael Grade argued, the BBC has always resisted the idea of catering merely to the educated middle class, yet in the context of a dwindling audience share, and a government committed to 'free market' economics, its delicate attempts to retain a balance between popular and minority tastes have inevitably been fraught with uncertainty.[16]

In this sense, the attempt to reconcile the popularity of *EastEnders* with the ethos of 'public service' represents a further shift away from the Reithian tradition. Although many of the basic Reithian tenets remain – the definition of 'quality', for example, or the idea that a popular programme might serve as 'groundbait', to lead viewers on to less popular, more 'specialised' programmes – there is a strong sense in which the agenda is being set from outside the BBC itself. Thus, the BBC has to 'prove things' in order to silence its 'enemies'; it has to produce programmes which will be 'good for its image' and thus 'create space' for 'specialised programming' (that is, for 'high culture'). What is perhaps most significant here is that these pressures on the BBC derive, not primarily from viewers, but from its critics in the press and in government, who for both economic and political reasons wish to see it privatised: in this sense, the BBC is becoming more accountable, not so much to the public, as to its powerful enemies on the political Right.

Educating the audience

If 'quality' is one key term in the definition of public service broadcasting, 'responsibility' is certainly another; and it is around *EastEnders*' responsibility in dealing with 'social issues' that further controversy has been generated. This theme will be discussed in greater detail in the following chapters; here I shall confine myself to considering some of the ways in which the producers themselves perceived it. Julia Smith and Tony Holland were very concerned to refute the idea that *EastEnders* was an 'issue-based' programme. Although it did cover social issues, they argued that this was merely an inevitable consequence of its commitment to realism, rather than something which they self-consciously set out to do. The programme did have an educational function, but it was one which they saw as, by and large, incidental to its main purpose of providing 'entertainment' and exploring 'dramatic conflict'. Such issues 'grew naturally' out of the characters and the story-line, rather than the other way round. Simply by 'showing people in the real world', the writers would inevitably 'fall over' issues that lay in their path.

JULIA SMITH   You can't live in this life and notice what goes on around you and not learn something. So hopefully you can't watch *EastEnders* and not learn something. Mary Whitehouse might prefer that 15-year-old children didn't learn about the pill. Some other mother, who's got a 15-year-old daughter she's rather worried about, might be very grateful that she learnt about the pill.

TONY HOLLAND   ... and because of the programme, be able to talk to her daughter about it, which she hadn't been able to do before. It is a focus. People do get information.

JULIA SMITH   But this is nothing new. *The Archers* did it. We don't sit down and say 'This week we're going to do this, or this week we're going to do that.' Out of the characters we invented, out of their predicaments in life, out of the situation of low welfare state, out of whatever, things are going to happen. Arthur's going to have to learn about unemployment. Maybe other people who are also finding out about it will learn about it. ... If anyone feels we are ever sticking anything on top, imposing a subject which wouldn't naturally come up, that doesn't come out of the characters we invented in Lanzarote three years ago, then we would be wrong, we would be imposing subjects on them.

In this respect, they sought to distinguish their own work from *Brookside*, which they felt 'went out of its way' to deal with social issues, and therefore tended to do so in an artificial and self-conscious way – what Tony Holland referred to as 'stick-on drama'. By contrast, *EastEnders* almost appeared to write itself:

TONY HOLLAND   Things do get raised, but only if the characters tell us to. We let the characters take us for a walk, we don't take them for a walk. I put a piece of paper in the typewriter and say, 'Talk to me!', and they do. So we are going to run into things, we are going to fall over what will eventually be called an issue.

On one level, these arguments might be regarded as an attempt to disclaim responsibility, at least for the kinds of issues which are raised, if not for the way in which they are dealt with. Yet on another level, they represent a strained response to the pressures which the programme-makers felt were being brought to bear upon them. The problem with being seen to be an 'issue-based' programme was that it made them more open to the demands of pressure groups and others who, they felt, wanted to influence their work.

In responding to Mary Whitehouse's criticisms, however, they used a very different argument, claiming that, on the contrary, their approach to 'social issues' was highly 'moral' and 'responsible' and that they 'cared dreadfully' about their audience. In the case of the attempted suicide of Angie Watts, for example – which had been followed by a series of 'copycat' stories in the press – Smith and Holland argued that the programme had been falsely accused, and was merely being used to sell newspapers. They expressed considerable concern at the possibility that viewers might confuse fact and fiction:

> TONY HOLLAND   We're make-believe. People can get involved, and terribly into *EastEnders*, and can sit there saying, 'I'm terribly into that, but thank God I don't have those problems!' They can switch it off and forget about it. They're not living in Albert Square. That's why we don't have guided tours around Albert Square. We don't want anyone to think it's real, because it isn't.

Conclusion

The very popularity of *EastEnders* thus highlights a number of tensions and contradictions in the relationships between the broadcasting institution, the programme-makers and the audience.

On the one hand, the programme has clearly served a very useful function for the BBC, in a period of increasing uncertainty. As a significant element within its early evening schedule, it has managed to maximise ratings, and to reverse the downturn in its audience share, thereby staving off a certain amount of public criticism. Yet, on the other hand, its success has also provoked further attacks on the Corporation from those on the political Right. *EastEnders* has been seen as a symptom of the BBC's abandonment of its 'public service' obligations, whereby 'quality' and 'responsibility' have simply been sacrificed in a cynical drive for ratings.

In this context, the degree of autonomy which appears to have been granted to the programme-makers is quite remarkable. A considerable investment, both of money and of reputation, was at stake, yet there seems to have been very little overt management interference in their work. As experienced programme-makers, Julia Smith and Tony Holland are used to working within extremely rigid industrial and institutional constraints. They are required to devise a product which can be manufactured regularly and consistently within a given budget and with fixed plant and resources, and which will attract a large and diverse market. Over and above this, they have to negotiate the broader institutional tensions, and to balance the requirement to be popular with the historical commitment to serve and to educate the public. Yet at the same time, they have their own very definite ideas about what the programme should contain, and the form it should take.

Although assumptions about the audience are a crucial element within this process, they are based largely on professional 'intuition' rather than on hard evidence. Broadcasters' knowledge of their audience remains at best impressionistic. To a certain extent, this is symptomatic of their relative insulation from the public they claim to serve. The extraordinary pressures which are placed upon them mean that the audience itself tends to be perceived as yet another distraction from the intensely demanding and difficult business of making programmes.

EastEnders was clearly designed to create, and to retain, a large audience. In this sense, it was the product of a series of quite specific calculations. Yet these calculations were based on an extremely limited amount of data about the audience itself – and it is for this reason that its eventual success was far from guaranteed. In order to explain its popularity, we therefore need to look beyond the intentions of the programme-makers, and to investigate the complex and ambiguous relationship between the programme and its audience.

2
THE AUDIENCE IN THE TEXT

Every act of communication – from brief verbal utterances through to literary and televisual texts – rests on a series of mutual assumptions. Readers inevitably make assumptions about the writer, or writers, of a text, even where they are not named. For example, they may infer motivations to the writer, or attempt to identify the nature of his or her 'designs' upon them; and on the basis of this, may seek to resist the effects of the text – or willingly abandon themselves to them. Likewise, writers inevitably make assumptions about their readers – about their existing knowledge, about their values and beliefs, and about their expectations of the particular text at hand. In both cases, these assumptions, inferences and expectations are subject to a process of change and negotiation. Readers build hypotheses about writers, which are constantly being revised in the light of new information, and in the process of reading itself. In the same way, writers are constantly – and perhaps in many cases unconsciously – adapting their image of their readers, both in the light of their own and others' readings of the texts they produce.

From the writer's point of view, the potential for failure in this process is fairly high. The greater the distance between writers and readers, the greater the possibility that one's assumptions about one's readers are inaccurate. As I have argued, this is particularly the case with broadcasting, where the relationship between programme-makers and audiences is highly institutionalised, and in general very remote. Programme-makers' conceptions of their audience are based on relatively inadequate data, and are therefore bound to be imprecise.

Nevertheless, the very detailed work which goes into writing and producing a television serial inevitably involves far more specific assumptions and calculations – for example, about how viewers are likely to relate to, and to judge, particular characters; about what they will remember of previous episodes; about what they are likely to want to happen next, and how far they will be able to predict it; and more generally, about what they will find amusing, moving or believable. Every decision – from killing off a character to selecting their wardrobe – entails making assumptions about viewers and the potentially diverse ways in which they may respond. As far as programme-makers are concerned, these assumptions are likely to be intuitive, rather than explicit; and the process of debate and negotiation which surrounds such decisions is one in which many of these assumptions are constantly being tested and redefined.

Over the past fifteen years, the analysis of film and literary texts has increasingly turned its attention to such questions. Approaches as diverse as psychoanalytic theory, semiotics and reception theory have variously sought to identify the ways in which texts 'imply' or 'position' their readers.[1] This 'reader-orientated' approach regards reading as a dynamic and reciprocal process: meaning is not something contained within the text, but something which the reader is actively involved in producing. Readers are seen to have a certain degree of autonomy in this process, although the text itself also exerts a series of constraints – both insofar as it uses specific linguistic or symbolic codes, and thus implicitly presupposes certain competencies and understandings; and also insofar as it enables readers to develop new competencies and understandings in the process of reading itself. Texts invite readers to read them in familiar ways, but they may also attempt to teach them new ways of reading.

Perhaps the most critical problem with these approaches, certainly in relation to soap opera, is of balancing the 'text' and 'reader' sides of the equation. On the one hand, there is a danger of favouring the text at the expense of the reader: certain kinds of psychoanalytic theory, for example, regard the text as having almost total power to position and even to 'construct' the reader, and leave readers very little room to negotiate.[2] Yet, on the other hand, there is a danger of favouring the reader at the expense of the text: certain reception theorists, for example, effectively deny that texts exist at all – instead, all we have to work with is an infinte multiplicity of individual readings.[3]

In terms of soap opera, it is this latter position which has become increasingly influential. Soap operas are regarded as 'open texts',[4] which offer multiple levels of interpretation, as opposed to 'closed texts', which are far more straightforward and inflexible. Certain writers have argued that soaps leave viewers free to choose from an infinite variety of different readings. Dorothy Hobson, for example, in her book on *Crossroads*, claims that:

> To try to say what *Crossroads* means to its audience is impossible for there is no single *Crossroads*, there are as many different *Crossroads* as there are viewers.[5]

There are certainly a number of reasons why soap operas might be regarded as 'open texts', as compared for instance with television documentaries. They contain a large number of characters, and thus a wider range of points of view with which the viewer may choose to identify. They typically lack a single 'hero' or a single authoritative voice, and although characters do pass judgment on other characters, they often do so in contradictory ways. Characters themselves are subject to change, and occasionally to dramatic reversals in their fortunes. Soap opera narratives are rarely finally resolved: 'happy endings' are always temporary, mere pretexts for further change and conflict. In many respects, therefore, soap operas would appear to permit, and indeed encourage, a variety of different readings, and to deny us the security of a single fixed position from which to interpret them.

If we look beyond the text, the picture becomes even more complex. On a very basic level, soaps are always unfinished texts, and as a result viewers are bound to discuss them in very different ways from more self-contained genres, like sitcoms or single plays. Much of the pleasure of talking about soap opera derives from its unfinished, provisional nature. In the periods between episodes, viewers may speculate about future developments, actively producing their own hypotheses and predictions, which are then tested against the text itself. Newspapers and magazines also extend the text in various ways, both by providing their own predictions and 'leaks' of future storylines, and by encouraging readers to compare and contrast the fictional lives of the characters with the real lives of the actors who portray them – although the fact that different viewers will read different material means that they will then bring different information and expectations to bear on the programme itself. Viewing patterns are also likely to vary; and as a result, regular viewers will read the text in very different ways from occasional viewers – although most viewers are likely to have gaps in their knowledge.

Soap operas can therefore be seen to possess a greater degree of 'openness' or 'indeterminacy' than many other television genres – and, indeed, many literary genres. It is at least partly for this reason that they have been able to appeal to such large and diverse audiences. Nevertheless, there are significant dangers in assuming that the meanings which audiences derive from soap opera are therefore infinite in scope, as Dorothy Hobson appears to do.

While I would agree that it is ultimately impossible to reduce a soap opera to a single 'meaning' – in effect to 'translate' it into a series of substantive propositions – it remains possible to specify the ways in which it invites its viewers to produce meaning. If one cannot say what *EastEnders* 'means' to its audience, one can at least say a good deal about how it *works*. For example, the ways in which the viewer is

36

allowed or denied access to privileged information – whether we are 'let into' secrets, or kept guessing – plays a significant part in determining our interpretation. Likewise, the extent to which we are invited to 'identify' with particular characters – and the different types of identification which are encouraged – also serves to orientate us towards the text, and enables us to make sense of it, in specific ways.

EastEnders also refers to, and draws upon, various kinds of knowledge which viewers are assumed to possess, and which they are encouraged to use in making sense of the programme. Some of this knowledge is specific to the text itself, and is derived from our previous viewing experience; some is derived from our experience of other kinds of texts, and our understandings of how they typically work; and some is 'commonsense' knowledge which derives from sources beyond the text itself, and which is specific to a particular social and historical context. Of course, viewers will inevitably bring different kinds of knowledge to bear on the programme, and to that extent their readings are bound to vary: although in several respects their knowledge is likely to be shared. Furthermore, the 'commonsense' knowledge which the serial draws upon is by its very nature partial: viewers may seek to apply other kinds of knowledge, but the text itself may in various ways make this difficult to achieve. Thus, while *EastEnders* cannot be said to embody a single, consistent ideological position, it does encourage viewers to produce meaning in certain ways and not others. To this extent, it becomes possible to talk about readings, not as infinitely various, but as differentiated in more or less systematic ways.

I

Everyday television

How does *EastEnders* attempt to 'position' its viewers? What assumptions does it make about their existing knowledge, both of the text itself and of the world beyond the text? How does it encourage viewers to go beyond the information given – to generate hypotheses, to draw inferences, and to make predictions? To what extent does it permit or encourage a diversity of interpretations?

In order to investigate these questions, I shall begin by concentrating in some detail on a short sequence taken from one episode (Episode 73, tx. 29 October 1985). I intend to describe, in as much detail as possible, the ways in which the text invites the viewer to make sense of what is shown. The total length of the sequence, which is taken from the beginning of the episode, is twelve minutes. For copyright reasons, I will provide a summary, with some extracts from the dialogue, rather than a complete script.

In some respects, this sequence is untypical of *EastEnders*, being based in and around a single location (the Fowlers' living room). While there are shifts of location, to the adjoining kitchen and to the front of the house, the whole sequence appears to take place in continuous real time. In a serial whose scenes rarely last longer than three minutes, this is certainly exceptional, although the rapidly shifting combinations of characters who traverse the Fowlers' living room in this scene do serve to break it up into a number of shorter sections, numbered here 1 – 15.

In other respects, however, the sequence is far more typical of the serial as a whole: it contains very little dramatic incident, yet manages to maintain a rapid sense of pace, by developing a number of parallel narrative strands simultaneously. The processes I shall identify here are, I would argue, representative of how *EastEnders* typically operates.

The sequence takes place on the morning of the christening of Pauline and Arthur Fowler's new-born child. The couple already have two teenage children, of whom the youngest, Michelle, is sixteen. This is their second attempt to christen the child, the first having been abandoned some weeks earlier when he was taken ill.

1. The scene begins with a close-up of Pauline Fowler's hands holding a number of photographs of (unidentified) young children. Church bells are heard ringing, and continue throughout the sequence. Arthur appears, wearing a suit and a blue and white football hat and scarf, chanting a supporter's song.

PAULINE You're not going to the ceremony like that, are you?
ARTHUR Yeah. How often does Walford Town win 5–2?
PAULINE As often as we have a christening, I suppose.
ARTHUR That's right. I'm going to celebrate both! Walford Town! Walford ...
PAULINE Arthur! If it's all the same to you, I prefer a quiet christening.
ARTHUR [*looking over her shoulder*] Are you OK? [*Taking the photographs*] Oh, I see ... Cup of tea help?
PAULINE Maybe.
ARTHUR Just remember that christenings are always better second time round.

This scene contains a number of references to past events, of two main kinds. Firstly, there are references to the *intra-diegetic* past – that is, to past events within the serial, which regular viewers are likely to remember. In addition, there are references to the *extra-diegetic* past – in this instance, to events which pre-date the beginning of the serial, and which have only ever been related – if at all – in the form of reminiscences.

38

References to the intra-diegetic past are both short-term and longer-term. Thus, although regular viewers will have been awaiting the christening of the Fowlers' baby, the church bells on the soundtrack serve to 'cue in' their memory of this before the event itself is directly referred to. Arthur's ambiguous reference to this being the 'second time round' reminds us more specifically of the failure of their previous attempt, and establishes a question: will the christening be successful this time around, or will there be another obstacle to prevent it? The main reference to the longer-term intra-diegetic past is fairly fleeting, but for regular viewers (and for Pauline herself, as the following scene reveals) it will carry a particular significance. This is contained in the opening shot, where we glimpse the photograph of the Fowlers' errant son Mark on the mantelpiece. Mark's sudden and mysterious disappearance several months before this episode has yet to be explained: and we infer that for Pauline his absence on this family occasion is particularly upsetting.

References to the extra-diegetic past are equally dependent on such inferences. We presume that the photographs Pauline is thoughtfully looking through are photographs of the previous christenings of her children, Michelle and Mark, although we are not directly told this. Arthur's knowing remark, 'Oh, I see', encourages us to empathise with what we take to be Pauline's emotions – a mixture of nostalgia and regret, perhaps. His reference to 'the second time round' is the first of a number of comments which invite us to draw parallels between the previous generation (Michelle and Mark) and the new generation represented by the baby about to be christened; and it invokes broader reflections about the continuity of family life, of which the christening itself is a significant ritual.

This scene also establishes a number of hermeneutic questions – that is, questions which invite us to speculate about future events. As I have indicated, the reminder of the failure of the previous christening generates some uncertainty about whether this one will eventually take place. Arthur's determination to wear the Walford Town colours at the ceremony, and Pauline's unwillingness for him to do so, establish a further question: will Arthur manage to get away with it, or will Pauline prevent him? Both these questions are short-term, in the sense that we can expect them to be resolved one way or another within the episode, although subsequent scenes also establish longer-term questions.

At the same time, the scene draws upon our knowledge of the characters gained from previous episodes. Pauline is in many respects the pillar of the Fowler household, who attempts to hold the family together in the face of conflict and misfortune – particularly those relating to her children, the now absent Mark and the pregnant Michelle. For this reason, the christening is clearly an important event for her, and her seriousness contrasts with Arthur's less respectful approach. At least at this stage in the serial, Arthur might be described as dependable, but as faintly immature and inadequate. His attachment to Walford Town – for whom, as he admits, a victory is a rare event – is symptomatic of the fact that he too is ultimately somewhat of a loser.

The contrast between Arthur and Pauline relates in turn to broader contrasts between men and women – in a sense, to a body of 'common-sense knowledge' or 'popular wisdom' about what men and women are, and the qualities they represent. These contrasting notions of masculinity and femininity are far from fixed or consistent within the serial, and only on certain occasions are they explicitly stated, for example in comments about what constitutes 'typical' male or female behaviour. Nevertheless, they do form a kind of moral backcloth, against which we are invited to assess the characters' behaviour. In this short scene, for example, Arthur is 'typically' rowdy and immature, while Pauline is 'typically' emotional and family-centred.

2. Pauline and Arthur move through to the kitchen adjoining the front room.

PAULINE   Oh dear. Here we go again.
ARTHUR   Yeah. It's Mark, isn't it.
PAULINE   Yeah. I woke up thinking about him …

After this brief exchange, Pauline and Arthur continue their argument about Arthur wearing Walford Town colours: Arthur asserts that Walford's victory is a 'miracle', and that the vicar himself will treat it as 'a sign from God'. Pauline, however, is adamant. Lou (Pauline's mother) enters, accusing Arthur in passing of looking 'a right wally'. She goes on to tell them of a 'dream' she had the previous night: her dead husband Albert had appeared, and told her that the baby should be named after him – 'It'll bring him luck'. Pauline, clearly tired of Lou's arguments, refuses; while Arthur suggests that he should be called Pele, after the Brazilian footballer. Lou exits in disgust, leaving Pauline and Arthur laughing.

The brief exchange at the start of this scene confirms our inferences about Pauline's state of mind, and in particular her thoughts about the absent Mark. Her comment 'here we go again', like Arthur's 'second time round' again invites us to compare this christening, both with the previous failed attempt, and also with the christenings of Mark and Michelle, and thus implicitly to reflect on the cyclical and continuing nature of family life.

The scene develops the hermeneutic questions established in the previous scene, and adds a further question, about the name of the child.

Lou's pressure on Arthur and Pauline to call the baby Albert (itself a reference to the extra-diegetic past, since it is the name of her long-since dead husband) has in fact been building up over several previous episodes. For *EastEnders* enthusiasts, Lou's reference may well call up memories of her young married life, as recounted in the *EastEnders* novel *Home Fires Burning*; while others may have entered a competition being run by the *Daily Star* newspaper at this time, which asked its readers to 'help Pauline out' by suggesting a name for the child. The idea that the name might bring 'luck' to the child is the first of a series of references to popular superstitions, and encourages us to speculate – albeit with no great urgency – about the child's future life.

What is particularly notable in this scene is the variety of points of view which are on offer, and the ways in which it is possible to shift between them. We may agree with Lou's summary dismissal of Arthur – 'You look a right wally' – but we may also join in his enjoyment in teasing her about the child's name later in the scene. Lou is one of the matriarchal figures common both in British and American soap opera, and in many situations she can muster an authority which few characters in the serial can match: yet this does not render her immune from criticism, or from being the butt of others' humour, as she is in this scene.

3. Exterior, front of house. The van belonging to Pete Beale (Pauline's brother) draws up outside the Fowlers' house. Michelle (Arthur and Pauline's daughter) is already waiting for them. Kath and Ian (Pete's wife and son) get out of the van. Michelle compliments Pete on being thoughtful enough to bring the video equipment, and helps him unload it from the van, rejecting his claim that it's too heavy for her:

PETE You're supposed to take care!
MICHELLE Don't be daft! [*She takes the video into the house*]
PETE All right. Well, don't blame me.

This brief scene draws on our existing knowledge of the two principal characters: the fact that Pete has brought the video equipment illustrates that he is dependable and considerate – qualities which have often been contrasted in the serial with those of his best friend Den Watts – while Michelle's behaviour illustrates her determination to make her own decisions. The brief exchange quoted reminds us that Michelle is pregnant, and, in Pete's final remark, plants a seed of doubt in our minds as to whether she will eventually have the baby. A number of popular newspapers at the time were in fact speculating about whether Michelle would have a miscarriage.

4. The Fowlers' living room. Kath, Pete and Michelle carry in the boxes from the car. Kath has brought a machine for making fizzy drinks. Pauline and Arthur express concern at the idea of the teenagers drinking alcohol, and Pauline says they will be limited to one glass of champagne 'to wet the baby's head'. Pete compliments Arthur on his outfit, but Pauline insists 'He's taking all that lot off before he sets foot in that church.' Wicksy (Pete's son) also compliments Arthur, but Pauline tells him not to encourage him. After Pauline and the others have left the room, Arthur and Wicksy are briefly left alone: Wicksy suggests to Arthur that it would be even better if the baby wore the Walford colours, and bets him a pound that he won't get away with it. Arthur accepts the bet.

This scene develops the hermeneutic question about whether Arthur will defy Pauline and wear the Walford colours to the ceremony, and in the final exchange between him and Wicksy, displaces it slightly: the question now is whether Arthur will be able to dress the child in the colours, and thereby win his bet. We are implicitly led to speculate about how he will be able to achieve this, and conceal it from Pauline. This theme is further developed by the way in which the gender differences are mapped onto it: it is notable that (with the comical exception of Ethel) it is the men, Pete and Wicksy, who compliment Arthur on his outfit, in a spirit of male camaraderie – while it is the women who can scarcely believe that he is serious.

The brief exchange about the teenage children drinking champagne introduces a further theme, which is referenced briefly at a number of points in this sequence. This concerns the extent to which adults are – or should be – able to retain control over their children's behaviour. As with the issue of Arthur and Pauline's argument over his football colours, certain forms of 'commonsense wisdom' are being invoked here. In this instance, these are concerned with age rather than gender – for example, the notion that young people left on their own are likely to behave 'irresponsibly'. At the same time, it is possible for the viewer to take different sides. In this instance, for example, we might agree with Pauline and Arthur's concern, or we might view them as being rather old-fashioned.

5. The Fowlers' kitchen. Saeed (the local Bangladeshi shopkeeper) has brought Pauline some gifts for the baby – a talisman, and a miniature Koran. Saeed says that the talisman will bring the baby luck, and keep him safe from the 'evil eye'; Kath remarks that she could do with one herself. Pauline is rather unsure what to make of the gifts:

PAULINE Oh, what is it? It's so tiny. Look Kathy. What is it?
SAEED It's the Koran.

PAULINE   Koran?
SAEED   Yeah, the Muslim bible.
PAULINE   Muslim?
SAEED   Yeah. Pin it to his vest always.
PAULINE [*still uncertain*]   Oh, right. I'll pin it to him later, thanks.

This scene is particularly interesting in that it can be read from a number of different points of view. On the one hand, it could be regarded as almost didactic: Pauline's ignorance allows Saeed to teach her what the word 'Koran' means – and, if the viewer is also unfamiliar with the word, to teach the viewer also. Yet at the same time, how we read Pauline's ignorance of these words will depend upon whether we ourselves know what they mean: for many – perhaps most – viewers, Pauline's apparent inability to understand the word 'Muslim' will make her appear rather stupid – which is surprising, given that she is a highly respected character, who consistently occupies a central and privileged role within the serial. Yet, on the other hand, the didactic intentions which might be discerned here may well be refused: Pauline's suspicion of the 'alien' Saeed might well be read as entirely justified.

Didactic moments such as this are comparatively rare in *EastEnders*, and, as this example illustrates, are distinctly 'risky'. They involve quite specific assumptions about the viewer's existing knowledge which may well be inaccurate. Such inaccuracies can lead us to regard the programme as patronising – we may well feel that it is trying to teach us things which we already know.

Kath's passing comment that she too could do with a talisman to protect her might be ignored by an inexperienced viewer; but to a viewer familiar with recent developments in the narrative, it is likely to be seen as an oblique reference to her persecution by Nick Cotton, who in recent episodes had begun a campaign of blackmail against her.

6. *Following a hint from Saeed, Kath leaves him and Pauline alone. He tells Pauline that he has received a letter from his father in Bangladesh, ordering him to sell the shop and return home. He needs to get in touch with his wife Naima, who has recently left him: he knows that Pauline has been in touch with her, and tries to pressurise her into telling him where she is. Pauline refuses, saying that she has promised Naima that she would not reveal her whereabouts. Saeed eventually leaves, depressed: the talisman, he says, has not brought him much luck – 'Maybe the baby will do better, eh?'*

This brief interlude serves to develop a further strand of the narrative, and to establish a number of hermeneutic questions. Saeed's arranged marriage with Naima appears to have failed, although there is a possibility that the pressure on him to return home to Bangladesh may bring them back together. On the other hand, this new development may push the already depressed Saeed over the edge, into more deviant behaviour – he has already been discovered frequenting a strip club, and in a subsequent episode is unmasked as the dirty phone caller who is pestering Debbie Wilkins.

The scene also draws upon, and develops, our knowledge of the characters: Pauline is sympathetic, but stands by her promises – at least partly out of female solidarity with Naima – while Saeed is increasingly fatalistic. Saeed's final remark draws us back to the christening of the new baby, and the hopes for his future life.

> 7. *Exterior, front of house. Pete is puzzling over the video equipment. Michelle, by contrast, says it's easy, and offers to help him; Pete is slightly affronted. Seeing Ethel Skinner approach, they comment on her bizarre appearance: Pete suggests she is wearing 'the gear for the Halloween haunt.' Ethel is excited by the presence of the video:*

ETHEL   Ooh. Am I going on television, then?
PETE   You know what, Et? If all goes well, I'm going to immortalise you today.
ETHEL   [*laughs*] That'll be nice. [*To her dog:*] Come on, Willy. [*She goes into the house, leaving Pete and Michelle laughing.*]

Pete and Michelle's brief exchange over the video equipment provides an interesting example of 'commonsense wisdom' being turned on its head. As the male adult, Pete might conventionally be expected to be able to handle the video, but it is Michelle, who is in fact the more capable of the two. This in turn draws on our character knowledge, in particular of Pete, whose self-esteem is very much based on his view of his own masculinity – yet it is precisely on these grounds that he is occasionally 'deflated', as he is in this scene.

The treatment of Ethel is more straightforwardly comic: we are encouraged to laugh at her eccentric dress by Michelle and Pete's opening comments (a reference to the Halloween preparations which had been shown in the previous episode), and at her failure to understand the word 'immortalise' by their laughter as she departs. This presentation of her thus depends upon a degree of distance – we see her from the other characters' point of view, and are rarely invited to take on her perspective.

> 8. *The Fowlers' living room, where Kath is doing Pauline's hair. Ethel enters, only to be told by Pauline that she has arrived two*

hours early – at eleven o'clock, rather than one o'clock. Ethel is
confused: 'I keep thinking it's yesterday. I've done all this before, I
think.' Kath compliments Ethel on her 'smashing' appearance, and
she herself agrees that her dress is 'dreamy'. Ethel goes through into
the kitchen, and in turn compliments Arthur on his outfit:

ETHEL   Oh, Arthur, you do look so fashionable.
ARTHUR   Oh, there's only a couple of us left, Et, only a couple
left.

Ethel is again positioned here as a comic character: regular viewers
will know that she is notoriously absent-minded. Her confusion also
reminds us again of the previous attempt to christen the child. The
series of compliments which follows draws attention to the characters'
appearance – a special occasion such as this provides an opportunity to
see an unfamiliar side to the characters – but there is also a degree of
irony here. We might suspect, for example, that Kath, true to character, is being nice to Ethel, rather than saying what she really thinks.
Ethel's lack of dress sense in turn tends to invalidate her compliment to
Arthur: and Arthur's jovial response suggests that he too recognises
that whatever else he may be, he certainly is not fashionable.

> 9. *Back in the living room, Arthur again tries to persuade Pauline*
> *to dress the baby in Walford Town colours: Pauline asks if he has*
> *been drinking, and rejects his idea, although she still suspects he is*
> *serious. Kath finishes Pauline's hair, and all compliment her on how*
> *attractive she looks. Kath suggests that they invite Arthur to take a*
> *look, although Pauline is reluctant. Nevertheless, Kath proceeds to*
> *usher everybody out of the room, and does the same in the kitchen,*
> *removing a bottle of beer from Ian's hand in the process: both*
> *Arthur and Pauline are confused by her behaviour.*

Apart from the brief exchange at the start of this scene, continuing
the question of Arthur's bet with Wicksy, the main focus here is on the
transformation of Pauline. Her appearance is normally somewhat
dowdy, indicating her low self-esteem and her harrassed lifestyle,
although scenes such as this serve to remind us that 'if only she tried'
she too could be glamorous and desirable. Here again, a form of 'commonsense wisdom' is being invoked – in this instance about the importance of women being physically attractive to men.

> 10. *Living room. Kath brings Arthur through from the kitchen into*
> *the living room, and then leaves him and Pauline together. Arthur*
> *marvels at Pauline's appearance:*

45

ARTHUR   You look lovely.
PAULINE [*bashful*]   Do I? [*They embrace*]
ARTHUR   You do, you do.
PAULINE   Oh, I feel all soppy.
ARTHUR   Well don't, don't. It's just like old times, innit?
PAULINE   Is it?
ARTHUR   Yeah. I feel like I did years ago. [*They kiss*].

This scene serves to mobilise a series of 'commonsense' assumptions about married life. Arthur's surprise at Pauline's transformed appearance, and his reference to 'old times', suggests that the romantic feelings which (we assume) the couple felt in the early days of their marriage have been submerged under their routine, unglamorous existence as a family. Yet the scene reassures us that, just as Pauline is 'really' beautiful underneath it all, so she and Arthur 'really' love each other just as they did years ago. We are thus given a rare 'behind the scenes' view, which reinforces our impression of the Fowlers' marriage – which at this stage in the serial served as a model of steady contentment, in contrast with that of Den and Angie Watts – and also, more generally, reassures us that marriages can be happy and even romantic at times, however briefly.

11. *Pauline and Arthur's brief romantic interlude is interrupted by Angie Watts, closely followed by Ethel. Arthur protests – 'We don't stand a chance, do we?' – but Angie goes on to make an announcement:*

ANGIE   Bad news, folks. Den can't be Godfather.
PAULINE   Oh, I knew it was too good to last.
ARTHUR   Why not?
ANGIE   Unavoidably detained, he says.
PAULINE   Oh gawd. Where does that leave us, then? [*Exit, shouting off:*] Mum, Pete, Kathy!
ANGIE   I'm so embarrassed, Arthur. I couldn't be more embarrassed.
ARTHUR   Well, where is he?
ANGIE   That's the point, innit. Where *is* he?
[*Lou, Michelle, Kath and others enter.*]
LOU   What's wrong?
PAULINE   Dennis can't be Godfather. He can't make the ceremony.
ANGIE   It can't be avoided, Lou.
MICHELLE   What's he up to?
ARTHUR   All right, Michelle.
MICHELLE   No, it's not all right.

46

ARTHUR   Michelle! If Den says it can't be avoided, then it can't be avoided. Isn't that right, Pete?
PETE [*reluctantly*]   Yeah. Sure.

Lou asks whether the christening will now have to be cancelled again, but Angie tells the family that she has telephoned the vicar, and that it is possible to have a proxy Godfather. There is some confusion over the meaning of the term 'proxy': Lou doesn't like the sound of it, but the term is eventually translated to mean a 'stand-in'. Ethel proposes that Nick Cotton could do it, but Kath is vehemently opposed to this. Ethel's claim that Nick is 'a very nice boy' is roundly dismissed by the assembled company. Ian volunteers himself, but Pete says he is too young, and proposes Wicksy instead. After some initial reluctance, he agrees, although Ian is rather aggrieved. This having been settled, the preparations continue.

This scene, which is effectively the climax of the sequence, is one which for experienced viewers is dense with implicit references to other narrative strands. Thus, we might well assume that Den Watts is not 'unavoidably detained', but is in fact with his mistress, Jan. Pete's grudging acceptance of his excuse indicates that he at least suspects as much – Pete being a character with whom Den regularly discusses his extra-marital relationship. We may in fact recall that in the previous episode, Den told Pete that he was planning to spend the evening with Jan, and failed to appear for a candlelit dinner which Angie had specially prepared for him. Den's absence thus feeds our ongoing speculation about these characters – for example, about the future of the Watts' marriage, and about Jan herself, whom we have yet to meet.

Michelle's particular irritation at Den's absence – captured significantly in close-up before she speaks – only makes sense if we know that Den is the father of her unborn child. Again, this relates to our broader speculation about whether this secret will be revealed to the other characters, and the effects this might have. Michelle's behaviour here might lead them to have suspicions about her relationship with Den, and thus increases the tension for the viewer.

A little later in the dialogue, Kath's rejection of Ethel's suggestion about Nick Cotton similarly refers to a hidden secret: the fact that he is blackmailing Kath because he has discovered that she was raped when she was a teenager. Here again, the implications of this secret being revealed are potentially very great: her husband Pete is under the impression that she had 'saved herself' for him before their marriage, and if he were to discover her secret might decide to leave her, or take his revenge against her or against Nick, potentially through violence. Ethel's claim that Nick Cotton is a 'very nice boy' on one level merely indicates her gullibility, but it also implies that for this very reason she too is at risk. Nick's attempts over the previous few episodes to in-gratiate himself with the community have been regarded by many of the characters with considerable suspicion.

Finally, Pete's rejection of Ian in favour of Wicksy as proxy God-father has implications in terms of the ongoing rivalry between them. Wicksy is Pete's son by his first marriage (or at least so Pete assumes), and his recent arrival in the Beale household has not been welcomed by Kath, his second wife, or their son Ian. Ian feels that Pete is no longer interested in him now that Wicksy is on the scene, and his behaviour on this occasion provides further evidence to support this view. Just as Arthur uses his paternal authority to silence Michelle's protests, so Pete uses his to override Ian's wishes – although in both cases, they clearly provoke resentment on the part of their children. Yet, as in each of the previous instances described above, the hidden feelings of the charac-ters concerned are largely left unstated: the viewer is left to draw inferences from facial expressions and significant close-ups.

This scene also revives, and subsequently resolves, the over-arching hermeneutic question about whether the christening will in fact take place as planned, or whether it will be cancelled yet again. The solution of the proxy Godfather again provides for a brief didactic moment, where the meaning of the term is explained – although here with comic effect.

12. *At the end of the scene, Pauline crosses the room to Arthur, who is engaged in a confidential conversation with Wicksy. Arthur reassures her that everything will be all right, and renews his attempts to persuade her about the football colours, but remains unsuccessful. He then continues his conversation with Wicksy: 'Thought I nearly had it then.' Pauline remains suspicious, although Arthur protests his innocence.*

13. *Exterior. Ali Osman starts his minicab, and pulls away from the front of his house to reveal his wife Sue walking down to the garden gate, looking thoughtfully after him.*

14. *The Fowlers' living room. Michelle announces the arrival of the cars to take them to the church. Everybody exits, leaving Pauline and Lou: Lou makes a last attempt to persuade Pauline to name the child Albert, but Pauline again rejects her.*

15. *Exterior. The family and their guests get into the cars. There is a brief cutaway to Sue Osman watching them, before the cars move away.*

These brief concluding scenes re-state the two short-term hermeneutic questions which recur throughout this sequence, and thereby set the viewer up for the christening scene which follows. Indeed, we may already be speculating beyond these questions – for whichever way they are resolved, there are likely to be implications for the characters' future relationships. In the event, Arthur manages to pin a Walford Town rosette on the baby, and thereby wins his bet with Wicksy; while the baby himself is named Martin Albert, a compromise which is much to Lou's pleasure, and which effectively prevents further conflict.

The shots of Sue Osman provide a further reference to past events within the diegesis. While an inexperienced viewer might attribute her thoughtful, sad expression to the fact that she does not appear to have been invited to the ceremony, regular viewers will infer that she is remembering her own child, Hassan, who died a few months previously. Yet again, this remains unstated, and must be deduced from her facial expression. As with previous such references, this may in turn set off further speculation: Sue and Ali's attempts to have another child have proved unsuccessful so far – although the reasons for this are unclear.

In analysing this sequence, I have attempted to illustrate the potential complexity of what might be occurring in the viewer's mind as the serial unfolds, even at relatively 'undramatic' moments. I am not claiming that the meanings and references I have detected were necessarily intentionally put there by the writers, nor am I suggesting that my account exhausts all possible readings. Even an experienced and highly attentive viewer would be unlikely to 'activate' the text in such detail, or to follow up all the references I have identified.

Nevertheless, the analysis does indicate a number of different processes which go together to make up the viewing experience. Viewers are invited to engage in many different types of activity: recollecting past events which they have seen; imagining ones which they have not; hypothesising about future events; testing and adapting these hypotheses in the light of new information; drawing inferences, particularly about the characters' unstated emotions and desires; and learning new facts, both about the characters and their fictional world, and about the world at large. In all these respects, the viewer is positioned as an active participant in the process of 'making sense' of the text, as a partner in an ongoing debate about how it will be understood.

These processes may be grouped under three broad headings, each of which will be considered in some detail in the remainder of this chapter. Firstly, there are processes which relate to *narrative* – that is, to the manner and sequence in which new information is revealed to the viewer. Three main processes are at work here, which I shall term *retension*, *protension* and *lateral reference*.[6]

49

Retension, refers to the process whereby viewers are given cues which invite them to recall past events, of two main kinds. Firstly, there are _intradiegetic_ events, which have been shown in previous episodes. These might be further differentiated according to how long ago they took place. Thus, short-term intra-diegetic events which are referenced in this sequence would include Den's conversation with Pete in the previous episode about his evening out with his mistress (scene 11). Long-term intra-diegetic events would include the fleeting references to the disappearance of Mark Fowler (scenes 1 and 2). Secondly, there are _extra-diegetic_ events, which have not been shown in previous episodes, and which we are implicitly invited to imagine or reconstruct on the basis of the characters' accounts of them. In this episode, these references are all to events which took place in the distant past – such as Lou's marriage to Albert (scenes 2 and 14) – although it is also possible, for example, for characters to refer to conversations which took place recently, but which were not shown to the viewer.

Protension describes the process whereby viewers are given cues which invite them to project into the future, and to speculate about coming events. These cues are primarily in the form of questions – what I have termed here 'hermeneutic questions' – although they are rarely explicitly stated in the question form.[7] Again, one could divide these into short-term and longer-term projections. In this sequence, short-term projections would include the possible name of the baby (scenes 2 and 14). Longer-term projections would include the question about the baby's future, and whether he will be 'lucky' (scenes 2 and 5–6).

In addition, the parallel narrative strands of soap opera make possible a form of _lateral reference_, which typically contains elements of both protension and retension. Scene 11 is particularly rich in such references – to the Den/Angie/Jan triangle, to Ian and Wicksy's rivalry, to Michelle's past relationship with Den, and to Nick Cotton's attempts to blackmail Kath. In each case, we are implicitly invited both to recall past events, and to speculate about future developments. In the case of the first two references, this may take the form of more general speculation about a future which is unknown both to the characters and the viewer: we do not know, for example, whether Den and Angie's marriage will eventually fall apart, and neither (at this stage) do they. The latter two references, however, carry a stronger hermeneutic 'charge' in that they refer to secrets which are shared by very few of the characters – and, of course, by the viewer. In these instances, our speculation is more specifically concerned with the likely implications of the secret being revealed – what will Pete do when he discovers that Kath was raped before they were married?

A second area which is important here is that of _character_. The viewer's concept of a given character is something which is assembled from a variety of indications or cues which are dispersed throughout the text. These cues include a number of different types of information: the way characters talk and behave; their physical appearance; what other characters say about them; what they say about themselves; and so on. On the basis of this information, the viewer begins to construct a more or less consistent notion of the characters' attributes and qualities. As the text proceeds, it may throw up contradictory indications, which render the original constructs unstable, and force the viewer to adapt them.[8]

This body of character knowledge forms a 'background' against which the viewer makes sense of the characters' behaviour, which is the 'foreground' in any given scene. Arthur Fowler's behaviour in this sequence, for example, makes sense in the context of what we already know about him, and the qualities we attribute to him – although for an inexperienced viewer his behaviour might appear a little bizarre.

However, characters are not generally seen in isolation, but in the context of a variety of relationships and interactions with others. The 'foreground' of a soap opera narrative is constantly shifting from one encounter to the next, and the viewer's point-of-view inevitably shifts with it. As we shift from one scene to the next, we retrospectively adapt our estimation of the characters we have already seen in the light of other characters' perspectives – a phenomenon which in reception theory is termed the 'wandering viewpoint'.[9] A fairly comical example in this sequence is the series of compliments which are exchanged about the characters' dress, and particularly Arthur's (most notably in scenes 2, 4, 7 and 8).

Even in this instance, however, it is clear that certain characters are consistently privileged over other characters. Pauline, for example, occasionally passes negative judgments on other characters, which they tend for the most part grudgingly to accept, but only has positive judgments passed on her. At the same time, her ignorance of basic information about other cultures (scene 5) might be interpreted negatively. Lou passes negative judgments, for example on Arthur, but we are also invited to laugh at her (scene 2), and, along with Pauline, to reject her obstinacy (scene 14). Ethel, on the other hand, is presented almost exclusively as a comic figure, whom the other characters laugh at, but whose own judgments carry little weight (scenes 7, 8 and 11). In other words, although we may 'identify' with different characters at different times, we tend to identify with any given character in a fairly consistent way – for example, as somebody we should admire, or pity, or laugh at.[10]

Ultimately, the important point about this process is not the specific judgments themselves, but the fact that we are implicitly, and constantly, being invited to consider a variety of characters' perspectives, and to rank these in a hierarchy – a hierarchy which will certainly be different for different viewers, and which will change, albeit gradually and over the longer term, but which we nevertheless retain as a kind of mental standard against which to assess the characters' behaviour.

A third and final area which may be identified here is one which I shall refer to as *discourse*. As I have indicated, where characters are brought together in conflicts and relationships of various kinds, we are implicitly invited to assess these in terms of a body of 'commonsense wisdom' or 'popular knowledge'. This is particularly true where the characters involved are different in terms of age, gender, race or social class. Thus, we may be encouraged to judge the behaviour or attitudes of male and female characters in terms of assumptions or discourses about what constitute 'typical' male or female qualities – although these discourses may not necessarily be coherent in themselves, or consistent with each other.

This process is more difficult to identify, compared for example with the operation of narrative, not least because these assumptions are rarely mentioned directly. Even where they are mentioned, they are often the subject of debate, in which different characters take different perspectives. Although certain perspectives tend to be excluded, or otherwise devalued by being represented by comic or unsympathetic characters, the viewer is left with a certain degree of freedom to choose between them.

In one sense, this is unsurprising: in order to retain its large and diverse audience, the serial cannot afford to offend too many viewers by appearing to adopt a narrow or unambiguous moral or ideological position. Only on rare occasions does *EastEnders* adopt a more ex-plicitly didactic mode, in which it attempts to 'teach' the viewer. Such instances are, as the dialogue between Pauline and Saeed in scene 5 illustrates, fraught with dangers, since they depend for their effective-ness on the accuracy of the writers' specific assumptions about the viewers' existing knowledge – in this case, whether viewers will already understand the words 'Koran' and 'Muslim'.

More typical are scenes in which these discourses remain as a kind of 'background', against which the 'foreground' action can be understood and evaluated. In this sense, they operate in a similar way to the char-acter knowledge identified above – although in another respect, this knowledge is far less certain or reliable, since unlike character know-ledge it is inevitably drawn from sources beyond the world of the serial itself. For example, the conflict between Pauline and Arthur over his football hat and scarf becomes the focus of a gender division, the men siding with Arthur, the women (for the most part) with Pauline. Arthur is 'typically' noisy and disruptive, while Pauline is 'typically' quiet and sensitive. In other instances, such assumptions may be inverted: Michelle is 'untypically' confident about using the video equipment, while Pete is 'untypically' confused about it – and somewhat disconcerted by his inability to perform the male, adult role. In both cases, depending on our own position, we may relish the 'victory' of the party who comes out on top – in these instances, Michelle and (eventually) Arthur – or we may share the exasperation of the injured party, and trust that things will go better for them next time around.

This potential for differential readings exists in each of the three areas identified here, since the readings which are produced will depend upon the knowledge which viewers bring to the text. One major variable is knowledge of the serial itself: the readings produced by experienced viewers are likely to be different, and in several respects, more complex, than those produced by viewers less familiar with the serial. Yet the knowledge which viewers bring from outside the text is likely to be even more variable, since it will depend upon their own social experience and the discourses which circulate within it.

However, this does not mean that the process is merely random, or that it is possible to produce an infinite number of readings. As I have suggested, *EastEnders* permits a range of differential readings, and actively invites viewers to debate and choose between the possibilities which are on offer. Nevertheless, the scope for differential readings is limited in ways which it is possible to begin to identify, and to describe, systematically.

Narrative pace and structure

The sequence analysed above contains very little of any decisive dramatic significance: it has a mundane, everyday quality which is typical of the serial as a whole, and which is rarely disrupted by melodramatic or violent action. Yet what is quite remarkable about it is the sense of rapid narrative pace which it generates. On one level, nothing much happens; but on another level, there is a lot going on.

The problem of achieving the correct narrative pace is perhaps the greatest which the writers and producers of soap opera have to deal with. Clearly, the narrative must not move too quickly: to do so would be to risk implausibility in what is essentially (at least in the British variety) a naturalist form. Furthermore, even soap opera 'fans' are unlikely to watch every episode of their favourite serial, and might become confused if events moved too fast. Yet if the pace is too slow, the viewer may simply get bored.

Certainly, *EastEnders* has not been without its dramatic incidents: since its inception, it has included a teenage pregnancy, an attempted suicide, a violent protection racket, a cot death, a mental breakdown, a fatal road accident, a suspected murder, as well as numerous muggings, disappearances, marital bust-ups and extra-marital affairs. Compared with other British soaps, it has covered a lot of ground in a very short time. Yet when one compares it, even with the American soaps, let alone with other genres such as police series, the frequency of such dramatic incidents is comparatively low. Sometimes months can go by in which very little seems to happen, and there are few major 'cliff-hangers'. What is interesting, however, is that even in such fallow periods, the serial manages to maintain a sense of rapid pace: it is as if it is running very fast, but not actually getting anywhere.

To some extent, this sense of narrative pace derives from the frequent shifts of location, and the perpetual comings and goings of the characters: in the sequence described above, no fewer than eleven characters have speaking parts. Although the sequence appears to take place in continuous 'real time' – at least, there is no detectable sign of time having passed between each scene – there is a certain amount of condensation which can be detected on a close viewing. Pauline's transformation from curlers and casual clothes to elegantly coiffed hair and a smart suit is little short of instantaneous, and her comment to Ethel that she has arrived two hours early is contradicted by the fact that they leave for the church less than ten minutes later!

The density of protensive and retensive cues adds to this sense of narrative 'busyness'. The number of lateral references to other story-lines is particularly significant: apart from the main story of the christening of the Fowlers' baby, at least six other storylines are referred to in this sequence, most of which have more far-reaching dramatic consequences than the main action itself. In fact, none of these stories is developed to any significant degree – with the possible exception of that concerning Saeed. All these references do is to re-state what regular viewers already know; yet they also serve to make viewers 'work harder' at reading the text – or at least invite them to do so – and thereby contribute to this sensation of narrative pace.

Obviously, protension and retension are common features in all narratives, and genres like soap opera which develop a number of narrative strands in parallel are likely to make lateral references of the kind I have described. Nevertheless, what distinguishes *EastEnders* from other British soaps is the *density* of these phenomena.

Compared with *Coronation Street* and *Brookside*, which usually have three main storylines running at any one time, *EastEnders*' average is closer to five or six. This profusion of narrative strands at times seems difficult for the serial to contain: any given story may take many months, or sometimes years, to reach fruition, occasionally moving into the foreground to take a central place in the narrative, and then withdrawing into the background to make space for other stories. Furthermore, where the other serials tend to develop these narrative strands quite separately, *EastEnders* interweaves its storylines to a far greater degree.

Thus, at any one time, any given character is likely to be involved in a number of different storylines – although the extent of their contribution will obviously vary. Each character is the focus of a tangled network of relationships. Den Watts, for example, has simultaneously been the father of Sharon, the husband of Angie, the lover of Jan, the best friend of Pete, the father of Michelle's baby Vicky, the business rival of Naima and the employer of Pauline, Ethel, Lofty (Michelle's husband), Wicksy (Pete's son) and Pat (Wicksy's mother). Developments in any one of these relationships are therefore bound to have implications for others, and the effects of major dramatic incidents will reverberate throughout the different levels of the narrative.

This interweaving of storylines is also made possible by the large number of different locations where characters can meet: the launderette, the cafe, the doctor's waiting room and, of course, the pub are 'social spaces', where different combinations of characters can be brought together, and connections forged between the narrative strands. The square itself serves a similar function: the fact that many of the houses look inward onto it makes it possible – and plausible – for characters to meet each other as they cross from one side to another, on their way from one location to the next. Compared with *Brookside*, which as Christine Geraghty has observed is significantly lacking in such 'common ground', *EastEnders* is positively overflowing with potential for the interweaving of narrative strands: yet despite the variety of locations, the fact that *EastEnders* rarely moves beyond the confines of Albert Square can make it appear almost claustrophobic.[11]

This sense of the interconnected nature of the characters' lives is reinforced by the camerawork and the use of background sound. In the square and the pub, there is often extensive use of mobile cameras, in the manner of *Hill Street Blues* and *St Elsewhere*: the camera will follow a character for a certain period, and then pick up and follow another in its travels, without editing between the two. Even in scenes which take place in more private interiors, such as the Fowlers' house or the upstairs rooms in the pub, the background soundtrack of traders' cries and music from the record stalls in Bridge Street market serves to remind us of the presence of the outside world. This soundtrack also fosters a sense of temporal continuity: it will often continue over from one scene to the next, even where there is a shift in location.

Other factors also contribute to this sensation of narrative density and pace. Again, as compared with other British soaps, *EastEnders* generally has a greater number of separate scenes, and features a greater number of characters, in any given episode. While characters, or indeed whole families, often disappear from *Brookside* or *Coronation Street*, sometimes for several weeks, this occurs far less frequently in *EastEnders*: where characters are not featured in an episode, their absence is nearly always referred to and explained, and it is comparatively rare for more than one or two characters to disappear in this way at any one time.

These points may be illustrated by considering a single episode in

Fig. 1

EASTENDERS EPISODE 67 (tx. 8 October 1985): Characters and locations

SCENES	1	2	3	4	5	6	7	8	9	10	11	12	13	14	15	16	17	18	19
LOCATION	A	B	C	D	B	E	F	DA	F	A	G	H	G	E	G	C	G	A	G
Pauline	x									x							x		x
Arthur	x									x								x	
Michelle	x				x					x			x					x	x
Martin	x							x		x								x	
Lou	x							x		x		x							
Nick		x	x			x	x										x		x
Ethel		x			x							x		x			x		x
Dr Legg		x			x														
Debs				x				x	x							x			
Angie				x							x		x		x		x		x
Wicksy				x		x	x	x			x							x	x
Kathy						x								x					x
Saeed							x												
Sue							x		x								x		x
Ali									x								x		x
Ian									x		x						x		x
Lofty		x									x					x	x		x
Kelvin											x					x			
Sharon											x		x		x		x		x
Den													x	x			x		x
Pete														x				x	x
Mary					x												x		x

Key to locations A = Fowlers' living room; B = Dr Legg's waiting room/surgery; C = Lofty's bedsit; D = outside Debs'/Fowlers' houses; E = Beales' fruit and veg stall; F = café; G = Queen Vic; H = launderette.

Fig. 2

EASTENDERS EPISODE 67 (tx. 8 October 1985): Storylines

SCENES	1	2	3	4	5	6	7	8	9	10	11	12	13	14	15	16	17	18	19
Michelle	X				X					X			X	x				X	
Nick/Ethel		X	X			X	x				x	X	X	X			X		
Wicksy				x		X	x	X	X	x	X	x		x			x	X	X
Debbie				X				x	X		X					X			
Darts							X					x				x	X		X
Saeed															X				
Angie															X				

Key X = major focus in this scene; x = minor focus.

more detail. Again, I have selected an episode which is in most respects typical, in that it does not contain any major dramatic incidents. This is episode 67 (tx. 8 October 1985): it contains nineteen separate scenes, and features a total of twenty-two characters. As fig. 1 indicates, the characters appear in a variety of combinations: some appear in as many as seven different scenes, although the average number of appearances per character is just below five. Three regular characters are absent, and in each case their absence is explained: in scene seven, for example, Saeed refers to his wife Naima, who left him several episodes previously, while in scene sixteen Debbie reports that she has had a telephone call from her boyfriend Andy, who is on holiday in Scotland. A total of eight different locations are used, although this does not include instances where the scene moves from the street outside into an interior (or vice-versa), nor does it allow for the fact that in certain locations more than one room is used (for example, Dr Legg's waiting room and surgery, or the bar and the back room in the pub).

As is normally the case, the episode uses a 'day in the life' structure, which is again similar to that used in *Hill Street Blues* and *St Elsewhere*. Thus, the episode starts early in the morning and ends in the evening with most of the characters gathered in the bar of the Queen Vic. The passing of time is registered by the opening hours of the pub, which opens for lunch approximately half way through the episode (scene 11), and by the frequent breaks for meals. This familiar structure serves to orient the viewer, and it is one which *EastEnders* has departed from only on rare occasions, sometimes following a major dramatic 'cliffhanger'.

Five major narrative strands are developed in this episode. As fig. 2 indicates, they recur in a number of different scenes, with some scenes featuring as many as three separate stories. Scene one introduces the first major story: Michelle's pregnancy. The initial hermeneutic question – will she decide to have the baby, or will she follow her parents' advice and have an abortion? – is carried over from previous episodes, and is re-stated in the first scene. The close-up of Michelle's troubled face in this scene, and the further close-ups in scene five – where she meets Mary in the doctor's waiting room, and listens to her complaints about the difficulties of being a single parent – serve to fuel speculation, although the issue is resolved in scene ten, when she reveals her decision to keep the baby. This question then gives way to others: will she be able to cope? Will her father support her? (Scenes 10, 18) Will she reveal the identity of the baby's father? (Scenes 10, 13, 14).

The second major story, introduced in scene two, concerns the villainous Nick Cotton and his relationship with Ethel Skinner. Again, a number of questions are raised as the episode progresses. What are Nick's motives in befriending Ethel? (Scenes 2, 3, 6) Has he stolen her keys, and if so what does he want them for? (Scenes 3, 17) Is it to steal prescriptions and thereby to obtain drugs, as he has done in the past, and as Dr Legg suspects (Scene 2), or does he have even more sinister motives?

A third story is initiated with the appearance of a young man in a sports car (scene 4), who is eventually revealed to be Pete Beale's son by his first marriage, Simon Wicks ('Wicksy'). Subsequent scenes (6, 7) show him searching for Pete Beale, who is (coincidentally!) away buying vegetables; the fact that the young man is not recognised by Pete's wife Kath adds a further dimension to our speculation about his identity. This is partially revealed in the following scene, where he meets Lou Beale, and refers to her as 'gran' – although a certain amount of uncertainty remains, since we have not previously been told of the existence of another grandson. Lou herself adds to this specula- tion by proceeding to tell the Fowlers (scene 10), Ethel (scene 12) and the patrons of the Queen Vic (scene 17) about a secret she is keeping; although it is not until scene 18 that Pete and Wicksy finally meet, and not until the last scene that his identity is finally confirmed for the viewer. Meanwhile, a number of hints are dropped about Angie's attraction to Wicksy, and a possible romance between them (scenes 4, 11 and 19), a development which would clearly have implications for Angie's ailing marriage. Wicksy's meeting with Kathy and Ian Beale (Pete's second wife and their son) in the final scene also encourages us to speculate about the effects of his reappearance on the Beale family.

The fourth major story is more straightforward comic, and con- cerns Debbie Wilkins' involvement with the knitting business ineptly run by Ian, Kelvin and Lofty. In Debbie's first encounter with Ian (scene 9) she touches his hand in a friendly way, a gesture which he misinterprets, and which leads him to become infatuated with her (scene 16). Sue Osman, observing this gesture, looks disapprovingly at her husband Ali, whom she suspects of fancying Debbie (a theme also briefly referenced in scene 19): this in turn connects with the ongoing speculation about the identity of Debbie's dirty phone caller, Ali being considered a likely suspect by Debbie herself.

The fifth and final story concerns the preparations for the trials of the ladies' darts team. These eventually take place at the end of the episode (scenes 17 and 19), although the climax is reserved for the meeting of Wicksy with Kathy and Ian Beale.

In addition to these major narrative strands, a number of minor stories are also interwoven into the episode – the forthcoming christen- ing of the Fowlers' baby (scene 1), Saeed's broken marriage (scene 7), Angie's planned visit to the marriage guidance council (scene 15), Mark Fowler's disappearance (scene 19), and so on.

The juxtaposition of these stories permits a constant shifting in tone, from knockabout comedy (Ethel doing the doctor's washing 'all the way from Islington', and accidentally dyeing it pink) to satire (Debbie's attempts to apply the language of cash-flow analysis to the knitting business, and Ian's doe-eyed looks in her direction) to intrigue (Lou's secretiveness about Wicksy's arrival) to intimate drama (Sharon and Angie discussing their family problems). It also enables a given theme to be treated in different ways, and encourages the viewer to compare the characters' situations. Thus, Michelle's position as a potential single parent is compared with that of Mary, whom she meets in the doctor's waiting room (scene 5), with Sharon, who urges her to retain her freedom (scene 13), and with her own parents, particularly in the penultimate scene, where Arthur is left to look after the babies while everybody else is at the pub. Over the longer term, a given theme may be approached in a variety of ways, and through a variety of storylines, across a number of episodes.

The density and complexity of *EastEnders*' narratives therefore serves a number of functions. On a basic level, it allows the viewer a certain freedom of choice, and enables the serial to appeal to a variety of audiences. Even if we find one story boring, or embarrassing to watch, we can be sure that it will not occupy the entire episode, and so we can tolerate or ignore it until we get to a story which interests us.

On another level, the constant interweaving of different storylines leaves the viewer to organise the action into a meaningful pattern. Given the extraordinary degree of fragmentation, the large number of characters and the constant shifts in location, it is surprising that the narrative does not seem incoherent. In several respects, the demands being made of the viewer are very great. Simply in order to make sense of what takes place, viewers have to assemble the different narrative strands out of the series of fragments they are shown. They must be able to recollect what has gone before, draw inferences about the characters' motivations and states of mind, and imagine events which have not been shown, in order to 'fill the gaps' between scenes. In addition, the narrative provides a series of cues which invite the viewer to 'move' in a number of directions at once: forwards, to predict future developments; backwards, to recall past events; and across, to connect and compare the storylines.

The extent of this activity depends upon the viewer's familiarity, both with the specific serial, and with serials in general. For a less experienced viewer, much of the narrative is likely to seem confusing, random, or simply meaningless. To watch a soap opera with which one is not familiar can be a profoundly alienating experience, simply because one is unlikely to recognise most of the cues which its narrative provides. The more time you invest, the easier it becomes to make sense of it, and the more meaningful it becomes. A significant part of the pleasure of watching soap opera derives from the fact that it allows one to develop a form of 'expertise', and therefore a feeling of 'mastery' – whence, perhaps, the popularity of the 'soap opera trivia quizzes', which feature regularly in newspapers and magazines. Soap operas flatter their regular viewers by inviting them to regard themselves as people who are 'in the know'. As I shall argue in the following section, this feeling of 'mastery' derives not merely from the gradual acquisition of knowledge, but also from the specific processes whereby information is revealed to the viewer.

II

The hermeneutic code

The term 'hermeneutic code' derives from the work of the French critic Roland Barthes, and in particular from his exhaustive analysis of Balzac's short story 'Sarrasine' in his book *S/Z*. The hermeneutic code is that element of narrative which is concerned with establishing (and eventually resolving) questions or enigmas. Barthes traces the development of the hermeneutic code in Balzac's story through a number of phases. The narrative begins by emphasising the subject which will be the focus of the enigma, and alerts the reader to the fact that an enigma exists. Once the enigma itself is formulated, the text then plays a complex game with the reader, holding out the promise of an answer, but also denying satisfaction. For example, the text may ensnare the reader by giving clues which lead in the wrong direction; it may suggest that the enigma cannot in fact be solved; or it may offer a partial answer and then refuse to provide further information – before it finally reveals the truth.[12]

It is by constantly deferring vital information in this way that the text lures the reader to continue reading. The hermeneutic code thus serves to invoke, and promises to gratify, the reader's desire to know. Yet there is a difficult balance to be maintained: if information is revealed too slowly, the reader may become frustrated, yet if it is revealed too quickly, the text will simply come to an end. The reader is suspended between two poles: on the one hand, wanting to discover information, and thereby resolve uncertainties, yet on the other, wanting the narrative itself to continue. At the same time, it is not simply that narratives manipulate readers: readers know that they are being manipulated, and in this sense their pleasure is highly self-conscious.

This process is clearly an important feature of all narratives, yet it is especially vital to soap opera. While the regular scheduling of soap operas may lead them to become part of the viewers' domestic routines – and thus, perhaps, 'habit forming' – the narratives themselves must offer strong inducements to viewers to tune in regularly. The viewers' 'desire to know' must be sufficiently powerful to sustain them across the substantial gaps between episodes: Thursday's episode must hold out enough promises if next Tuesday's is to be worth waiting for.

61

Cliffhangers and snares

One straightforward way in which this is achieved is of course through the use of *'cliffhanger' endings*, which interrupt the narrative at moments of high drama, leaving crucial enigmas unresolved. *EastEnders* has tended to use cliffhangers in this way particularly in its Thursday episodes, thus leaving a longer period between episodes for speculation. The arrival of Den's lover Jan at the Queen Vic, Angie Watts' suicide attempt, and Michelle and Lofty's abortive wedding all engendered major cliffhangers, complete with lingering close-ups. In each case, the subsequent episode resumed on the following Tuesday almost immediately where the narrative had been interrupted (or shortly afterwards), thereby disrupting *EastEnders'* normal 'day in the life' structure, and enabling viewers to see the immediate aftermath of the incident.

The storyline which featured a series of attacks on women in the early months of 1987 also relied on this cliffhanger approach. A number of episodes concluded with hand-held shots of potential or actual victims – Hannah Carpenter, Sharon Watts, Sue Osman and Pat Wicks – fleeing from an unseen attacker. In each instance, viewers were left to speculate about whether they would be caught, although it was only in the case of Pat Wicks that the attack was actually perpetrated. This storyline, like that concerning the rape of Sheila Grant in *Brookside* in the summer 1986, provoked widespread criticism: it was felt that the repeated (and commonplace) use of violence against women as a narrative 'tease' was tasteless and misogynistic – although the subsequent development of both storylines may possibly have defused some of the criticisms.

In this instance, the narrative also deferred information by laying a series of *snares* designed to encourage viewers to speculate about the identity of the attacker, and (at least potentially) to throw them off the scent. In the episode following the attack on Pat Wicks, for example, there was evidence to point to no fewer than five of the regular characters; and although Pete Beale eventually emerged as the prime suspect, he too was eventually found to be innocent.

This device was also used in the story of Debbie Wilkins' dirty phone caller in late 1985: a number of hints in the narrative pointed towards Ali Osman as the likely culprit, most notably some deliberately deceptive editing which cut from a shot of him lifting a receiver and dialling to a shot of her responding to an offensive call. Yet the climax of the story, when it eventually came, revealed that it was Saeed, the other major suspect, who was in fact to blame. The episode which revealed the identity of the father of Michelle Fowler's baby was also particularly devious in this respect. A series of shots of Michelle telephoning the father to arrange a meeting were intercut with shots of Ali Osman, Andy O'Brien, Tony Carpenter and Den Watts all speaking on the telephone. In the following sequence, each suspect in turn departed, ostensibly for quite innocent reasons; and it was only in a subsequent scene, after a good deal of waiting around on the part of Michelle (and the viewer!), that the guilty party was revealed.

What is particularly notable about these devices – the cliffhanger, and the laying of narrative snares – is that both are highly contrived and, I would argue, are perceived as such by the viewer. The pleasure they afford is based on a degree of distance from the narrative: we are aware that the text is encouraging us to play a game with the characters and their destinies, and inviting us to test out a series of alternative possibilities, and that it may even be breaking a few rules in order to do so. Thus, for example, experienced viewers will have been aware that the chances of Angie Watts being killed off in her suicide attempt were extremely slight, given that she was such a central character: the main enigma here was not so much whether Angie would survive, as the effect her behaviour would have on Den. Likewise, the editing which was designed to lead us astray in the episode about Michelle's baby was, in terms of the conventions of realist drama, fairly unusual: it clearly depended upon the viewer recognising that a game was being played, and being willing to join in with it.

Keeping secrets

Although *EastEnders* has used these devices as a means of denying information to the viewer – and probably to a far greater extent than other British soaps – it has done so comparatively rarely. While episodes normally build to a climax, it is often in these moments that information is *revealed*, rather than withheld. Viewers are left to speculate, not so much about hidden information, but about what will happen when the other characters discover what viewers themselves already know.

In this sense, the hermeneutic code functions in soap opera in ways which are rather different from other genres. Unlike a typical detective story, for example, which is based on a single character's attempts to trace the solution to a single hermeneutic enigma, soap operas have multiple (and often interconnected) enigmas which emerge and develop at different rates. Perhaps most crucially, soap operas do not possess a central character from whose point of view we can watch the narrative unfold, and with whom we learn new information. While information is occasionally withheld, as in the cliffhanger, it is rarely withheld for long. In fact, it is relatively uncharacteristic of the serial to deny the viewer vital information: on the contrary, the viewer is often given privileged access to information which is denied to the characters themselves.

As a result, the narratives of soap operas tend to place the viewer, not in a position of relative ignorance – as in most detective stories –

but in a position of knowledge. We are enabled to look down upon the characters and speculate about their potential reactions to information which we already possess. The pleasure of 'gossip' about soap opera is essentially the pleasure of sharing secrets to which only 'a select few' are privy.

hence
gossip

Perhaps the most remarkable example of this phenomenon in *East-Enders* was the way in which the serial consistently concealed the identity of the father of Michelle Fowler's baby from the other characters. From October 1985 through to Christmas 1986, this was a secret which was shared between the viewer and the two characters involved. Despite his feelings of guilt and responsibility, Den was obviously concerned to avoid the secret being revealed, and the public disapproval which would be likely to follow. Michelle's loyalty to Den meant that she too was unlikely to reveal his identity, despite the considerable pressures upon her to do so, and despite her resentment against him.

Thus neither character was fully able to express their feelings about the matter, except to each other – although the fear that other characters would guess their secret meant that they had to stay apart as far as possible. Although Michelle was able to discuss her feelings with her mother, her grandmother and her friend Sharon (Den's adopted daughter), she could only do so obliquely and in fairly general terms. Den himself had fewer outlets – he did discuss the issue briefly with Jan – and could only attempt to assuage his guilt by buying Michelle presents, which she tended to refuse. In this context, viewers were mostly left to infer the characters' emotions from a very restricted range of signals: occasional nods of recognition, significant glances and tortured close-ups.

The fact that viewers themselves knew the truth, while the other characters did not, was exploited in a variety of ways: as a means of creating suspense, as a source of irony, and as a means of explaining behaviour which appeared 'illogical' to the other characters. Michelle's anger at Den's absence from the christening (described above), or her blunt and apparently unreasonable refusal of his offers to pay for her wedding dress and her honeymoon might have led one to speculate about whether her emotions would 'give her away', and lead the other characters to guess the true nature of their relationship. Den, on the other hand, was more the butt of humour – as when he was almost run over by the van taking Michelle to hospital to give birth, or when Lofty's enthusiasm about the birth reduced him to tight-lipped irritation.

At the same time, our knowledge of the guilty secret served to set the other characters' ideas in perspective. Arthur's suspicion of Lofty, for example, appeared faintly absurd, while Sharon's suggestion that Michelle should give birth in the Queen Vic as an alternative to the hospital was highly ironical.

The moment at the climax of the Christmas Day episode in 1986 when Pauline Fowler saw Michelle accepting money from Den and at last appeared to realise the truth was quite startling, not least because it came so unexpectedly. Yet while it marked the end of one phase of the secret drama of Den and Michelle, it also began another: the fact that Pauline knew Den's secret while Den himself did not know that she knew gave her a unique power. Rather than simply spreading the information around, Pauline was now able to make hints about her knowledge as a means of exerting power over Den, although he himself was unwilling to confront her for fear of confirming her suspicions. Here again, Pauline's knowledge was not immediately exploited in the narrative, but could be kept in reserve for future storylines.

As this example illustrates, knowledge in the serial is a significant form of power. Yet the viewer's position here is somewhat paradoxical. We are powerful in the sense that we are generally far more knowledgeable than the characters: not only do we know their secrets, but we also know who else knows them, even though this may not be apparent to the characters who have secrets to hide. Thus, we typically see characters discovering secrets by chance – through accidental observations, as in Pauline's case or, more frequently, through overhearing conversations – and subsequently using this knowledge against the characters concerned. For example, when Angie got drunk on the journey back from her disastrous 'second honeymoon' in Venice and told the barman her guilty secret – that she had lied to Den in telling him that she had only six months to live – we saw that Den had overheard her, although Angie herself did not. This knowledge in turn led Den to take his revenge, by preparing to serve divorce papers on Angie, while leading her to believe that he was planning a surprise treat for Christmas.

Yet although viewers generally possess a considerable amount of knowledge, there remains very little that they can do with it, since they are obviously powerless to influence the development of the narrative itself. This may give rise to a variety of responses. By allowing the viewer to share secrets, the text may invite us into a complicity with the characters concerned, yet it may also distance us from those who remain ignorant – enabling us to feel superior to them, or to take pity on them, or to become frustrated by their inability to realise the truth.

The disparities between the knowledge possessed by different characters, and between the characters and the viewer, often generates irony. Thus, in one episode when Dr Legg (the local GP) made a passing observation to Den Watts about people who get involved in crime which is 'out of their league', he did not know about Den's anxiety over a deal he had recently made involving stolen fur coats. Here, it was the disparity between Den's knowledge and Dr Legg's which was the source of the irony. At other times, the viewer is privy to information which neither of the characters knows. Thus, in a conversation in the bar of the Queen Vic between Tony Carpenter and Andy O'Brien, both characters referred to their past involvements with a married woman: what the viewer knew, and what neither character was aware of, was that the woman in question was in fact the same woman, namely Angie Watts, whom we saw looking over at the two men from her place at the bar. A rather different use of this device is where characters appear to be talking about other people, while in fact they are also implicitly talking about themselves. When Angie discussed Dot Cotton's shoplifting with Dr Legg, and interpreted it as a 'cry for help' on the part of a woman who had been 'badly hurt', she was also indirectly referring to her own 'cry for help' in that she had recently told Den that she had contracted an incurable illness. Dr Legg of course did not know this – and would soon have been able to disprove it if he had – although the viewer did, and was able to interpret Angie's comments as a veiled explanation of her own behaviour.

Perhaps paradoxically, the fact that secrets tend to be known to the viewer can also help to increase suspense. The tension is focused, not on the question of the secrets themselves, but on the potential implications of them being revealed. A fairly dramatic example of this was the storyline which preceded Arthur Fowler's mental breakdown. In order to pay for his daughter Michelle's wedding reception, Arthur withdrew the Christmas Club money which he had been saving on behalf of his friends and neighbours, and subsequently faked a burglary in his own house in order to make it appear that the money had been stolen. Although we were not shown the fake burglary itself, our suspicions were aroused by Pauline Fowler's reactions to it; she eventually confronted Arthur, and forced him to confess to her. In the following episode, the tension mounted to fever pitch as Arthur was taken into the police station. Significantly, Pauline was unable to get in touch with Arthur; he was left in a room with a police constable who failed to respond to his conversational overtures, with occasional visits from the investigating officer who pointed out a number of discrepancies in his statement. Arthur was therefore left to think his way out of the situation in silence, and without support – except, that is, from the viewers, who shared his secret, and could be presumed to understand and sympathise with his motivations. In this sense, the mounting pressure on Arthur to reveal his secret was also placing a similar burden on the viewer, with whom the secret was shared.

It is notable that the device is used more frequently with certain characters than others, and particularly in relationships which are based on deception. In the case of Nick Cotton, for example, we have often been shown the details of his criminal behaviour – for example when he stole Kathy Beale's medical records, or removed cheques from his mother's cheque book – before it is made known to the characters whom it is likely to affect. His mother Dot has repeatedly been a victim of deception, both on the part of Nick and her husband Charlie, and although it is always made clear to the viewer what is going on, she refuses to believe it even when she is given clear evidence. By distancing us from Dot, the narrative invites us to regard her as hopelessly gullible, and therefore to take pity on her.

In the case of Angie and Den Watts, we have again typically been placed in a position of knowledge rather than ignorance – we have seen the actions of the deceiving husband, and have thereby been distanced from the delusions of the deceived wife. Thus, when Angie discovered a set of golf clubs hidden in a cupboard and assumed they were a present for her, the viewer knew full well that they were in fact intended for Den's lover Jan. Likewise, viewers were aware for many weeks beforehand that Den would serve divorce papers on Angie on Christmas Day 1986, and although Angie herself had some suspicions about his plans, she was clearly anticipating a more pleasant surprise. As with Dot Cotton, the fact that we knew more than Angie tended to distance us from her, and thus allowed us to take pity on her. Yet the fact that we were shown Den's behaviour does not necessarily mean that we were being invited to adopt his point of view: if anything, seeing the contrast between the lies he told Angie and what he was in fact doing may well have made for a more negative estimation of him than if we had learnt about his behaviour indirectly, or at a later date. Here again, the fact that the viewer is privy to information which is hidden from the characters who would be most immediately affected by it may well result in a considerable degree of frustration, which can only partially be relieved by shouting at the television screen.

Inviting speculation

Much of the pleasurable tension which derives from 'keeping secrets' in this way is implicitly based on speculation about what would happen if the secrets were to be revealed. Sometimes, this speculation amounts to a kind of foreboding: in the instances described above, we know that Angie, Dot and Arthur are doomed to suffer. At other times, our knowledge leads us to expect violent confrontations – 'just wait until Pete finds out that Nick has been blackmailing Kathy!' Other, less urgent, speculations are invited by more ironical instances – 'if only Dr Legg knew about Den's connections with the Mob!'

Of course, the narrative also invites speculation by withholding information – for example, about the name of Pauline and Arthur's baby, or the identity of Debbie Wilkins' dirty phone caller – although in order to do so, it must also, as Barthes points out, signal to the viewer that an enigma exists, and provide a certain amount of information about it.

However, many significant developments in the narrative are less easy to predict, since they are not essentially based on enigmas; and in such cases, enigmas are often constructed around them, in order to encourage the viewer to speculate. Angie Watts' suicide attempt, for example, which took place in February 1986, was prefigured for many months beforehand by a series of seemingly off-the-cuff and even humorous remarks about death and suicide. In the episodes immediately preceding it, Angie was shown borrowing pills from a number of other characters, and buying aspirin from the shop. Meanwhile, Den's contempt for her had become even more vicious, and when Angie promised to prove to him that he needed her, Den responded by suggesting that he might help her throw herself off a tower block. Indeed, the beginning of the episode preceding the suicide attempt itself began with Angie's daughter Sharon banging on her bedroom door in an attempt to wake her – a clear premonition of what was to follow, since we had already seen Angie knocking back the pills and gin at the end of the previous episode.

Major dramatic incidents of this nature are often preceded by a trail of information which serves to prepare the viewer, although in certain instances the signs may lead in the wrong direction. The return of Nick Cotton in April 1986 was preceded by a number of scenes in which Ethel Skinner read Dot Cotton's palm and predicted that a 'tall dark man' would come into her life. Dot herself was convinced that the man in question was her husband Charlie, and she at least was surprised to bump into the leering figure of Nick as she left the Queen Vic one night.

Viewers may also be prepared for unpredictable events by quite fleeting clues – both in the characters' behaviour, and in the narration itself (for example, by means of close-ups or editing). In the episode which preceded Lofty's proposal to Michelle, for example, there was a scene in the launderette in which the characters discussed Michelle's future prospects. Dot Cotton's comment 'No man's gonna want a woman with a baby' was followed by a brief but 'significant' close-up of Lofty. Throughout this and the following episode, Lofty was involved in a series of conversations with other characters, in which he talked in fairly general terms about his attitudes towards relationships, occasionally making reference to Michelle, although without revealing his intentions. In this way, the viewer was invited to speculate about Lofty's feelings, and the ground was prepared for his proposal.

More sudden and less predictable events may also be prefigured in similar ways. Thus, the episode in which Debbie Wilkins was mugged at the very end of 1985 began with Sergeant Quick issuing a series of warnings about the rising crime rate in the area. As we saw Debbie preparing to leave her house, we were shown a (seemingly irrelevant) close-up of the diamond engagement ring which she had recently been given by her boyfriend Andy – this being the ring which was of course stolen when she was mugged minutes later.

The principle of 'pride coming before a fall' which was apparent in this instance – the theft of the engagement ring marked the beginning of a period of uncertainty in Debbie's relationship, and her involvement with Sergeant Quick – has also been a repeated feature of the narrative. Arthur Fowler's loss of his job in April 1986 was preceded by him unwisely buying a new living room carpet, and a ring for Pauline, having failed to heed his mother-in-law's warning that 'famine follows feast'. The bad news was brought by Dot Cotton, interrupting Arthur and Pauline as they danced a waltz on their new carpet.

The narrative thus often provides information which is designed to encourage the viewer to predict future events. As with other such devices, this is a process which viewers expect and understand. Far from being lulled into regarding the text as a 'window on the world', viewers are aware that it is a fictional artefact which tends to work in certain ways and to obey certain rules. The text invites the viewer to play a game with the characters' lives and destinies: and viewers know that it is, in the end, just a game.

At the same time, the text has to avoid becoming too predictable, since viewers also expect the unexpected. Although regular viewers are likely to become more adept at spotting the clues, it is vital that the text does not give away too much information, and thereby lose its capacity to surprise. It is for this reason that, on occasion, the text reserves the right to bend or even break the rules.

The way in which Michelle Fowler left her husband-to-be Lofty standing at the altar was certainly a significant example of this. Although the viewer was clearly made aware of Michelle's doubts about Lofty, and her lingering affections for Den, these had appeared to fade into the background as the preparations for the wedding gathered momentum. Despite her family's initial uncertainty about the wedding (and, in the case of Arthur, outright opposition to it), there was a growing consensus among the more trusted characters that marriage to Lofty was a sensible and viable proposition. Michelle's doubts only resurfaced in the episode of the wedding itself, and her decision was not made any easier by a last-minute meeting with Den, who had returned from the church and crept into her bedroom unobserved.

The episode thus concluded on a classic cliffhanger, with a close-up of Michelle hesitating just as she was about to enter the church. Yet despite the resurgence of Michelle's doubts, and the cliffhanger itself, my own prediction at this point was that the marriage would go ahead nevertheless, and that the doubts were simply being re-stated in order to lead viewers astray. This prediction was informed by a number of different kinds of data. On the one hand, my understanding of the development of Michelle's character led me to feel that she would, in time, come to assume the 'tentpole' position occupied by her mother Pauline, and that she could scarcely do this as a single parent. I also reasoned that the presence of another single parent in the serial – in addition to its existing one, Mary Smith – was unlikely, since it would be difficult to avoid repetition of stories. A newly-married couple, on the other hand, would make a whole new set of stories possible. I had also seen the *Radio Times* feature article on the wedding, which included a full-page colour picture of Michelle in her wedding dress. Finally, I was particularly concerned about the likely impact of Michelle calling off the wedding on Lofty and Arthur, both of whom I regarded as essentially good but vulnerable characters, whom it would be callous to hurt.

My predictions in this instance proved incorrect – although I felt partly vindicated when Michelle and Lofty were subsequently married in a private registry office wedding. In a sense, the serial was able to have its cake and eat it, and it had to bend the rules slightly in order to do so – particularly through its use of the *Radio Times* feature. While it clearly cannot afford to do so frequently, the ability to generate surprise and even shock in this way is crucial if the narrative is to retain its hold over the viewer.

Secrets from beyond the text

One further aspect of this phenomenon, which will be discussed in greater detail in the following chapter, is the role of information which derives from sources beyond the text itself. My incorrect predictions about Michelle and Lofty's wedding, for example, were partly informed by my reading of the *Radio Times* – not that the *Radio Times* directly confirmed that the wedding would take place, although of course if it had *not* featured an article about it, I would certainly have reached a different conclusion!

Predictions of future events in *EastEnders* have featured regularly in the popular press, and although not all viewers will read them at first hand, many more will hear about them from those who do. Thus, the news that Ross Davidson (Andy O'Brien) would be written out of the programme in the summer of 1986 led to considerable speculation about the likely cause of his departure. The fact that his relationship with Debbie Wilkins appeared to be developing particularly well at the time, after several months of uncertainty, meant that his departure was likely to be involuntary, and perhaps quite sudden. Viewers familiar with the principle that 'pride comes before a fall' might well have noted the tell-tale signs of complacent happiness which accompanied the couple's announcement of their engagement. Nevertheless, the only direct clue in the text itself came when Andy and Debbie had a brief argument, which concluded with her telling him to 'drop dead' – which he of course did in a road accident shortly afterwards.

In other instances, the text appears to presume that readers possess such knowledge, and plays with the fact, often for ironic purposes. The arrival of Colin Russell followed a series of front-page predictions that *EastEnders* was about to feature a gay character. For some months, the programme itself gave no indications that Colin was gay, although for viewers who assumed that he was, there were some rich ironies. Thus, Tony Carpenter approved of Colin, and wanted to sell him his flat: he had a 'man to man' feeling about him – 'You can tell when someone is straight'. Meanwhile, Colin was judged fanciable by a number of the female characters, and assumptions were made about his 'girlfriend'. To the knowledgeable viewer, Colin was clearly attempting to pretend that he was not gay, although the fact that he was not making a particularly good job of it seemed lost on the majority of the other characters.

Finally, false predictions may serve to introduce suspense where the text itself gives little indication of any potential dramatic incidents: the widespread rumour that Michelle Fowler would lose her baby, for example, could well have made her excursions on her motorbike appear more dangerous to many viewers than they were intended to do. Yet the fact that several such predictions have proven inaccurate means that viewers are likely to treat them with a degree of scepticism, as potential 'snares' which might lead them in the wrong direction.

Moving across the text

In various ways, then, the hermeneutic code draws the viewer onward through the text. While it may occasionally invite viewers to look back, for example to assemble clues or to draw upon past knowledge of the characters, it primarily seeks to encourage them to look forward, to predict and speculate about future events. At the same time, the development of multiple narrative strands which is characteristic of soap opera also enables viewers to move *laterally* across the text, in order to compare and contrast different characters and storylines.

Perhaps the most straightforward aspect of this phenomenon is the way in which the viewer is invited to draw analogies between the various characters and their situations. Any given character will come into contact with other characters whose circumstances are in certain ways similar to their own, although in other respects they may well be different. In some cases, the comparisons are implicit, although in others they are made directly by the characters themselves.

Michelle, for example, is the same age as Sharon, although their family backgrounds are rather different. Events in Michelle's life have meant that she has had to assume an adult role at an earlier age than Sharon, although she has also had to surrender some of the freedoms which her friend still enjoys. On the other hand, if we compare Michelle's situation with Mary Smith's, as Michelle herself has done on many occasions, she has in several respects been more fortunate. During her pregnancy, when she was facing the possibility of becoming a single parent, this comparison acted as a powerful disincentive, although it was one which she chose to ignore. At the same time, both characters have suffered as a result of their romantic involvements with married men, although Mary's response was significantly more vindictive than Michelle's. After the birth of her baby Vicky, and her marriage to Lofty, Michelle found herself in a similar position to her mother Pauline, who had given birth to a child only a few months previously. Yet Michelle appeared more determined to call the tune in her marriage, and to ensure that she maintained a degree of independence within it. Our concept of Michelle as a character, and our judgment of her, are thus informed by a series of comparisons with other characters who are similar to her but who have had different experiences, or who have been in similar situations, but have responded differently. Thus, we might conclude that Michelle is more sensible and mature than Sharon, for example, and a good deal more fortunate than Mary.

The potential which the serial offers for such comparisons is vast, and changes constantly as the characters' situations change. The decline and eventual collapse of Den and Angie's marriage, for example, was consistently contrasted with a number of other marriages in the serial, both those which appeared to be stable (Pauline and Arthur, Pete and Kath) and those which were similarly ailing (Tony and Hannah, Dot and Charlie). Pete and Kath in particular served as a norm of the happy marriage which many of the characters contrasted with that of Den and Angie. Meanwhile, comparisons were also drawn on gender lines, between Den's friendship with Pete and Angie's friendship with Kath: according to Kath, the men regarded friendship as a matter of covering up for each other – for example in the case of Den's extra-marital relationship – rather than being honest, as when Kath refused to collude in Angie's affair with Andy.

By encouraging viewers to look for similarities and differences between characters, such comparisons also invite us to move beyond the level of the individual, and to interpret and to judge the characters' behaviour in terms of broader moral and ideological discourses. The comparisons between Den and Angie's marriage and Pete and Kath's are implicitly *normative* – they invoke assumptions about what a 'good' marriage should be, and the kinds of behaviour which should be acceptable within it, which ultimately derive from a relatively traditional morality. The comparison between the two friendships also implicitly refers to assumptions about the differences between 'typical' male and female behaviour, which are clearly weighted towards a female perspective.

Of course, viewers will perceive these comparisons in different ways, and may bring different discourses to bear on the text – which in this instance might lead them to reject the 'norm' represented by Pete and Kath, or to delight in the men's guilty cameraderie. Nevertheless, in doing so they will have to reject the alternative perspectives offered by the text – and as a result, they are likely to be aware of the conscious ideological choice which informs their own judgment.

As these examples suggest, the criteria for such comparisons are extremely diverse. Most characters possess qualities, or have had experiences, which can form the basis of comparison with others, so that even the most unlikely characters can be brought together. Thus, Dot Cotton and Colin Russell have discussed the tragedies which have blighted their lives, although in other respects they have very little in common.

Such comparisons can also form the basis of new allegiances or rivalries. The first indications of Sharon and Wicksy's romance, for example, which developed early in 1987, were contained in a conversation they had about their shared experience as children going through their parents' divorce. On the other hand, Sue Osman's loss of her child in a cot death and her subsequent inability to have children led her to become extremely jealous of Mary Smith, whom she felt was an inadequate mother: her eagerness to look after Mary's child was regarded with suspicion by Mary herself, and provoked a series of bitter conflicts.

Finally, the comparisons between different characters can also generate irony. For example, Michelle's depression at the prospect of single parenthood was contrasted in one episode with Sharon's attempts to identify the characteristics of her 'ideal man' using a book entitled 'How to Achieve Meaningful Relationships'. In a subsequent scene, Michelle sat alone in the cafe as Cassie Carpenter read Mary's daughter Annie a story about a handsome prince and a princess. In both scenes, the reality of Michelle's dilemma and the limitations on her future were set against the superficial fantasies associated with childhood. A similar contrast took place in a later episode, where an argument between Kelvin and his girlfriend Tessa was intercut with shots of Sue Osman receiving the results of a pregnancy test, and learning that she was not in fact going to have the child she had desperately been trying to conceive for many months. In both cases, 'real' problems were seen in stark relief, against a background of trivial or imagined ones.

In addition to inviting viewers to compare and contrast the characters and their situations, the interweaving of a number of different storylines enables the serial to vary its mood and tone. On a basic level, this helps to prevent it becoming boring, yet it also suggests that the narrative demands an extraordinary flexibility of response on the part of its viewers. Different storylines call on different expectations, and encourage different types of response – different degrees of involvement with the characters, different criteria for judging plausibility, and different levels of seriousness.

EastEnders certainly tends for the most part to adopt the 'transparent' naturalist style characteristic of British soap operas. The lighting is usually flat, without harsh shadows; the camerawork is generally static and unobtrusive, with close-ups and tracking shots used only rarely; the editing follows the rules of standard continuity editing; and there is no extra-diegetic music, apart from the opening and closing theme. There is a density of naturalistic detail in the background sound and in the design of sets and costumes, and a distinct lack of opulence. Above all, much of the action is resolutely mundane: the characters do their laundry, go shopping, cook and eat their meals, go to the lavatory, take their dogs for walks and make endless cups of tea.

Nevertheless, *EastEnders* often moves beyond this naturalistic mode, in the direction both of comedy and of melodrama. In the case of the former, there have been many storylines, and occasionally whole episodes, overflowing with witty one-liners, running jokes and slapstick comedy which would not have been out of place in a sitcom. A few episodes have verged on high farce – as in the one which featured Den and Angie's increasingly desperate attempts to avoid the brewery discovering their irregular use of cheap booze.

Certain characters tend to be presented more consistently as objects of comic ridicule, and in particular the older female characters – a fact which certain critics have found offensive: Ethel's malapropisms, Dot's hypochondria and occasionally even the eccentricities of the matriarchal Lou Beale have regularly been used as sources of light relief. All three have featured in more serious storylines, but on occasions when they have worked together, the dialogue and performances have sometimes seemed closer to music hall than naturalistic drama.

Other characters have functioned more consistently as the initiators of comic repartee – when Den Watts is 'on form', the manic sarcasm which he directs at his customers and employees resembles the routine of a vicious stand-up comedian. As with other characters who occasionally function in this comic mode, such as Ethel, Dot or Lofty, there is a self-consciously stylised quality about the performance – a quality which also distinguished certain characters in *Coronation Street*, such as Ena Sharples and Hilda Ogden.

The comparison with *Coronation Street* is particularly relevant here. As Marion Jordan observes, the *Street*'s use of caricature and comic dialogue marks a departure from its predominantly naturalistic approach: by combining elements from genres which depend upon the open and self-conscious display of artifice and convention, the serial reminds viewers of the unreality of the fiction.[13]

A similar argument has often been used in relation to melodrama, and in particular to the films of Douglas Sirk. Jane Feuer applies this

74

approach to US prime-time soap operas: she argues that they possess a kind of melodramatic 'excess' – for example in the exaggerated styles of acting, the over-emphatic camerawork, and the opulence of the *mise en scène* – which serves to distance the viewer, and prevent any naive belief in the 'reality' of the fictional world.[14]

Although *EastEnders* clearly aspires to naturalism in a way that *Dallas* and *Dynasty* do not, it has on occasion ventured into the territory of melodrama, and at times with a degree of relish which is similar to the 'excess' which Feuer identifies. Angie Watts' suicide attempt, and the expulsion of Nick Cotton in November 1985 both exemplified this – although in the latter case, the visual style perhaps owed more to *The Godfather* than to Douglas Sirk. *EastEnders*' use of emphatic final close-ups often recalls those of its US counterparts; and the fact that episodes usually reach a climax at night means that the most dramatic sequences are often shot in semi-darkness, or in more lurid artificial light.

Certain characters are more clearly melodramatic 'types' than others. Nick Cotton's leering eyes and curling lip, not to mention his swaggering walk and his compulsory leather jacket, combine to make him closer to a stage villain than a mere juvenile delinquent. Angie Watts' artificial smile, heavy make-up and flashy clothes mark her out as the tragic clown, although the vicious snarl which she occasionally throws at Den makes it clear that she is capable of giving as good as she gets. Den himself, in his dark lounge-lizard suits and loose thin ties, has the air of the urbane 'rotter', the man women love to hate.

These movements – between naturalism and comedy, between naturalism and melodrama, and in particular between comedy and melodrama – inevitably disrupt the viewers' attempts to settle into a secure position from which to read the text. Naturalist elements can undercut high melodrama, and thereby defuse some of the tension which it generates. A clear example of this was the episode in which Angie played her last, desperate card – responding to Den's announcement that he was finally going to leave her, she told him that she had contracted an incurable illness and had only six months to live. In what was certainly unprecedented in British soap opera, the entire episode was given over to these two characters. Yet the melodramatic revelations, the tears and the shouting, were consistently interrupted by the intrusion of a window cleaner who appeared (by chance) to be following the characters as they moved from room to room.

In other instances, the intrusion of mundane images into the dialogue restrains the movement towards melodrama: in the scene in which we discovered Den's responsibility for Michelle's pregnancy, she described her emotions, in a characteristic *EastEnders* line, as being 'like a bunged-up sink'. A similar movement 'back to reality' took place on the morning after Jan's first visit to the Queen Vic – a night which had been the occasion of a good deal of melodramatic excess. As Jan left, we saw Ali Osman removing his rubbish, and the mundane daily life of the Square resuming, almost as if the stage were being cleared for the next act. Sharon reassured a hesitant Lofty that life would go on as normal, while Ethel commented, 'It's like *Dynasty*, isn't it?'

Other such movements have been rather more uncomfortable, however. Occasionally, this has been because relatively minor characters (and less than adequate actors) have had to bear the weight of a major melodramatic role and to work 'against the grain' of the rest of the narrative. The episode which intercut the (rather ineptly staged) Walford Carnival with the flight of Hannah Carpenter from her violent boyfriend Neville, and the episode which showed Debbie Wilkins attempting to come to terms with the sudden death of her fiance Andy, both contained a deliberate, but nevertheless uneasy mixture of melodrama and comic absurdity. *EastEnders'* big production of 1986, which took Den and Angie on a doomed second honeymoon to Venice, faced similar difficulties. Transposed from the tawdry and claustrophobic confines of the Queen Vic to the grand expanse of St Mark's Square, and endowed with rather pretentiously 'arty' metaphors about masks and deception, Den and Angie's relationship appeared almost trivial.

In employing elements of comedy and melodrama in this way, *East-Enders* draws upon viewers' knowledge of a wide range of other genres, which in different ways are less concerned to conceal their own artifice than the naturalistic style of television drama in which the serial is predominantly based. This shifting between genres disrupts the illusion of naturalism – the belief that we are looking through a 'window on the world' – and increases the distance between the viewer and the text. Indeed, this distance may sometimes be so great as to enable viewers to perceive the performances as self-parody or 'camp'. As I have suggested, the operations of the hermeneutic code may have a similar effect: viewers know that they are being manipulated, or at least invited to participate in a 'guessing game' which has its own artificial rules and conventions. In both respects, *EastEnders* constantly draws attention to the fact that it is, precisely, a *fiction*.

Character

The building of characters is a process which requires a considerable degree of activity on the part of the viewer. Characters are not fixed properties 'contained' within the text: rather, they too are the products of an interaction between the text and the viewer. Viewers actively assemble networks of character-traits from a variety of indicators which are dispersed throughout the text, progressively building a stable and coherent concept of the character's unique 'personality'.[15] These indicators or 'cues' may be implicit in the character's appearance or behaviour, or explicit in the judgments they make about themselves, or those which other characters make of them. In assembling these cues, the viewer moves along the protensive/retensive axis – recalling past events, piecing together disparate items of information, drawing inferences, generating hypotheses, and adapting these in the light of new developments. In addition, the viewer moves laterally between the different storylines, comparing characters in similar circumstances, and identifying their differences and similarities.

In order to encourage viewers to participate in this process of character building, the text has to leave 'gaps' or indeterminacies which the viewer is invited to fill.[16] The indicators provided may in themselves be inconsistent, and viewers have to compare and evaluate them in order to select those they are prepared to trust. In doing so, the viewer attempts to guess what is going on in the characters' minds, and thereby infers a degree of psychological consistency which will explain their behaviour. Thus, viewers are often enabled to make distinctions between a character's outward appearance – that is, how they present themselves to other characters – and the underlying essence which constitutes their 'real feelings': here again, the viewer is placed in a position of knowledge, observing all the different facets of a character as they are presented in a variety of interactions, rather then being confined to observing them in a single relationship, or through the eyes of one character alone.

In many situations, however, the characters are unable to articulate their 'real feelings' – either because the consequences of doing so would be potentially disastrous, or because the characters themselves are confused or uncertain. In the case of Den and Michelle, for example, they were rarely able to express their feelings to each other for fear that others would see them together and guess their guilty secret. Nevertheless, the judgments of other characters often alerted us to their real state of mind. Jan, for example, divined that the real reason for Den's depression was more to do with Michelle's child than with Angie; and Lou suggested to Michelle that the real reason for her doubts about Lofty was that she was still in love with the father of her child. In the case of Debbie Wilkins, her romantic prevarifications between Andy O'Brien and Roy Quick derived from her own state of confusion, although the reasons for this were never fully clear: Roy Quick's charge that she was simply using him to make Andy jealous was perhaps not entirely fair, although the fact that her inconsistent behaviour was left unexplained can scarcely have added to the viewer's sympathy for her.

Over time, as these indicators accumulate, they begin to cohere into relatively stable constructs, which in turn serve to introduce a degree of order to the fragmented and constantly changing narrative. As we begin to perceive consistencies in their behaviour, characters increasingly appear to be 'known quantities' – and as a result, our ability to predict their reactions and behaviour improves. This is not to suggest that characters cannot change, or behave unpredictably: but if they do so, the viewer must be carefully prepared for this, lest their actions seem merely implausible. As I have described above, major dramatic events, such as Lofty's proposal to Michelle, Angie's suicide attempt, or Arthur's mental breakdown have to be *made* predictable by means of the clues which precede them in the narrative. Without careful preparation, such behaviour may appear 'out of character' – that is, it may prove impossible for viewers to integrate it into their developing constructs of the characters concerned.

In addition to developing more or less coherent definitions of the characters, we also inevitably pass judgments upon them. In many respects, soap opera is a genre which positively invites the viewer to make moral and, to a lesser extent, ideological judgments of its characters. This is one of the major functions of 'gossip' within the narrative: as new information is passed from character to character, we are shown a wide variety of responses, and thereby encouraged to formulate our own. Certain characters habitually function as bearers of gossip, particularly Ethel and Dot, with the latter in particular often combining moral disapproval with a prurient fascination for 'forbidden' behaviour.

Major developments are typically accompanied by a series of judgments, which form a kind of chorus. Thus, Jan's first appearance at the Queen Vic was followed by a sequence of short scenes giving the other characters' reactions: Angie and Sharon were outraged; the Fowlers were surprised that she was so 'posh' and 'classy'; Michelle went away to have a good cry; Sue Osman reflected on Den's 'mean and moody' sex appeal; Lofty and Wicksy felt sorry for Sharon; while Dot, of course, condemned the sinful couple. In certain situations, the viewer is left to infer such judgments: thus, in one scene when Mary discussed her work as a stripper with the drag artist who was briefly featured in the Queen Vic, Lofty and Dot were shown overhearing their conversation, and functioned as a kind of silent chorus, whose views did not need to be stated. The arrival of new characters, such as Simon Wicks and Colin Russell, has also occasioned a chorus of judgment and speculation. In the case of Pat Wicks, Pete Beale's first wife, the comments of other characters – which, with the significant exception of Angie, were largely negative – helped to establish a powerful new character very rapidly.

The judgments passed within the serial are often extremely varied, and even contradictory, and in many cases the characters concerned have strongly rejected them. Pat Wicks, for example, fought back against the criticisms directed at her by seeking to undermine Pete Beale's masculinity – he was 'boring, selfish and terrible in bed' – and by suggesting that he was not the father of their child Simon.

Nevertheless, just as our concepts of the individual characters tend to become more stable and resistant to change as the narrative progresses, so do our judgments of them. These judgments tend to coalesce into relatively fixed hierarchies, arranged on a moral and/or ideological basis. Thus, for example, viewers may rank characters according to a scheme of moral values: certain characters may consistently and deliberately violate moral norms, while others may do so through no fault of their own. Some characters may come to embody the norms themselves, and their perspectives will thus be regarded as more authoritative, although others may overtly espouse the 'correct' moral principles, while behaving rather differently, thus potentially exposing the limitations of the moral code itself.

Although these judgments obviously depend upon the criteria which the viewer brings to the text, there are a number of ways in which the text itself promotes certain characters above others. Some are more consistently respected than others, and rarely attract negative judgments: others tend to look to them for advice, and to accept it when it is given.

Dr Legg, for example, often acts as a 'father confessor' to characters with emotional, rather than simply medical, problems. He often performs a didactic role, providing information and offering advice which is in the other characters' best interests. He has even on occasion attempted to confront the villainous Nick Cotton. At the same time, although he has worked in the community for many years, he lives elsewhere, and clearly comes from a different class background from most of the characters, and is occasionally satirised as a result. More recently, his authority has been undermined as he has been shown having difficulty coping with the demands of his practice.

By contrast, Lou Beale's authority derives from her position as the matriarch of the Beale/Fowler extended family. She too is a character whom others have turned to for advice when in difficulty, and who has been seen to 'lay down the law' with troublesome characters such as Den Watts and Pat Wicks. At the same time, she has often been accused of obstinacy and selfishness by others, particularly Arthur and Pauline Fowler. These qualities have been highlighted by her illness, which itself served to undermine her authority – although even in this case only Dr Legg has been capable of persuading her to take advice.

The fact that Dr Legg and Lou Beale tend to be endowed with a degree of authority by the other characters would suggest that the viewer is implicitly being invited to regard them in a similar light – although in neither case is their authority absolute or unchallenged. Indeed, neither age nor class background is in itself sufficient to guarantee such deference: on the contrary, the majority of the older characters (such as Dot and Ethel) and the more middle-class characters (such as Debbie Wilkins, or Den's lover Jan) tend to meet either with contempt or with ridicule from the other characters. In certain cases, it is the judgments which are made by younger characters such as Kelvin Carpenter and Sharon Watts, particularly those which are directed against their own parents, which are seen to carry considerable weight.

Although certain of the more middle-aged characters – most notably Tony Carpenter and Kathy Beale – are widely respected, it is Pauline Fowler who has come to occupy the 'tentpole' position in the serial, routinely acting as confidante and adviser to the other characters. Significantly, although she does occasionally criticise other characters, she does so relatively sparingly – unlike characters whose judgments are more freely given, and therefore tend to carry less weight, such as Dot Cotton. At the same time, it is very rare for other characters to pass negative judgments on Pauline, and these are rarely sustained for long: after the news of Arthur's fake burglary had spread through the community, Pauline rallied the family together, urging them to stand up with pride and face their critics.

Clearly, this process is subject to change as the narrative progresses – although, just as changes in the characters themselves tend to be signalled to the viewer, and take place over a relatively long period, so the viewers' personal hierarchy of judgment is unlikely to tolerate sudden and unpredictable alterations.

To a certain extent, *EastEnders* conforms to Wolfgang Iser's model of the 'counterbalancing text', in which the qualities and deficiencies of the various characters' perspectives are graded in a definite hierarchy – a phenomenon which Iser argues is common in didactic or propagandist texts such as Bunyan's *Pilgrim's Progress*.[17] Nevertheless, unlike such texts, the serial lacks a single hero, and thus a single 'preferred' perspective: although certain characters' perspectives are clearly respected by a majority of other characters within the text, the multiplicity of perspectives available nevertheless offers the viewer a considerable freedom of choice. Indeed, in many cases, the text itself may make a number of different, and even contradictory, sets of criteria available, thereby denying the viewer the security of a straightforward and simple judgment.

The character of Mary Smith provides an interesting example of this phenomenon. On the one hand, Mary has clearly violated a number of moral norms: she has been a stripper and a part-time prostitute, she has neglected her child, and has been discovered stealing from the local shops and from her workplace. Her often surly manner and alienating punk appearance are not designed to endear her to others. As a result, she has inevitably attracted negative judgments, not merely from Dot Cotton, but also from more authoritative characters like Pauline.

Yet it has also been argued that Mary has been led astray and exploited by 'bad influences' – such as Sheena Mennell the stripper, Nick Cotton, Pat Wicks and Mehmet Osman. More crucially, however, Mary's circumstances clearly mitigate her moral failings. She is a single parent, living in a cramped bedsit, with no prospects and very little money. She is also illiterate, and on the one occasion when she managed to get a 'proper' job, was forced to resign when she was given more responsibility, and was required to read. As a result of this, Mary has been able to fight back against her critics, accusing Dot of hypocrisy and the Fowlers of complacency – charges which neither were fully able to refute.

The text has thus made available two distinct sets of criteria on which the viewer's judgment of Mary might be based – criteria which are broadly either moral or political. On the one hand, we can conclude that Mary alone is to blame for her actions; while on the other, we might choose to blame 'society', or the government. Yet these different criteria are not available in all instances: while one could make a similar argument about Arthur Fowler's theft of the Christmas Club money, for example, it would be difficult to do so in the case of Nick Cotton, whose moral villainy is far more 'personal' and straightforward.

The fact that viewers may 'identify' with different characters in different ways, or to different degrees, will also have implications in terms of how they are judged. This can be seen most clearly in the way in which certain characters are consistently held up to ridicule on the basis of their personal eccentricities. Dot Cotton, for example, is an obsessive hypochondriac, while Ethel Skinner is prone to absurd malapropisms: both characters often verge on caricature, a quality which is accentuated by the comic display of the performances. To a lesser extent, Lofty Holloway has also been ridiculed by the other characters on the basis of his naivety and gauche behaviour: as Arthur Fowler exclaimed, Lofty is 'an accident looking for somewhere to happen'. At the same time, each of these characters has been featured in stories which have given them a more serious, or even tragic dimension, although the 'shift in register' tends to require a certain amount of adjustment on the part of the viewer. While Dot's problems with her son Nick and her husband Charlie have been relatively sustained, Ethel's tragic grief over the loss of her dog Willy was rather more difficult to take seriously. In the case of Lofty, this shift from a comic to a more serious role was an essential prerequisite of his integration into the Fowler family as Michelle's husband.

In the case of other characters, comedy has been used more intermittently, as a means of undermining their self-estimation and thereby reducing their authority. Thus, Den Watts' dealings in stolen property have been consistently unsuccessful, either because the goods themselves have been faulty, or because he has been unable to get rid of them. Although Den's connections with 'the Mob' have given him a certain degree of status in Albert Square – for example when he expelled Nick Cotton – it has also been made clear that he commands little respect within the broader criminal fraternity. In his brief stay in the Watts household, the Walford bank robber repeatedly undermined Den's masculine self-image – although Den himself was powerless to respond. As I shall indicate, Pete Beale is another character whose masculinity has consistently been questioned in this way.

Comedy is thus a fairly obvious means whereby the viewer's identification with particular characters may be disrupted. Nevertheless, even with more consistently 'serious' characters, there remain significant differences between the types of identification which the text invites.[18] Identification may not necessarily coincide in any straightforward way with the moral or ideological hierarchies which viewers construct. It is clearly possible to identify with characters whom one would judge very negatively, and to fail to identify with characters whom one would judge positively.

Ultimately, the concept of 'identification' is itself rather imprecise, and has barely been theorised in relation to television. In several respects, the characteristic forms of television drama and the conditions in which it is typically viewed may well serve to dilute, or even actively militate against, the kinds of identification which are invited by cinema, for example. Many of the formal qualities of soap opera in particular may also disrupt the viewer's identification with individual characters – the fragmentation of the narrative, and the constant shifting between storylines; the intrusion of comic and melodramatic elements within the predominantly naturalistic style; the self-conscious contrivance of the hermeneutic code; the multiplicity of characters and diversity of personal judgments; and the influence of factors outside the text itself, most notably the press coverage of the actors' private lives and the predictions of future developments.

This would suggest that our identification with particular individuals may well be short-lived and relatively weak, and that our primary identification is with the process of narration itself. In certain instances, we may adopt the privileged role of the voyeur, who can intrude into the lives of the characters without being seen, observing the revelation of hidden secrets and 'forbidden' behaviour without fear of reprisals. Alternatively, as Charlotte Brunsdon has suggested, the text may invite the viewer to cast a more caring or even 'maternal' eye over the characters and their problems.[19]

On the other hand, soap opera is unique in providing its viewers with the opportunity to get to know characters over a long period; and it is likely that simply as result of this familiarity we may come to regard them in a very different way from characters whom we encoun-

82

ter for only a short time. Furthermore, the concentration on the minutiae of everyday life which is typical of British serials means that they may enable viewers to relate the characters' experiences to events in their own everyday lives to a much greater degree than is possible in other genres of television drama.

In the absence of any more detailed theoretical or empirical work in this area, it is difficult to do more than simply generate hypotheses. The ways in which viewers are invited to construct, evaluate and identify with characters, and the ways in which they are likely to respond to these invitations, are potentially extremely variable and, in many cases, contradictory.

III

The teacherly text

EastEnders was intended from the outset to be a programme which would be committed to representing the realities of inner-city life, and which would therefore inevitably confront 'social issues'. Early press coverage of the plans for the new serial tended to present these issues in the form of a 'shopping list' – unemployment, racism, sexism, urban deprivation and single-parent families were among the topics included on the programme's agenda. As the serial has evolved, this list has certainly been extended, with storylines on homosexuality, rape, prostitution, law and order, illiteracy, adoption, divorce, arranged marriages, and conflicts between the generations. *EastEnders* has also featured a number of 'public health' issues, such as mental illness, vaccination, the blood donor service, AIDS, the Samaritans, cot deaths, drugs and alcoholism.

Despite the extraordinary number of issues which the programme has raised, it would be false to suggest that these have all been 'dealt with' explicitly. As I have indicated, Tony Holland and Julia Smith were concerned that the programme should not be regarded as 'issue-based'. While they felt that a soap opera could be a useful vehicle for providing information, and could provoke valuable discussion of such topics among viewers, they felt it was crucial to raise questions rather than to provide answers, and to avoid being 'moralistic'. Their central concern, they stressed, was with 'dramatic conflict' and with 'entertainment', not with 'issues'. Rather than consciously deciding on the issues they wished to cover, and developing the storylines out of these, they claimed that issues arose 'naturally' out of the storylines and the characters.

To some degree, this argument represents an attempt to deflect criticism: qualities like 'dramatic conflict' and 'entertainment' clearly cannot be seen as unproblematic. Furthermore, many of the issues which

83

have been raised in the programme have not arisen 'naturally' out of the characters, and in many cases have been dealt with in very didactic ways. Nevertheless, as Smith and Holland implicitly acknowledged, there are distinct dangers in this approach: if the programme is seen to 'preach' to its viewers, or consistently and explicitly urge them to adopt a particular point of view, it may be rejected as contrived or as patronising. For this reason, *EastEnders*' didactic moments have been comparatively rare and short-lived, and have tended to focus on a fairly restricted range of issues.

One approach which is typically adopted in such instances is for the more trusted or authoritative characters to function as 'teachers'. Thus, there was considerable speculation surrounding the relationship between Dr Legg and the social worker Ruth Lyons, with whom he was spotted on a number of occasions early in 1986, most notably by the disapproving Dot Cotton. Yet the characters' (and the viewers') assumptions about a possible romance were finally quashed when Legg revealed to Pauline Fowler that Ruth was in fact a lesbian: 'Don't be shocked, Pauline. She's not a bad person, at least I don't think she is. But you have to be honest to be unconventional, sometimes far more brave. They're not bad assets in these days.'

As with the dialogue between Saeed and Pauline quoted earlier in the chapter, Pauline functions here as a kind of surrogate for the viewer, who is thereby 'taught' a brief lesson. Yet with her didactic function thus accomplished, Ruth Lyons was promptly written out of the programme – suggesting that, like Pauline, the viewer was assumed to be not yet ready for a character so 'unconventional', despite her many assets.

On the 'public health' issues mentioned above, both Dr Legg and Andy O'Brien (who was a children's nurse) have occupied this 'teacherly' role. Andy, for example, advised Mary to have her baby vaccinated against whooping cough, informing her that the risks had been greatly exaggerated, and later persuaded most of the population of Albert Square to attend the local blood donor clinic. He was also one of a number of characters who advised Angie to seek help for her alcoholism, giving her leaflets about Alcoholics Anonymous. Meanwhile, Dr Legg has been seen to advise the characters on a range of medical and psychological problems – angina, mental illness, alcoholism, the menopause, impotence, and so on. It was in response to his suggestion that Kathy Beale became a counsellor for the Samaritans: and while her decision to do so was opposed by her husband Pete, his argument that it was a job for middle-class people was clearly shown to be invalid. Kathy in turn has increasingly come to adopt the role of 'expert' adviser, for example condemning Dot for her bigoted and hysterical response to the threat of AIDS.

Other problems have occasioned advice from a variety of 'helping agencies' from outside the community. For example, during her pregnancy and immediately after the birth of her child, Michelle Fowler was regularly seen in the company of her health visitor, her educational welfare officer, her home tutor and her social worker, all of whom offered information about her rights and entitlements. However, such representatives of the welfare state have occasionally met with considerable suspicion and resentment. Lou Beale, for example, has often railed against the interference of her social worker and her doctor, arguing that she would much rather be left to look after herself. Pauline Fowler and Sue Osman have also mounted similar attacks, arguing that social workers simply 'create problems', and make decisions about people's lives without taking account of their effects on those concerned. The character of Carmel, a health visitor who became rather more integrated into the community through her relationship with Kelvin Carpenter, is generally regarded more sympathetically, although she too has come under attack from a number of the more established characters for very similar reasons.

In dealing with racism, *EastEnders* has adopted a similarly didactic approach. The few characters who are consistently seen as racist have tended to be the more unsympathetic ones: thus, Nick Cotton's racist attitudes are simply further evidence of his deviant status, while Dot's are a function of her general bigotry and ignorance. In both cases, they have regularly been questioned and corrected by more authoritative characters – and, in most cases, by white characters such as Kathy Beale and Andy O'Brien. Thus, in a typical exchange, Kathy informed Dot that she should not refer to 'nigger brown', since this was 'rude to black people'. In this respect, the programme would appear to imply that racism is simply a question of individual prejudice, a matter of the odd 'rotten apple'. Nevertheless, in other instances, the question of institutional racism has been raised: Kelvin Carpenter, for example, has occasionally been critical of the police on these grounds, and his parents have supported him. In one extraordinary instance, Dr Legg gave an extended monologue on his experience as a Jew being brought up in the East End, and his memories of the anti-fascist demonstrations in Cable Street, which led into a direct attack on the Government:

> D'you know what worries me, Lou? A vacuum. I think about things, like everybody does. And things that are happening now were happening then. I mean, Jews were having a bad time – and now it's the Asians. You have to ask yourself how that happens. But that's not what I want to say. Then, there wasn't the vacuum. People knew. But now ... What I decided is, you have to identify the enemy for yourself. Not the enemy the newspapers tell you, nor the enemy that the Government tells you, but the real enemy, the vacuum. What I'd

like is a Prime Minister who stands up and condemns racism as strongly as she condemns terrorism.

Nevertheless, this approach remains comparatively rare, and tends to appear jarring as a result. It may disrupt the illusion that we are being shown a 'window on the world': viewers may feel that the fiction is being used 'illegitimately', as a vehicle for the educational or political intentions of the writers, who are simply putting words into the characters' mouths which they would not normally use. Once viewers perceive that the text has 'designs' upon them – that it is attempting to change their attitudes or behaviour – it becomes significantly easier to reject.

As a result, this approach runs the distinct risk of alienating viewers, precisely because it relies on specific assumptions about their existing knowledge and attitudes – assumptions which may turn out to be false. In attempting to 'teach' viewers, it implicitly assumes that there are deficiencies in their knowledge which need to be made good, and that viewers themselves will recognise this, and will therefore be willing to submit to being taught. For all these reasons, an explicitly didactic approach may be one which a popular television drama simply cannot afford to adopt if it is to retain a large and diverse audience.

Knowledge and discourse

The fact that *EastEnders* rarely adopts a didactic approach does not, of course, mean that it does not 'teach' – it is simply that most of its 'teaching' is implicit rather than explicit. By virtue of what it represents and does not represent, and by virtue of the ways in which it invites viewers to make sense of what they watch, the serial inevitably encourages certain kinds of readings, and thereby makes others more difficult.

Nevertheless, the text cannot be seen to 'contain' an ideology which it simply imposes on its viewers – even a 'hidden' ideology which viewers are not consciously aware of, but which can be recovered from the text by means of analysis. On the contrary, making sense of the text is an active and often self-conscious process, in which viewers draw on a whole variety of different types of prior knowledge. If only in order to maintain its popularity, the serial has to allow for the diversity of its viewers, and the diversity of the knowledge which they bring to it. Rather than fixing the viewer in a single position, the text provides a multiplicity of positions from which it may be read and understood. At the same time, that multiplicity is finite; in this sense, the text may be seen to construct, not an ideological position, but an ideological *terrain*, on which a limited range of meanings may be negotiated.

In using the term 'discourse', I am referring to the body of 'social knowledge' which viewers are invited to bring to bear on the text. As I

86

shall indicate, the serial routinely invokes certain 'commonsense' discourses, by means of which the characters' behaviour can be understood and evaluated. These discourses may provide norms or stereotypes of what constitutes good or acceptable behaviour – although they are not necessarily as rigid or as consistent as this. However, discourses are not primarily bodies of attitudes or beliefs; they are more accurately seen as means of generating knowledge, as ways of understanding the world. As well as claiming to present 'what is known', they also define 'what it means to know'.

Nevertheless, it is comparatively rare for these discourses to be referenced directly; on the contrary, they typically remains as a 'background' against which the 'foreground' of the action can be understood. In seeking to identify them, I shall therefore inevitably focus on instances in which they are made more explicit – instances which, like the didactic 'moments' already described, are relatively untypical of the serial as a whole.

I intend to concentrate on two major areas – the community and the family – which condense many of the broader social tensions which are at stake in *EastEnders*, and thereby to indicate a number of the discourses which circulate within it. In a sense, it is inevitable that these areas should perform such a central function within the serial. Both provide means of bringing a variety of characters together, and thereby generating new relationships. Both function as spaces within which broader social differences and inequalities are negotiated on an interpersonal level. Thus, the inner-city community brings together individuals and groups from different ethnic and, increasingly, class backgrounds, who will themselves define the notion of 'community' in different ways. Likewise, the family is also a site of conflict in which the tensions and inequalities between men and women, and between the generations, are constantly being renegotiated.

Both the community and the family have an important function in terms of narrative. Potential threats to their stability will inevitably lead to conflict, yet both hold out at least a promise of harmony and equilibrium to which the narrative must constantly seek to return.[20] Nevertheless, the fact that both are founded on basic differences and inequalities means that any resolution can only be temporary – a provisional truce or compromise which nevertheless contains the seeds of further disruption. In this sense, neither are seen as unproblematic values which are simply to be celebrated; while the happy family or the harmonious, integrated community may be regarded as ideals, they are ideals which can be attained only in fleeting moments.

At the same time, neither the community nor the family are timeless qualities; on the contrary, they have specific meanings within a given social and historical context. Both have been significant sites of change within British society over the last thirty years, and are central themes in contemporary political debate, which focus more general anxieties about social and moral decline.

As far back as the late 1950s, sociologists were drawing attention to the collapse of the traditional working-class inner-city community, based around the matriarchal extended family. Upward mobility in the 50s and 60s had enabled many families to migrate to the outer suburbs and new towns, leaving a growing concentration of people living on the economic and social margins – a phenomenon which many politicians have viewed with considerable alarm. The effects of the decline of traditional manufacturing industries, and of the increasing cuts in public spending which began in the 70s have been particularly severe in the already deprived urban areas. The need for cheap labour, which had resulted in successive waves of immigration in the post-war period, has also declined; yet the presence of black workers is perceived by many whites as a further threat to their livelihoods. More recently, the shortage of property in more traditional middle-class areas, at least in London, has led many young professional people to colonise hitherto working-class areas, forcing rents and property prices out of the reach of the local inhabitants. In several respects, the inner-city community of the mid-1980s may be seen as a site of considerable social tension – between the white working-class and the first- or second- generation immigrants who have increasingly been the victims of racist attacks; between the (rapidly declining) employed working class and those who are unemployed, or operating in the so-called 'black economy'; and, most recently, between the indigenous community and the middle-class intruders who have sought to 'gentrify' their areas.

The inner-city disturbances of 1981 and 1985 brought these tensions to the surface, although in many respects they simply marked the culmination of a period of growing unrest, dating back at least to the mid-1970s. Despite the fact that the disturbances themselves had largely been provoked by heavy-handed policing, the government's primary response was to instigate tougher 'law and order' legislation, which merely increased police powers. Yet at the same time, the traditional urban working class has been particularly vulnerable to the appeal of this authoritarian 'law and order' rhetoric, as a result of the collapse of its own structures of self-help and social organisation, such as those provided by the extended family.

Meanwhile, the family itself has also served as a focus of broader social tensions. The increasing entry of women into the labour market, and their greater economic independence, together with the collapse of industries which have historically relied on male workers, have led to changes in the traditional division of domestic labour. Feminism and gay politics have also contributed to a broader questioning of stereotyped gender roles within the family, and, indeed, of the family itself.

88

Although the conventional nuclear family is no long statistically the norm, its image has repeatedly been invoked by politicians seeking a return to more traditional moral values. The Conservatives have declared themselves 'the party of the family', and have been at the forefront of a growing backlash against the perceived 'permissiveness' of the 1960s; on moral issues, as in the political sphere, the social-democratic consensus of the 50s and 60s has increasingly come to be undermined. The kind of moral and religious authoritarianism represented by figures like Mary Whitehouse, with their belief in the essential sacredness of family life, has increasingly come to set the agenda for debate, and to inform legislation. Meanwhile, the gradual dismantling of the welfare state has led to growing pressure on working-class families, and in particular on those which may be classified as 'deviant', such as single-parent families.

Here again, the disturbances of 1981 and 1985 brought many underlying tensions to the surface, and particularly those which focused around the problematic category of 'youth'. The disturbances were interpreted by many on the Right as a result of the collapse of traditional family values, and the failure of parents to exert sufficient discipline over their children. The existence of a growing population of unemployed young people was perceived by many as a considerable threat to the social order, and led to increasing central government intervention under the guise of 'youth training'.

Notions of 'family' and 'community' thus condense a whole range of broader changes and conflicts which characterise contemporary British society. Both are widely perceived to be 'in crisis', although responses to this crisis clearly vary. On the one hand, both are regularly upheld as embodying social and moral values which obtained in a past era, and which many regard as preferable to those which appear to have replaced them. On the other hand, many have welcomed these changes as offering the potential for new, more progressive forms of social organisation – for different definitions of 'family life', and for 'communities' which are diverse and multicultural. To talk about the family or the community is thus inevitably problematic: the terms no longer possess a fixed meaning, but are, on the contrary, the site of a number of broader political struggles.

The community: class and ethnicity

PAULINE FOWLER [*reading a press report about the death of Andy O'Brien*] His death comes as a sudden blow to the residents of Albert Square, who are devastated at the loss of such a highly regarded character in what is held to be one of the closest-knit communities in London.

LOU BEALE Do they mean us?

On one level, *EastEnders* would appear to hark back to a notion of the traditional working-class community which is highly anachronistic. The Beale/Fowler extended family, which is at the centre of the serial, bears a remarkable resemblance to those described by Willmott and Young in their book *Family and Kinship in East London* as long ago as 1957. Their central thesis, however, was that this kind of matriarchal working-class family was already beginning to die out, as a result of the gradual depopulation of the inner city; and subsequent developments have certainly accentuated this.[21]

Insofar as this notion of community is directly invoked in the serial, it tends to be identified with the older characters, and particularly with Lou Beale. For example, in organising the women in the community to support Angie Watts, Lou criticised the 'uncaring' attitudes which she felt had come to prevail:

> LOU   I've been round this square longer than any of you. And in the old days, we used to be in and out of each other's houses and in and out of each other's business.
> ETHEL   That's right. You couldn't sneeze in the Square without everyone knowing about it.
> LOU   But now, all that's changed. You're supposed to keep yourself to yourself. That's progress, eh? It means that an old geezer like Reg Cox can lay dying in his flat and nobody notices.

Nevertheless, Lou and Ethel's version of 'the good old days' has been questioned by many of the characters, not least by Dr Legg, and what they regard as being 'a good neighbour' is seen by many as an invasion of their private lives. The need for community support which Lou emphasises here is seen to be in conflict with the need for privacy which is so vital for many of the characters, if their secrets are to be kept hidden.

At the same time, *EastEnders* also refers to more modern notions of urban community, which emphasise social diversity, both in terms of class and ethnicity – in a sense, to the notion of the multicultural community which informed the policies of the Labour metropolitan councils of the early 1980s. Yet if the older definition of community is seen to be under threat, if not simply redundant, this concept of the multicultural community is also highly fraught. Although *EastEnders* does seek to provide 'positive images' of co-operation between different ethnic groups, the racial harmony of Albert Square is constantly threatened by forces both from within and without.

Like *Coronation Street*, *EastEnders* occasionally provides brief moments of respite amid the ongoing dramatic conflict, in which these notions of community are celebrated.[22] Festivals such as Halloween and Christmas, and family occasions such as the christening of the

90

Fowlers' baby, have provided opportunities for the re-affirmation of traditional 'community spirit'. The Walford Carnival which took place in March 1986 (ironically almost at the same time as the abolition of the Greater London Council) was at least partly a celebration of the notion of the multicultural community – although despite the presence of a significant number of black extras, the major roles were taken by the white characters. At the same time, such affirmations of community have not always proceeded without difficulty – Michelle and Lofty's abortive wedding, for example, and the Christmas celebrations of 1986 were both community occasions which failed disastrously.

Despite the conflict between these two notions of community, they have increasingly come to merge. Conflict was certainly apparent in the very first episode, for example, when the body of Reg Cox was discovered in his bed-sit after he had not been seen for several days. Lou Beale saw this as symptomatic of the decline of the community, and was particularly outraged that it was the Bangladeshi couple, Naima and Saeed Jeffery, who had first alerted them to the fact that Reg was missing. Yet when Saeed offered to help, Lou waved him aside: 'We'll look after our own'. Lou's definition of 'community' was clearly seen to be confined to the white population: yet when Saeed left the neighbourhood less than a year later, it was Lou who provided his epigraph: 'You're part of us, and we never turn our back on our own.' This inconsistency may partly derive from a general 'softening' of Lou Beale's character, which early audience research suggested many viewers found unduly abrasive. Nevertheless, it is also symtomatic of a broader attempt within the serial to effect a compromise between the two notions of community identified here.

As I have already suggested, the notion of community performs a central function in terms of narrative. The 'closeness' of the community enables the various narrative strands to be interwoven to a far greater extent than is possible in serials where the community is less coherent, such as *Brookside*, or indeed the US soaps. The notion of community also serves an important role in generating the forward movement of the narrative. The basic structure here is similar to that of many Westerns: threats to the community, often deriving from sources outside it, serve to disrupt the basic equilibrium, which then has to be reasserted by the forces of law and order. Yet the differences between this and the serial are nevertheless significant. In the serial, the narrative itself never reaches a final closure: although some threats do derive from outside the community, they can only be expelled temporarily. Furthermore, the community itself is also characterised by division; and in this sense the forces of disruption are as likely to be found within the community as outside it. Finally, the law within the serial is far from absolute: the 'official' forces of law and order which operate outside the community may have very little power within it, and they may also conflict with the 'unofficial' forces of law and order which prevail inside the community itself.

Nevertheless, the most significant sources of disruption come from the world outside the community. If one considers crime, for example, there is an effective distinction between petty crime, which can be tolerated within the community, and major crime, which derives from outside it. Thus, many of the regular characters have been involved in receiving stolen goods – not merely characters like Den Watts, but also more respected characters like Pete and Kathy Beale. Others have defrauded the social security – again, not merely characters like Mary Smith, but also Arthur Fowler and Debbie Wilkins (in her case, encouraged by Detective Sergeant Quick). Nevertheless, serious crime is seen to derive exclusively from outside the community. Thus, the protection gang featured early in 1986, or the attacker who assaulted Pat Wicks a year later both came from outside Albert Square to terrorise its inhabitants. Although Den Watts has connections with big-time criminals, he is clearly in a minor league by comparison; and Mary Smith's involvement in prostitution was also very much on an 'amateur' basis.

The more obviously deviant characters often straddle this divide between 'inside' and 'outside': Mark Fowler and Nick Cotton are both 'temporary' characters of this nature, who often disappear from Albert Square for extended periods, and return bringing further disruption. In both cases, they have been expelled from the community as a result of their actions. Thus, Mark was forced to leave on one occasion after Cassie Carpenter had been discovered smoking dope which she had taken from his hippy friend Owen. Yet if Mark's deviance tends to derive more from his unwillingness to 'fit in' with family life, Nick Cotton's is more clearly based on a contempt for the community – as shown in his overt racist insults, and his sarcastic remarks about 'the caring community'. As a result, he has tended to be expelled in more violent ways, by the combined forces of the male members of the community. In both cases, however, the fact that they are related to regular characters – and, at least in the case of Mark, to characters who are central to the community itself – means that their status remains ambiguous.

This is also true to a lesser extent of Den Watts, whose deviance is more of a moral than a criminal variety. He is associated with disruptive elements which derive from beyond the community, not merely with his criminal connections, but also with his lover Jan, who clearly comes from a different social class. On the rare occasions when the serial has moved beyond the confines of Albert Square, it has often done so in order to record his illicit liaisons. Thus, we have occasionally seen him in the company of Jan, either in a wine bar or in her flat; and in order to meet Michelle, he has occasionally had to go outside the neighbourhood, to the canal bank or to the hospital. Meanwhile, his response to community rituals has been cynical, or down-right misanthropic; and his self–interest sets him apart from other members of the community:

> What's it they say? If you can't get what you want, want what you can get. Well I've tried that, and it doesn't work. I'm going to get everything I want all right. And that's the difference between me and the people round here. They want what they can get.

Nevertheless, Den's attempts to get what he wants have been far from successful: although he has aspirations beyond the community, he appears likely to remain, albeit reluctantly, constrained within it.

Where more serious deviance arises within the community, it often has to be removed from it – Saeed's sexual deviance, for example, was resolved by his return to Bangladesh, while Arthur's breakdown led to him being removed to a mental hospital. In both cases, it was notable that the characters became increasingly alienated from those around them before their eventual removal – Saeed, for example, was seen getting very drunk in the Queen Vic, and sitting alone in the cafe at Christmas wearing a party hat. Yet he too was critical of the lack of community support, compared with that of his home country.

However, the relationship between the community and the 'official' forces of law and order remains ambiguous. A number of the charac-ters – most notably Lou Beale, but also more middle-class characters such as Hannah Carpenter and Debbie Wilkins – have expressed con-cern at the collapse of law and order in the local area. Yet the police have generally been regarded with considerable resentment and suspi-cion, as intruders whose attitude to the community is essentially hos-tile. Although Detective Sergeant Quick occupied a fairly prominent role in the serial at one point, he was generally distrusted by the other characters, and his attentions to Debbie Wilkins (herself a far from sympathetic character) were ultimately rejected. Following the burg-lary of Dr Legg's surgery, Quick was involved in confrontations with Kelvin Carpenter and Lou Beale as he attempted to investigate the crime. Kelvin accused him of racism – 'he can't see beyond the colour of a man's skin' – although he later appeared to accept that he was 'just doing his job'. Lou argued that he was 'persecuting respectable people', and again harked back to 'the old days':

> LOU If you'd been doing your job properly, we'd all be able to leave our windows open. We always did in the old days. The old police used to keep the youngsters in check.
> QUICK Well, the world's changed, hasn't it?
> LOU Not for the better in my opinion.

QUICK   And the old police used to get a bit more co-operation, didn't they? Everyone I go to see now seems to think I'm accusing them.

Despite this claim, Quick's attitude to the community seemed to be that it was guilty until proven innocent:

> I've had Walford up to here. I don't need it, right. Nine out of ten of you are bent. You stick up for each other, you lie for each other, and you expect mugs like me to sort out the mess.

Rather than 'community policing', he argued, Walford needed 'taking by the neck and shaking'.

In its representation of the police, as in its representation of the 'helping agencies' of the welfare state, *EastEnders* would appear to connect with a widespread resentment against the state regulation of community life. In both cases, there is a corresponding emphasis on community 'self-help'. Thus, in the absence of any effective policing, the re-assertion of law and order has often been left to the representatives of the community itself. The expulsion of Nick Cotton in November 1985, for example, was carried out by a 'posse' effectively led by Den Watts, supported by Pete Beale, Tony Carpenter and Ali Osman. As they confronted Nick in the bar of the Queen Vic, Sergeant Quick remained out of sight in the back room, condoning their action without participating in it himself. Through his criminal associations, Den effectively has the role of an 'unofficial' community leader.

In various ways, then, the narrative of the serial is structured around a basic binary opposition, between the forces which maintain the community and those which seek to disrupt it. As I have indicated, many of the latter emanate from outside the community, although their relationship with it is often rather ambiguous. At the same time, it is clearly part of the function of the concept of community that it emphasises qualities which are shared between people, and thereby minimises their differences. In a sense, to insist on these differences, and in particular to insist on the inequalities which accompany them is to call into question the very notion of community itself. To what extent does *EastEnders* seek to construct an artificially harmonious community, and thereby to efface fundamental differences and inequalities, particularly those based on class and ethnicity?

The representation of working-class London in *EastEnders* can partly be seen as a modern manifestation of a long literary and dramatic tradition – a tradition which can be traced from Shakespearean characters like Mistress Quickly, through Dickens' Sam Weller and Mrs Gamp, via Victorian music hall, to Shaw's 'Pygmalion' and Somerset

Maugham's Liza of Lambeth. In addition to these fictional representations, generations of social commentators and journalists, from Mayhew onwards, have sought to define the specific characteristics of 'Cockney' culture. The term 'Cockney' does not merely refer to the speech-patterns of London dialect: the Cockney is also seen as a specific character type, whose primary quality is that of cheerfulness in the face of adversity. Cockneys are typically described as 'chirpy' or 'cocky': they possess an indomitable spirit and a high degree of self-reliance. Despite their occasional involvement in petty crime, Cockneys are fundamentally honest, the women in particular having 'hearts of gold'. Cockneys are essentially sensual people, with little interest in intellectual matters: their values are primarily sentimental and conservative, derived from a deep attachment to their local environment and to their nation.[23]

Gavin Weightman and Steve Humphries have traced the origins of the modern definition of 'the Cockney' back to the early nineteenth century, when the building of the docks led to an influx of working-class labourers and their families from the City of London.[24] As industry declined in the latter part of the century, there was considerable anxiety among middle-class Londoners about the threat of 'the dangerous classes', the 'outcasts' concentrated on the margins of the City – anxiety which was fuelled by the riots which took place intermittently from the 1840s onwards. The growth of philanthropic social work in the 1880s and 1890s was partly designed to defuse this threat of social disorder – and it was at the same time that this image of the East End as 'a kind of music-hall place, full of chirpy Cockneys' began to emerge. Indeed, as Michael Chanan has observed, music hall itself may be seen as a form of commercialised popular culture which came to displace more authentic forms generated from within the working class itself.[25] Historically, then, 'the Cockney' may be seen as an image of a loyal, patriotic working class which accepted its station in life and therefore posed little threat to the established social order. Cockneys may occasionally have been insolent, but they were also far from revolutionary; the harshness which they cheerfully endured resulted not from exploitation, but simply from the blows of fate.

Although this sentimentalised, fundamentally 'harmless' image of the cheerful Cockney remains influential – for example, in the work of the popular singers Chas and Dave, or the comedian Jim Davidson – it has increasingly come to be replaced by a more abrasive image of London working-class life. Series like Hazell and The Sweeney in the 70s and The Bill and Prospects in the 80s have drawn on the traditional image of the Cockney, but have given it a sharper edge, accentuating the Cockney's opposition to authority and to middle-class tastes and values. Even a series like Minder, which in many respects derives from the Cockney music-hall tradition, often gives voice to these 'oppositional' sentiments – although, like the other series I have mentioned, it remains almost exclusively male.

EastEnders might also be aligned with these more abrasive representations of working-class life. While it does pay homage to the traditional image of Cockney wit and fortitude, and to its association with notions of patriotism – whence Albert Square, the Queen Vic and the Churchill bitter which it serves – its definition of working-class identity also has a distinct oppositional edge. While this is apparent in its representation of the community's relationship with the police, it is particularly true of its articulation of class difference.

class

Although *EastEnders* has few middle-class characters, their relationships with the other characters have often drawn attention to their class differences. In a sense, the middle-class characters are largely seen from the point of view of the working-class characters. They remain on the margins of the community, for the most part defined by their inability to 'fit in': we rarely see them together, or have the opportunity to hear their judgments of the other characters.

Debbie Wilkins, for example, was routinely mocked by the other characters for being 'stuck up' and 'posh'. In the early stages of the serial, her attempts to integrate herself into the community were seen as absurd or patronising. During a brief spell as a barmaid in the Queen Vic, for example, she attempted to improve the presentation of the food by decorating the meals with alfalfa sprouts and other salad vegetables, causing consternation and ridicule among the punters: Den was eventually obliged to dismiss her with the memorable line 'Tell Fanny Craddock to go home to Johnny!' Likewise, when Arthur Fowler saw her doing her own washing in the local launderette, he condemned her 'pretend poverty' – 'Let's get all trendy and join the working class.' In the case of Sue Osman, Debbie's attitude provoked outright resentment, although this was at least partly caused by Sue's suspicion of her relationship with her husband Ali. In return, Debbie accused Sue of behaving like a 'fishwife', although she also attempted to defend herself by proclaiming her East End roots:

> S U E   I can see right through you. You're nothing special. Even if you think you are, with your fancy gear and your lah-di-dah. You're a conniving bitch ... Why don't you go back where you came from?
> D E B B I E   Where I came from? I came from round here, Sue Osman. You don't have any special rights to the East End.

Debbie did eventually manage to integrate herself into the community to a certain extent by taking a job in Naima's shop – although she was clearly embarrassed by having to do this, feeling that people would have 'a field day' seeing her in such a lowly position. Nevertheless, her romantic associations with policemen – both with Sgt Quick and with the even more unsavoury Sgt Rich – did little for her popularity: she consistently remained marginal to the serial's main network of relationships, and was eventually written out altogether.

Class difference has also been a significant issue in other relationships. The conflicts between Tony and Hannah Carpenter, for example, were at least partly a result of their different class backgrounds. Thus, Tony accused Hannah of being a 'snob' and 'Lady muck', while Hannah's mother had described Tony as her 'bit of rough'. These differences became particularly significant when Hannah decided to send their daughter Cassie to a private school: both Tony and Kelvin opposed her 'middle-class aspirations', although Hannah argued that teachers in state schools did not expect or encourage black children to do well. Hannah also received advice and support from Den and Angie Watts, whose daughter Sharon attended a private school, and for whom education was a significant means to upward mobility out of Albert Square. Ultimately, Tony and Kelvin were forced to agree with Hannah's argument: Kelvin advised Cassie that attending a private school would give her 'a chance of winning for a change'. Nevertheless, in the break-up of the Carpenters' marriage it was clearly Tony's point of view which was privileged, and Hannah who eventually left him (and the serial).

Colin Russell is another character who has been defined very clearly in terms of his class difference. The sparse, 'tasteful' decor of his flat, for example, has attracted comment from a number of the characters – as Dot said, 'It'll be nice when it's finished.' Perhaps the key signifier of class differences in Colin's case, however, is the Filofax which he habitually clutches, and which in one episode was stolen 'for a joke' by his boyfriend Barry, causing him considerable (and comic) anxiety. The difficulties in his relationship with Barry have been partly a result of their class difference, although there are a number of other factors. Barry has occasionally satirised Colin's use of language – for example, his concern about his 'space' being invaded – and violated his cultivated 'designer' tastes, for example by filling his flat with lurid Christmas decorations.

In the case of Den's relationship with his lover Jan, class was also a major issue. Here again, the fact that Jan is middle-class has constantly been emphasised, at times to the point of caricature – as on her first appearance in the Queen Vic, when she attempted to order a Glenfiddich and Malvern Water. For many of the characters and, one would suspect, for many viewers, the discovery that Jan was not working-class came as a considerable surprise. Lou Beale, for example, had expected her to be 'tarty, with loads of make-up', and was intrigued to find out that she was, in Arthur's terms, 'classy' – 'She'd look out of place in Albert Square'. The contrast between Den and Jan led to considerable speculation as to what she saw in him: Angie for one

97

argued (or hoped) that the relationship could not last, for this very reason – 'Think about it: she reads books!'

The contrast between Jan and Angie was also repeatedly defined in class terms, not least through visual signifiers such as make-up and dress. This contrast was particularly apparent in the episodes featuring Den and Angie's disastrous 'second honeymoon' in Venice. While Angie toured the gift shops buying tacky souvenirs and naughty underwear, Den sloped off to meet Jan in a restaurant, where they enjoyed authentic Venetian delicacies. While Angie rushed to get on a gondola, Jan clearly knew the 'correct' middle-class codes of behaviour – 'Nobody goes on a gondola!' When Angie ultimately confronted Den, it became clear that much of her bitterness stemmed from her feelings of class inferiority: 'You think I'm common, don't you? It's 'cause you've been with her. You always see my bad points when you've been with her.' Yet here again, although we were often given Angie's judgments of Jan – she was an 'ageing Sloane Ranger', for example – we were rarely given Jan's judgments of Angie, except in the form of a rather condescending pity.

Class boundaries within the serial tend to be clearly marked and strongly policed. On the rare occasions when working-class characters have attempted to cross these boundaries, they have been seen as absurd, or as having ideas above their station. Kathy Beale's decision to join the Samaritans, for example, was criticised by her husband Pete for this reason, although he failed to prevent her; and Angie's attempts to 'go upmarket' have failed miserably – as Den argued, 'Angie's flash. All she ever wants is class, and all she ever gets is a kiss-me-quick hat.' Characters who attempt to move in the other direction are also rarely successful – Jan's brief stay at the Queen Vic being one clear example. While Dr Legg is occasionally found playing darts in the Queen Vic, he remains a 'worker priest' character who is in the community, but not of it. Colin has partially succeeded in integrating himself into the community through his relationship with Barry, although it is significant that his work (as a self-employed graphic designer) does not take him away from the Square. Nevertheless, it has remained difficult for the serial to integrate the more middle-class characters into the community, and thus to generate storylines around them.

Although class differences have certainly been emphasised, the question of inequality has rarely been explicitly raised. The vast majority of characters who are employed work in and around Albert Square, and either run their own businesses or are employed in businesses run by the other characters. This clearly contributes to the sense of narrative 'density' I have identified: most of the characters can plausibly be seen around the Square for most of the time, enabling the storylines to be constantly developed and interwoven. Yet at the same time, it means that Albert Square begins to assume the dimensions of a Thatcherite paradise, in which everyone has a small business.

However, the situation is rather more complex than this. Admittedly, there are few employer/employee relationships in the Square, although Den's occasionally tyrannical approach to his bar staff perhaps compensates for this lack. More crucially, the 'small business' ethic often conflicts with loyalty to the community. There have been a series of rivalries between the different businesses – between the cafe and the pub, after Den's decision to provide bar food, and between Naima's shop and the other businesses after her decision to upgrade her facilities by acquiring a drinks license and starting to sell coffee and hot snacks. In Naima's case, her commitment to running a successful business also led her, at least temporarily, to abandon her own principles by selling pornographic magazines. Yet her growing economic independence was eventually constrained by the involvement of her family, and the arrival of her cousin Rezaul. Similarly, Kathy Beale's success in running her own market stall was seen as a threat by her husband Pete – although she was subsequently defrauded by a rather less scrupulous small business entrepreneur, Mehmet Osman.

One storyline which demonstrated the ambiguity surrounding the small business ethic very clearly was the one concerning Naima's attempts to buy the flat in Tony Carpenter's house, which he had recently converted. Hannah Carpenter was initially very keen for Naima to buy the flat, at least partly because of a sense of solidarity:

> I'm a black woman, and I know what it's like to be the wrong colour in this country ... And how important it is to have a place to live where you feel safe. I know exactly what it's like trying to be a woman who is not dependent on her family or a man to see her through.

Yet when Colin offered to pay a further £1,000 above Naima's bid, Hannah's loyalty to Naima disappeared instantly: the extra money, she argued, could be used to pay for Cassie's school fees. Hannah assured Tony that Naima would understand, because she was a 'businesswoman' – and 'business is business'.

The small business ethic is thus far from being one which is simply celebrated: yet again, it comes into conflict with other discourses circulating in the programme, such as those concerned with women's financial independence, with loyalty to the community and with racial solidarity.

If questions of class inequality are raised explicitly in the serial, therefore, they almost inevitably refer to the world beyond Albert Square. The story of Arthur Fowler's unemployment was occasionally presented in such terms: for example, his discovery that there was a 'Professional and Executive' job centre with wall-to-wall carpet provoked Michelle to observe, 'it's us and them even when you're out of a job'. Arthur has sometimes come into conflict with other characters over political issues: in one instance he rounded on Den for having voted Tory:

> You know, it's cynics like you Den that have put me where I am today – on the bloody dole queue ... You may be a high and mighty landlord now, but you're working-class like the rest of us. And how a working-class boy can vote for the Tories, I'll never know. You're dancing on your father's grave, you are.

Nevertheless, Arthur's situation has predominantly been explained in individual terms: he has simply been 'kicked in the teeth', and is now seen by most employers to be too old for the jobs which are available.

Overt political comments of any kind remain extremely rare in the serial. To its credit, *EastEnders* was alone among British soaps in featuring the 1987 General Election, although (perhaps understandably) the political alignments of most of the characters were left vague. In general, however, more explicit forms of 'class politics' have been positively marginalised. Kelvin Carpenter's friend Harry, who was featured for several months in 1986, remains the only explicitly socialist character who has appeared thus far, and he was presented quite unambiguously in a negative light. Significantly, Harry was identified very clearly as a middle-class character who was pretending to be working-class: although he was rejected by most of the other characters as a 'fake' and a 'poser', he was tolerated mainly because he owned the equipment which they needed for their band. Harry's eventual betrayal of the band effectively confirmed his hypocrisy, and was followed by his final departure from Albert Square.

If the explicit discourses of class politics are thus rarely visible in *EastEnders*, those of class identity and class difference are certainly emphasised in many of the key relationships and storylines. The same could not, however, be argued in relation to issues of race and ethnicity. Although on one level the serial does represent a multicultural community, it has tended to efface cultural differences and inequalities in favour of 'positive images' of interracial co-operation. Nevertheless, this process is not without its contradictions.

Perhaps the most significant fact about *EastEnders*' black characters is simply that they exist: compared with other British soaps, and indeed with much British television in general, their mere presence is unusual. Furthermore, the black characters are often given central dramatic roles within the narrative: far from being marginal, they are embedded in its complex network of relationships, and in certain cases (most notably Tony Carpenter) occupy privileged and authoritative positions within it.

On the other hand, *EastEnders* could be (and has been) accused of simply reproducing a limited range of racist stereotypes. Thus, until the recent introduction of an Asian doctor, its sole Asian characters were shopkeepers. Naima has been one of the primary representatives of the small business ethic within the serial and has come into conflict with the other characters as a result of her assertive approach to developing her business – although this may not necessarily mean that she has been judged negatively as a result, particularly since her main business rival has been Den Watts.

However, it is clear that her commitment to her business has not been entirely a matter of choice – as she once said, 'Just because I'm Bengali doesn't mean I like working in a shop' – but it has been linked to her desire for economic and personal independence. It would therefore be wrong to suggest that she has been represented as a money-grabbing capitalist, out to exploit the local community for all she can get – and in this sense, she is not an 'Asian shopkeeper' stereotype.

Nevertheless, the implicit equation 'Asian' = 'shopkeeper' is a mis-representation – as is the more 'positive image' of the Asian doctor. The majority of Asian workers in Britain are in fact employed as un-skilled and semi-skilled waged labour. Yet to assess 'stereotypes' in terms of their accuracy to the real world leads to a very reductive form of analysis which ignores the specific constraints and conventions of the genre.[26] In fact, there are very few characters in *EastEnders* employed in waged labour – and this is at least partly a result of the need to maintain narrative complexity and development. If Naima were employed in a factory, it would be far more difficult to involve her in the storyline. One could make a similar argument about the representa-tion of black family life: the collapse of Saeed and Naima's arranged marriage and the break-up of the Carpenter family could be accused of conforming to inaccurate racist stereotypes – although it is clearly one of the requirements of soap opera as a genre that marriages cannot last, and that the narrative must constantly be regenerated by combining the characters in new relationships.

At any one point in the narrative, there are bound to be systematic imbalances in the representation of particular social groups, although this is not to say that these will always remain. The presence of an Asian shopkeeper today does not preclude the introduction of an Asian doctor, or perhaps an Asian publican or an Asian graphic designer in the future. In many ways, the existing characters fail to connect with dominant stereotypes, and even deliberately oppose them: Kelvin, for example, is very far from being a troublesome black youth. Because the black characters in *EastEnders* have to stand in for groups which are themselves extremely diverse, they are bound to be read against a 'background' of racist stereotypes which are constantly being reasserted in the culture at large, and which viewers will inevitably bring to the programme. Particularly for viewers whose social experience does not bring them into contact with black people, they will therefore tend to be highly 'charged'. In this sense, the degree of 'accuracy' of a representation may be less important than the *discourses* which surround it. The crucial question is not whether *EastEnders*' black characters are 'realistic', but how the serial invites its viewers to make sense of questions of ethnicity – and in particular, how it defines ethnic difference and inequality or racism.

In fact, *EastEnders*' stance towards racism is often explicitly didactic. Racist characters such as Dot and Nick Cotton are routinely 'corrected' and attacked for their beliefs by the more authoritative characters. Although there have been a few cases of the other white characters expressing racist views, the vast majority would appear to be completely lacking in prejudice.

Thus, as I have shown, although Lou Beale began life in the serial expressing some hostility towards Saeed and Naima, her attitude appeared to have magically changed by the time Saeed departed for Bangladesh. Yet again, although Pete and Kathy Beale disapproved of Wicksy going out with Naima – and were condemned by him for their prejudiced views – there has been no evidence of racism on their part since that time.

More extreme forms of racism have tended to derive from outside the community, for example in the form of the protection gang which terrorised the 'ethnic minority' characters of Albert Square in the early months of 1986, extorting money and daubing their shops with paint. Yet this storyline was very ambiguous, not least because Beresford, the leading villain, was himself black. Although the harrassment was clearly directed at the black characters, the fact that a black person was carrying it out meant that the racial dimension was simultaneously emphasised and effaced, making for some bizarre contradictions:

BERESFORD We're acting as agents on behalf of Mr Jesper Scannell, who is offering a new neighbourhood scheme to tradesmen of the minority persuasion, particularly aimed at integrating them into the cultural majority. We live in a desperately racist society. No doubt you've noticed this, sir. I've suffered myself. This may surprise you, but I have suffered, particularly when a boy. An unfortunate trick of colouring and feature giving me a somewhat Hebrew appearance. Sufficiently so that the yobs of my youthful day sought constant pleasure in bouncing my head against a wall. So I know, believe me, I know what our immigrant friends go through. Now, thankfully, Mr Scannell is going to eliminate all this: eliminate petrol poured through letter boxes, excrement smeared on door handles, racist abuse daubed on walls and windows. But this will inevitably incur some heavy expenses.

In response to the harrassment, it was Tony Carpenter who assumed the role of black community leader. For him, the issue was clearly to do with race: and when Pete Beale questioned whether Ali Osman (who was another of the victims of the gang) could really be described as black if he was a Turkish Cypriot, Tony asserted that he was still an 'outsider', 'an ethnic minority' – 'To a lot of your people he will never belong.' Here again, the police were seen as unable to defend the community, leading Naima to accuse them of racism: 'They don't care when it's us'.

Nevertheless, as with its representation of class, the serial rarely makes reference to broader structural inequalities – in this case, to institutional racism. Racism is predominantly defined as a question of individual prejudice or discrimination. While this might be regarded simply as a further consequence of the focus on interpersonal relationships which tends to characterise soap opera as a genre, it is also a significant element within the serial's broader 'multiculturalist' approach.[27] Through their disavowal of individual racial prejudice, the white characters effectively disclaim the inequality between themselves and the black characters, and the possibility that they might benefit from institutional racism. The fact that racism is generally located outside the community or in the prejudices of individual deviant characters thus allows the serial to construct an oasis of multiracial harmony.

In order to do this, it must also seek to efface the signs of racial difference, to construct white characters with black faces. While the ethnicity of the white characters remains unproblematic, that of the black characters is rarely emphasised. This is largely because each of the 'ethnic minorities' represented in the programme is personified by a few individuals: although Naima and Ali occasionally refer to their families, for example, we rarely see them in the company of large numbers of other characters from the same culture. Thus, if they do bear specific cultural values, they do so as individuals: and they are constantly having to adapt to the values of the dominant white characters.

In an interview conducted shortly before the launch of the serial, the producer, Julia Smith, made a remark which seems to me to encapsulate this 'multiculturalist' approach very clearly:

We have got a couple of very nice young Bengali characters whom I think everyone will like, and I hope that people won't even realise they're Bengalis.[28]

In this respect at least, the serial would appear to be premissed on the idea that we all possess an 'essential humanity': if only we would recognise that we are all the same under the skin, the inequalities between us would simply fade away.

The family: gender and generation

If the notion of community in *EastEnders* thus condenses and, in certain respects, effaces broader social tensions, so also does the notion of the family. Like the community, the family is constantly threatened by forces from outside which seek to undermine it; yet the fundamental reasons for its instability are contained within it. The survival of the family depends upon it retaining a delicate balance of power, between men and women, and between adults and children. When this balance is disturbed, the family is thrown into a crisis which can often result in its total destruction. Perhaps to an even greater extent than the community, the family within the serial is seen as a site of inequality, and therefore of perpetual struggle. It is vulnerable precisely because its 'enemy' is within: outsiders may precipitate the crisis, but if families collapse, it is because they tear themselves apart, and not because others have the power to destroy them.

As with the community, the family performs a central function in terms of generating narrative. On one level, the narrative of the serial is based on a conflict between two opposing drives, one tending towards the destruction of the family and the other towards its reconstruction. Yet it is the former which more often prevails: moments of resolution are comparatively infrequent, and are rarely sustained. As a result, happy families are very much the exception. It is suffering which motivates the narrative: joy and contentment are fundamentally static, and therefore cannot endure.

This basic conflict which characterises the role of the family in the serial was illustrated in almost schematic terms in the two episodes broadcast on Christmas Day 1986. In the weeks leading up to Christmas, there had been considerable discord within the Beale/Fowler extended family, as a result of Pete and Kathy Beale's decision to break with the family tradition, and to have Christmas lunch in the Queen Vic, rather than with the Fowlers. Pete's attempt to heal the rift with Pauline had been in vain:

> PAULINE This family is falling apart, Pete. It's on its knees. Only you don't realise that, do you? You think everything's going to be all right. You have to work at being a family. You can't just coast through it. Things have to be renewed. There have to be shared times, good times.

Nevertheless, Pauline's appeal to family loyalty proved ineffective. Her final judgment was delivered in a classic *EastEnders* line – 'If you can't sit down when I serve dinner at the Queen's speech, then you can bugger off!'

Yet this was only one of many tensions which surfaced on Christmas Day. Pete's meal was spoilt by the presence of his ex-wife Pat Wicks, who had recently been tormenting him by suggesting that he was not in fact the father of their son Simon. Simon himself decamped to the Fowlers', where Pauline was bemoaning the absence of Pete and Kathy, her husband Arthur and her children Michelle (who had recently got married) and Mark (who was in a detention centre). Meanwhile, Kelvin Carpenter had had an argument with his parents over his relationship with Carmel, and had stormed out of the house; Dot had been abandoned by her errant husband Charlie; and Colin had had a quarrel with his boyfriend Barry and was spending Christmas Day alone talking to his computer. Angie was looking forward to Christmas Day – 'We'll be the happiest family in Walford' – not knowing that for weeks beforehand Den had been preparing to serve the divorce papers on her.

Across the two episodes, there was a constant interplay between scenes of reconciliation and scenes of disintegration. The Carpenters were reunited; Colin got back together with Barry; Arthur awoke from his mental torpor and came downstairs to carve the chicken for Christmas lunch; and Pete made up with Lou. Meanwhile, Den served the divorce papers, and Angie and Sharon left the family home; Sue appeared at the Fowlers' house, where Arthur was babysitting, and told him about the failure of her application to adopt a child; Arthur had a mental breakdown and proceeded to wreck the Fowlers' living room; and, as if this were not enough, in the final shot Pauline learned the truth about the father of Michelle's baby. Throughout, thirty million people across the country sat transfixed in front of their television sets.

The discourses which define the family have been particularly explicit in the case of the Fowlers, who in many respects are at the centre of the serial's network of relationships. Both Arthur and Pauline have repeatedly dwelt on the significance of the family, and sought to hold it together in the face of imminent destruction. Nevertheless, the family is not seen as something which can be taken for granted: it requires work if it is to be maintained. Thus, when Michelle was facing the prospect of becoming a single parent, Arthur advised her against taking this course:

ARTHUR I think we were made to be in families. The system seems to have lasted for a few thousand years.
MICHELLE Then why is the divorce rate so high?
ARTHUR Because they're not prepared to stick at it. I know they say 'in sickness and in health' and all that sort of thing. But the first sign of trouble, they want to quit. That's no good, is it? You've got to work at it, like everything else.

Nevertheless, the Fowler family has shown considerable signs of strain on numerous occasions. The sudden disappearance of their son Mark, for example (which apparently occured as a result of the actor being dismissed for refusing to speak 'racist' lines), was explained in terms of his desire to 'lead his own life'. The Fowlers eventually found Mark by tracing him from a postmark on a letter he had written – although, significantly, he had now become part of a new family, through his relationship with an older woman and her two children. Although Pauline reluctantly accepted Mark's need for autonomy, and the fact that he would eventually 'grow away' from the family, it was clear that he himself found the family 'too close'.

Similar issues were at stake in Michelle's quarrels with her parents over her pregnancy. Indeed, she explained her brief misdemeanour with Den in the first place as a result of a lack of affection in the family, particularly on the part of her father, and the fact that she was treated like 'a little girl'. She also resisted her parents' attempts to force her to have an abortion, arguing that they were trying to make decisions for her, and not taking account of her wishes. Her eventual marriage to Lofty offered a potential reconciliation of the family, although it was not without its problems. Arthur's initial suspicion that Lofty was the father of the child led him to be extremely hostile towards him, although his discovery that he was not meant that Lofty's status became rather ambiguous. Lofty's attempts to initiate a father/son relationship with Arthur thus met with resistance, and some relatively comic confrontations:

ARTHUR   You're not my son!
LOFTY   Then you're not my father!
ARTHUR   You're worse than Mark!
LOFTY   You're worse than my dad was!

Lofty's own family background was clearly problematic: his marriage to Michelle meant that he could acquire the family he was lacking – as his Aunt said, 'He's seen all the mistakes, mostly from his own mum and dad. All his life, he's just wanted a chance to make them right. Now he can.'

In the case of Arthur, it was his unemployment which precipitated the family into crisis. On a personal level, unemployment was a blow to Arthur's masculinity – 'I don't feel like a man anymore!' – yet it also had implications in terms of his status within the family. After he had been laid off, for example, his mother-in-law Lou issued him with a list of jobs she wanted doing, leading him to complain that the women in the house were ordering him around. This disruption of the traditional balance of power within the family led to an increasing sense of confusion and resentment:

106

It's a topsy-turvy world, Tom, when a man can't provide for his family. They used to be rock-solid, families did. You knew what your role was, what was expected of you. The man was the bread-winner, and the woman the home-maker. Now it's all arse about face, isn't it? I'm sitting at home with Martin. I've even learnt to cook. While she goes to her Creative Expression classes.

Most crucially, Arthur's inability to provide for his family meant that he was unable to pay for Michelle's wedding reception. As the 'head of the household', it was his responsibility to give Michelle a day to remember, and if he could not 'bring money into the house' by earning it, he was bound to steal it. His eventual breakdown was thus at least partly a result of his inability to perform his allotted role within the family – a fact which was repeatedly played upon by Lou:

You're tearing your family apart. You're not the only one who's out of work – there's others in the same boat. Besides, you've got to think of Michelle and Pauline. They rely on you. You've got to snap out of it, for their sake.

Michelle's wedding in turn became a focus of considerable discord within the family. Pauline favoured a church wedding, on the grounds that it would be a 'family occasion':

Those are the shared memories, with all your family around you, and that's what keeps us together. And without your family round you, and their support, you wouldn't have the luxury of talking about independence.

Michelle, however, did not want the wedding to be 'another Fowler show of strength', and argued against it with Arthur. Eventually, Lou herself intervened in truly matriarchal style to silence the dispute:

I'm ashamed of this family ... It doesn't matter what troubles you have. It doesn't matter what troubles you have either, my girl. But this family does not fight cat and dog in this house ... Now just you take this to heart. Family comes first. And that means family loyalty. We do not fight among ourselves.

Nevertheless, the principle of family loyalty is one which Michelle at least has questioned. After Cassie Carpenter was discovered smoking dope which she had taken from Mark Fowler's friend Owen, the Fowlers were heavily criticised by the Carpenters for lacking 'parental responsibility'. Michelle, however, refused to participate in this inter-family feud, and rejected her mother's attempts to 'stand by the family' – 'we are a family, and there are rules, and you have to stick by them'.

On several occasions, therefore, the Fowler family has been thrown into crisis as a result of threats from outside – most notably by Arthur's unemployment and by Michelle's relationship with Den and the pregnancy which resulted from it. These threats have in turn disrupted the balance of power within the family, between the different generations, and between the man and the women in the household. The task of holding the family together has largely fallen to Pauline: as Dr Legg once observed, she is the 'prop of the family'. While she has occasionally shown signs of cracking under the strain, her periods of crisis have been quickly resolved. Pauline has also rallied the family together against criticism from outside, and sought to enforce 'family loyalty'. Arthur's inability to perform the traditional male role has deprived him of much of his power, leaving Pauline to be both 'breadwinner' and 'homemaker'. The lineage within the family can thus be seen as matriarchal, with power being transferred from Lou to Pauline – and perhaps eventually to Michelle.

The presence of strong central women characters in soap opera is clearly a significant reason for the genre's traditional appeal to a female audience. As Terry Lovell has observed in relation to *Coronation Street*, it is through its strong middle-aged women characters that the serial offers a 'validation and celebration' of women's interests and concerns.[29] The conventions of the genre require that women remain independent in order to retain their dramatic interest: while there may be interludes in which they are contained within marriage, these remain temporary. Lovell argues that, as a result, soap opera has a rather ambiguous relationship to patriarchal ideology: it provides a context in which women can express '*both* good-humoured acceptance of their oppression *and* recognition of that oppression, and some equally good-humoured protest against it.'

This account also applies to *EastEnders*, although there are some significant differences. Although Lou certainly occupies the matriarchal role, the other older female characters are generally regarded, not with respect, but with ridicule. Pauline's strength is very much centred on the family: she has often seemed to be buried under the weight of domestic oppression, and rarely offers a protest against it, good-humoured or otherwise. Some of the other middle-aged women characters – such as Angie Watts and Pat Wicks, who in some respects are equivalent to the *Street*'s Elsie Tanner and Bet Lynch – seem to be more torn apart by the contradictions of patriarchy than 'good-humoured' about them. In this respect, *EastEnders* is considerably harder-edged than its rival. While Angie's fatal attraction to Den could be interpreted as a form of masochism, her attempts to get revenge, particularly since the break-up of their marriage, have been characterised by an inspiring degree of vitriolic hatred.

Pat Wicks is another character who could scarcely be described as passive, and her attitude towards men – particularly towards her ex-husband, Pete Beale – is often little short of contemptuous. Although the alliance between Angie and Pat is certainly formidable, both are essentially, in Angie's terms, 'lame ducks' who have been betrayed by their desire for men:

> PAT   It's the only thing that's ever made me feel real, safe. That short time in the dark when they want you. Before you see that look in their eye when they've got what they wanted. They despise you … The only thing that's ever given me any pleasure – and look where it's got me!

Pat's relationship with Mary Smith was also defined in terms of female solidarity – 'Us girls should stick together' – and as a matter of getting revenge on men by using their power as women, in this case as 'amateur' prostitutes. In this instance Pat clearly saw herself as a kind of surrogate mother, and chastised Mary when she went too far – 'You weren't supposed to turn professional, make a career out of it! You're a silly kid. I ought to put you over my knee and spank you.'

Mary herself is another character who has been seen to pose a potential threat to men, although again she has repeatedly been undermined by her own desires. Thus, her infatuation with Andy O'Brien led her to soften her aggressive punk appearance, in a kind of ritual unmasking: as a result, many of the men in the community expressed approval, and began to pay her romantic attention, although she failed to attract Andy himself. In the case of Mehmet Osman, her response was more forthright: when she discovered that he had bet his brother Ali £10 that he could get her into bed, she began a campaign against him, smashing up his car and pestering his minicab business with a series of hoax calls and deliveries.

Mary, Pat and Angie are all characters who have been driven to desperation as a result of their treatment by men. Yet in other instances, the serial has provided more 'positive images' of female independence. For example, Pat's conflicts with Kathy Beale have repeatedly drawn attention to the differences between them. While these are partly a matter of social class – the difference between the 'rough' and the 'respectable' working class – they have also been defined in terms of their power as women. Although Kathy's attempts to gain independence have certainly been opposed by her husband Pete – for example, when she decided to join the Samaritans, and to set up her knitwear business – she has usually won the arguments. As Pat argued, 'You're always in charge. Men always want women like you.' –

although, as her statement implies, Kathy's independence has been achieved within the confines of a relatively stable and conventional family life. Thus, Pete ultimately supported her knitwear business because it provided a useful extra income for the family: as in Pauline's case, the woman becoming a 'breadwinner' does not of itself pose any major threat to the family.

Although the serial has featured bitter rivalries between women over their rights to men, it has also emphasised female solidarity – for example in the 'women's support group' which Lou organised for Angie, and in the form of the women's darts team. Arthur's masculinity was further threatened by Pauline's decision to attend 'Creative Expression' classes, particularly when she told him that she had been drawing male nudes. Kathy supported Pauline, and exploited the men's anxiety, while Pete urged Arthur to assert himself:

> PETE There's only room for one boss in any house. And my Kathy knows that. And you should tell Mum that too, and Pauline.
> ARTHUR Oh yeah? Do you think you'd be boss in your house if Mum lived with you?

Nevertheless, as in the representation of 'class politics', more explicit forms of feminism have largely been marginalised. Naima's rejection of her arranged marriage and her subsequent 'Westernisation' were accompanied by an engagement with feminist politics: marriage, she argued, was all about 'property, possession and making men the head of everything'. The arrival of her cousin Rezaul was seen as a constraint on her developing independence – 'Time for the boys to take control.' Nevertheless, the main representative of feminism within the serial has been Debbie Wilkins, who was often rejected by the other characters on class grounds. The relationship between gender and class attitudes was clearly illustrated in her arguments with Sue Osman:

> DEBBIE I'm sorry, I've got a class to get to.
> SUE What's that, middle or upper?
> DEBBIE Self-defence, actually.
> SUE If you stayed at home with your man, you wouldn't need that, now would you?

Likewise, Debbie's attempts to offer advice to Angie were forcefully rejected: she claimed that since breaking off her relationship with Roy Quick, she felt a 'great sense of freedom':

> DEBBIE Perhaps you should do the same. I'm serious. Den's no good for you. You'd be better off without him.
> ANGIE I see. How would you know about that?

DEBBIE I'm speaking from experience.
ANGIE Yeah, all five minutes of it. You don't know what you're talking about, girl.

By marginalising and undermining explicit feminist politics in this way, the serial effectively confines women's 'protest against oppression' to the level of interpersonal relationships with men. While it clearly does provide 'positive images' of female solidarity, and of women gaining economic independence, and even gives voice to a powerful resentment against men, there is a sense in which the serial positively refuses the possibility that gender issues can be posed in *political* as well as personal terms.

EastEnders' construction of masculinity has been significantly more innovative, however. If traditional representations of men have tended to take their masculine identity and sexuality for granted, *EastEnders* has consistently posed masculinity as a problem. As I have indicated, Arthur's unemployment precipitated a crisis in which his sense of his own masculinity and his male role as 'head of the household' were severely undermined. Other characters have also come in for similar treatment. The death of Sue and Ali's baby Hassan resulted in Ali becoming impotent; and although this was subsequently overcome, their failure to have children led Ali's brother Mehmet to accuse him of not being man enough. Meanwhile, Mehmet himself was threatened by Mary's assertive approach to their relationship – 'I like to do the running. I like to be in control.' – and Sue condemned him for his hypocritical attitude towards English women. On a more comic level, even Den's masculinity was undermined by the arrival of the Walford bank robber – causing Sharon, for example, to refer to him as a 'poodle' – and his attempts to assert himself led to the suggestion that he might hit back with his handbag.

However, it is through the character of Pete Beale in particular that traditional definitions of masculinity have been called into question. On the one hand, Pete clearly regards himself as a 'real man' and as 'the boss' in his family – a self-image which is partly supported by his wife Kathy. He also feels he is an expert on women, advising his son Ian on the best strategies for 'pulling birds'; Ian himself was having little luck in this direction, and his recourse to a book entitled 'Increase Your Self-Confidence' provoked Pete to exclaim, 'There's no need to read rubbish like this. There's no mystery about women!' The discovery that Ian had been reading pornographic magazines led Kathy to become extremely concerned, although Pete reassured her that it was 'just a laugh'.

On the other hand, however, Pete's masculine self-image has been repeatedly undermined. The arrival of his ex-wife Pat Wicks, for example, provided a view of Pete which had not hitherto been heard in the serial: she told Pauline that Pete was 'boring, selfish and terrible in bed', and went on to torment him by revealing that he was not in fact the father of her son Simon – 'you're not man enough to make Simon'. Pete has also been publicly humiliated on a number of occasions: his taunting of the drag artist who played the Queen Vic resulted in him being pulled on stage, his embarrassment causing much amusement among the audience; and his attempt to gatecrash the women's lingerie party left him considerably deflated. Perhaps the most remarkable example of this came early in 1987, when Pete was under suspicion by the police for the attack on Pat Wicks. Den had organised a 'cross-dressing' party at the Queen Vic – although Ian had played a practical joke by telling everybody except his parents that the party had been called off. Pete arrived in full drag, and on seeing that he had been tricked, rushed out of the pub; only shortly afterwards, it was announced that there had been another attack, causing Sue to suggest that Pete was responsible. The episode concluded back in the Beales' flat, with a close-up of Pete's tear-stained, luridly made-up face.

Although Pete was not in fact to blame for the attacks, he was found guilty of hitting a policeman, and he has also had recourse to violence on a number of other occasions, particularly when defending his wife Kathy. In many ways, then, Pete's definition of his own masculinity has come into question; and the connection between masculinity and violence, far from being celebrated, has been seen as a problem.

Nevertheless, the serial cannot be said to have provided many significant alternative definitions of masculinity. Pete's son Ian, for example, is training to be a chef, yet he was tormented for a long time by his inability to succeed with women. Lofty might be said to represent a softer, more caring form of masculinity, although he has often been held up to ridicule as a result: on seeing him carrying a bag of nappies, Den mocked him for being a 'reconstituted man', while his disapproval of Mary's stripping act led her to suggest that 'a real man would like it'. The gay characters, Colin and Barry, clearly embody a different definition of masculinity – and in several respects also fail to conform to gay stereotypes; although again, with the exception of Dot and Nick Cotton, they appear to have been accepted by the community with magical ease.

The focus on men's domestic and 'personal' lives which characterises soap opera is unique in terms of popular television, at least outside the realm of comedy. In dealing with this area, there are clearly considerable constraints, not least of plausibility. While it can be acknowledged that men have problems with their relationships, it remains unusual for them to be shown actually talking about them, particularly with each other. Although *EastEnders*' female characters are often seen discussing their feelings, and offering mutual support, it is comparatively rare for the male characters to do so.

Ultimately, the problem with 'positive images', which embody alternatives to the dominant discourses, is that they run the risk of appearing implausible. A character like Colin, for example, clearly performs a didactic role – and does so more effectively, I would argue, not by making speeches about AIDS, but simply by being part of the community in the serial, and by failing to correspond to many viewers' expectations. It is precisely for this reason that he may be rejected – as Mary Whitehouse's attacks on the serial's representation of homosexuals clearly indicate. Yet the main problem is not so much that Colin himself may appear implausible, but that the other characters' reaction to him does. Here again, Albert Square appears to be devoid of homophobia, in the same way as it appears devoid of racism. Only a small minority of deviant characters dissent from the dominant view, and they are clearly and forcefully corrected for their sins. The central contradiction of the 'positive images' strategy is that it cannot give voice to the attitudes which it seeks to confront, for fear that it will merely encourage them.

Although the family is primarily a site of conflict between men and women in the serial, it also serves to focus differences and inequalities between the generations. *EastEnders* began life with a group of young characters who were all approaching the school-leaving age, and thus about to embark on the transition from childhood to adulthood. In the case of the Fowler family, Mark and Michelle's conflicts with their parents were largely defined as a struggle for autonomy, which led them to question and at least partly to reject the notion of family loyalty. Yet if Mark has remained outside the family, Michelle's marriage to Lofty has enabled it to survive into another generation.

A similar process has occurred in the case of Kelvin Carpenter. His attempts to achieve independence have brought him into conflict with his parents, whose morality has often been typified as relatively strict. His parents have occasionally been outraged to find him entertaining girlfriends, and, in one instance, being serenaded by a 'strippogram' girl at a party. Yet Kelvin has also achieved a degree of equality with his parents: he has advised his father about his marital problems, and has been able to criticise them for their handling of his sister Cassie. This ambiguity in their relationship has been particularly apparent in their disputes over his involvement with the health visitor Carmel. It was made clear on her first introduction into the serial that both Tony and Kelvin were attracted to Carmel, so that when Tony attempted to prevent Kelvin from staying the night with her, Kelvin was able to accuse him of jealousy. Furthermore, Kelvin also argued that his parents had no grounds on which to criticise him, given the difficulties in their own marriage: 'You and dad leave a lot to be desired... I want something better than you and dad have got out of life. I want a relationship where there's love and affection.' The fact that Kelvin has been able to question his parents' authority in this way has meant that he has not had to reject the family completely in order to attain his autonomy.

Sharon Watts' criticisms of her parents, and particularly of her father, have carried a similar degree of credibility. Perhaps even more clearly than the other teenage characters, Sharon was kept suspended between childhood and adulthood. While Den has often described her as 'just a child', she herself has sought to assert her status as an adult, rejecting the other teenagers' behaviour as 'immature' and 'childish', and even, on occasion, describing her parents in similar terms: thus, she argued that Den had tried to keep Angie like a baby, and that he himself was a child – 'I behave more like an adult than you've ever done.' Like Kelvin, she has been able to question her parents' ability to offer advice, and they have had difficulty in refuting her arguments: 'How come you two always know what's best for me? You haven't exactly made a good job of your own lives!'

To some degree, then, parental authority has been called into question in many of the families. In these conflicts, it is the children's perspectives which appear to be privileged: they can criticise their parents for their mistakes, although they themselves remain comparatively free of blame. Even in the case of the more deviant children, the responsibility for their behaviour has often been placed with the parents. Thus, Cassie Carpenter's problems arose largely from her anxiety over her parents' break-up; Mark Fowler had to escape from a family which he found 'too close'; and even Nick Cotton's behaviour was blamed on his mother, at least by Kathy Beale – 'You smothered him from the day he was born ... He never had a chance to become a man with you as his mother.' Yet even here, what is significantly lacking is any sense of an autonomous and distinctive 'youth culture', let alone one which poses any real threat to adult authority. The band which a number of the teenage characters formed in mid-1986 clearly epitomised this: despite the considerable disputes which surrounded it and eventually broke it apart, it remained anonymous and completely anodyne.

EastEnders' construction of its teenage characters also appears to be informed by the 'positive images' strategy I have already identified: it deliberately refuses dominant definitions of 'youth' as a 'problem', yet in the process wishes away fundamental differences and inequalities. While this might possibly serve a didactic function for older viewers, it runs the risk of appearing implausible, or at least merely bland – and was certainly perceived as such by the young people whose responses are recorded in Chapter Four. Indeed, it is signficant that *Eastenders* applies this 'positive images' approach more consistently in some areas than in others. While the teenagers, the black characters and the gay couple have tended to receive this treatment, the areas of gender and class have been dealt with in more complex ways, which may account for the fact that they were seen as more authentic.

Conclusion
In this chapter, I have attempted to analyse the ways in which *East-Enders* seeks to 'position' its viewers. I have argued that this process is characterised by diversity and, in many cases, by contradiction. Simply in order to retain a large popular audience, the serial must allow for a multiplicity of potential readings. Rather than confining the viewer to a single position from which it may be read and understood, it must provide a range of different positions, and enable the viewer to shift between them. Yet this diversity is not infinite in scope: if only by virtue of the discourses which it excludes, the text inevitably tends to resist certain types of readings.

Ultimately, textual analysis has distinct limitations: while it may provide a useful means of generating hypotheses, it is clearly incapable of accounting for the ways in which real audiences actually make sense of television. Viewers are not merely 'positioned' by television: they are also positioned in society and in history, and will therefore bring different kinds of prior knowledge to the text. As a result, they may refuse to accept, or indeed fail to perceive, the 'invitations' which the text offers.

Furthermore, there is also a significant difficulty in defining and isolating the text itself. Indeed, it may well be false to regard any television programme as a discrete self-contained 'text': the experience of television viewing may more accurately be seen as one of 'flow', in which the boundaries between programmes have increasingly become blurred.[30]

In the case of soap opera, this problem is compounded by the fact that the text always remains unfinished. As a result, the kind of generalisations I have made here are inevitably provisional. Recent developments in *Crossroads*, for example, where most of the regular characters have been written out, must provide a salutory warning to anybody seeking to make definitive statements about the ways in which a given soap opera represents the social world. Although generalisations about the ways in which soap operas typically 'work' may be a good deal safer, it would be false to regard the constraints and conventions of the genre as fixed or unchanging.

Finally, it may also prove difficult to separate the text from the variety of other texts which surround and mediate it – from the ways in which it is marketed and promoted, defined and criticised, extended and exploited. It is these processes which I shall consider in more detail in the following chapter.

3
BETWEEN THE TEXT
AND THE AUDIENCE

The relationship between a text and its audience is never direct. On the contrary, it is always mediated in various ways. Literary texts, for example, are mediated by critics and reviewers, and by the ways in which they are marketed and promoted. Readers never come to texts without expectations about what they are likely to encounter – even if these come simply from reading the dustjacket of a book.

With popular television programmes, this degree of mediation is often extensive and in the case of *EastEnders*, it has been unprecedented in the history of British television. On a daily basis, millions read the newspapers' latest exclusive predictions of future developments in the plot, along with 'intimate secrets' of the love-lives of the cast, and shocking revelations of their criminal past. Pin-ups of 'soap studs' taken from women's magazines adorn bedroom walls. Members of the cast appear on chat shows and phone-ins, and are caricatured as rubber puppets in *Spitting Image*. Their records reach number one in the pop charts, and promotional videos are screened on *Top of the Pops*. The 'stars' open supermarkets, meet members of the royal family, and are mobbed in nightclubs. *EastEnders* books, calendars, teatowels, computer games and knitting patterns are sold by the thousands in high street shops.

The popular press and official merchandising represent only a fraction of this phenomenon. On a recent visit to Brighton, I was sorely tempted to buy an 'unofficial' *EastEnders* T-shirt featuring a picture of the notorious East End criminals, the Kray Twins, and to have my photograph taken on the pier standing next to life-size cardboard cut-outs of Den and Angie Watts. Meanwhile, a pub near my home in North London has been promoting a series of *EastEnders* 'hen nights', just like those organised by Angie in the 'Queen Vic'.

In this context, the producers' claims that *EastEnders* has become 'public property', that it has 'gone beyond the screen' and entered into the culture as a whole, do not appear exaggerated. The programme has become a part of the texture of many people's daily lives, about whose 'effects' we can only begin to speculate. Inevitably, the kinds of phenomena described here do have an influence, not merely on the audience's relationship with the programme, but also on the programme-makers themselves; yet this influence is likely to be complex and ambiguous. To what extent, for example, does knowledge of the private lives of the cast undermine belief in the realism of the programme's fictional world? Or does it, in certain instances, reinforce it? What is the meaning of *EastEnders* merchandise for those who purchase and consume it – for those who wear *EastEnders* sweatshirts, or sleep under *EastEnders* bedspreads or duvet covers? Is the process simply one of 'exploitation' – both of the programme and the audience?

This chapter will consider two main aspects of this mediation process, namely marketing and press coverage. In a concluding section I shall describe a rather different form of mediation, on the part of Mary Whitehouse, the programme's most vociferous public critic.

Marketing

EastEnders arrived at a time when the BBC was already under considerable financial strain. Although its main source of income, the annual licence fee, had been increased to £58 in 1985, this was well below the £65 figure which the Corporation itself had argued was necessary to maintain and enhance its present level of service. The new fee would remain in force for the following three years, and would require the BBC to make substantial economies, as well as looking for new sources of revenue, such as merchandising. The amalgamation of BBC Publications and Enterprises in plush new offices near Television Centre in 1985 was the first stage in a determined attempt to enter the market place, which saw a series of high street outlets for BBC products being opened in 1987.

The success of *EastEnders* clearly represented a golden opportunity for generating income. As a long-running serial, it obviously lends itself to commercial exploitation in a way that programmes with a shorter life do not. As Michael Grade argued:

> The BBC has a duty to capitalise on it: it's our creation, and if anybody's going to make any money out of it, we should... The BBC knows a commercial opportunity when it sees it. It's the same as anybody. You've got to be a fool not to see that there is money to be made out of the right kind of exploitation of *EastEnders*. Whether it's mugs, pens, books, records, whatever. If we don't do it, somebody else will, so we might as well do it, and that way we can control it, and have quality control.

The range of *EastEnders* products available has grown rapidly. At the time of writing, the following are either in the shops now, or due to be launched: calendars; postcards and greetings cards; an annual, largely focusing on the younger characters; novels, aimed both at a general adult market and specifically at teenagers; records, including a 'singalong' album of Cockney favourites, as well as singles by at least six of the cast; a home video, in which Den Watts reminisces about his tortuous love-life; a computer game (in Amstrad, Spectrum and Commodore versions) involving simulated interactions between the characters; sweatshirts, T-shirts and knitting patterns; a 'party pack', complete with balloons; a board game; model houses; duvet covers, rugs and bedspreads; jigsaws, diaries, pens and mugs. With the exception of the home video and some of the records, which are marketed by the BBC itself, these items are all produced by commercial companies under licence from the BBC.

In addition to this 'official' merchandise, there is also a plethora of unofficial products, which the BBC can do very little to prevent. Only in cases where images of the cast are used – for example on 'Dirty Den' coathangers – is it clear that copyright has been infringed. In other instances, there are considerable opportunities to 'cash in' legally. Thus the *Sun* (28 April 1986) can offer 'a ring like Michelle's' with a zirconium oxide stone for 'only' £4.50; and a group called Whisky and Sofa can issue a 'Dirty Den' record (with the memorable refrain 'Dirty Den, he's a man among men, a ten out of ten, he does it again and again') with little fear of legal restraint. Members of the cast have also attempted to capitalise on their success, although they are only contractually permitted to do so under their own names: thus Peter Dean (Pete Beale), June Brown (Dot Cotton) and Tom Watt (Lofty Holloway) have all released singles, while 'Love Riding High' by Oscar James (Tony Carpenter) was promoted with a picture of the actor bearing the legend 'TWENTY ONE MILLION OF YOU KNOW THIS MAN'.

By comparison with American soap operas, particularly *Dynasty*, this remains relatively small-scale merchandising. In the United States, there are over two hundred *Dynasty* products available, including thirty different items of lingerie and forty of silverware, which together apparently gross over $200 million each year. Many of these are extremely expensive: while the more modest consumer can purchase *Dynasty* wallpaper, dolls or bedlinen, not to mention 'Forever Krystle' perfume, the more affluent can splash out $10,000 on a *Dynasty* fur coat. According to a report in *The Times* (20 November 1985), twenty-six thousand women stormed Bloomingdales, the New York department store, when a new range of *Dynasty* products was launched.

Nevertheless, by the more restrained standards of British television, the marketing of *EastEnders* products has certainly been unprecedented. In terms of BBC programmes, only the long-running children's series *Doctor Who* and, more recently, *Postman Pat* have generated significant amounts of income from 'spinoffs' such as books and toys. Indeed, the BBC's reported refusal to screen *She-Ra* and *He-Man*, two American cartoon series with extensive spinoffs in children's toys, indicates its past unwillingness to exploit programmes for commercial gain, or simply to allow others to do so.

If the marketing of *EastEnders* products has been unprecedented, then, it has not been wholly unrestrained. To begin with, this was simply a matter of economic calculation: the initial uncertainty and, at least in certain quarters, lack of confidence about the programme's success meant that manufacturers were understandably reticent about making bids for licences. The first rush of applications did not arrive until September and October 1985, which was rather too late to hit the Christmas market, although the first calendar just managed to make it in time. BBC Enterprises itself was also reluctant to flood the market, particularly once it became clear that the programme was likely to have a longer life than some had predicted. With a long-running serial, it seemed appropriate to wait until the market was ready, rather than attempting to create it through merchandising itself. As Judy Niner, the marketing executive with responsibility for *EastEnders* products, explained, it was important that BBC Enterprises and BBC Publicity should devise a co-ordinated strategy:

> If you have got ten years, or five years, or three years in which to exploit it, you don't necessarily need to rush in on that first year: particularly not when the Press Office did. You didn't need to have merchandising to get viewers... Marketing hasn't really played a part in gaining viewers. We have come in on the back of it, and we're using the market that has been created for us.[1]

At the same time, there have been additional constraints, partly concerned with 'taste' and 'quality' and partly with preserving a certain 'image' for the programme, and thereby for the BBC itself. As Judy Niner explained, any product connected with *EastEnders* would inevitably be perceived as a BBC product, even if it had in fact been produced by an outside contractor. For this reason, it is important that the products themselves should be well-made, and that the companies to whom licences are granted are capable of manufacturing and distributing them.

In order to ensure that these licensed products are consistent with the 'image' of the programme, the producer, Julia Smith, is asked to check all applications for accuracy, and in instances where 'copy' is required – for example to accompany the illustrations on the calendar, or in the computer software – this is produced by *EastEnders* writers themselves. The novels are largely based on the biographies written by Julia Smith and Tony Holland, who retain a joint copyright with the authors.

This requirement to involve the producers and writers acts as a further constraint on the amount of commercial exploitation, since their priorities must lie with the programme itself. Smith and Holland certainly regarded this aspect of their work as an additional source of pressure, which was in danger of detracting from their commitment to the programme; as Smith put it, there was a distinct danger of 'the tail wagging the dog'.

One specific requirement which is worth noting here is Julia Smith's concern that the cast should be regarded as equals, and that particular actors are not to be seen as 'stars'. Given that the public might get bored with a limited number of 'stars', this policy is clearly in the interest of maintaining the programme's longer-term popularity. Yet according to Judy Niner, this made it more difficult in terms of marketing than, for example, a programme like *Doctor Who*, which is based on one central character:

> It's much more difficult with *EastEnders*, where Julia is very anxious that [the cast] are treated like a theatrical repertory company. Obviously Den and Angie to the public are the stars, at the moment. But we have to be careful not to jeopardise Julia's position... If we were simply satisfying consumer demand, we'd have Den and Angie plastered on T-shirts, on everything. But we're not: we're trying to marry the two. Which means our range is much more limited than it could be.

Ensuring that the 'image' is correct is not merely a question of checking that the characters are consistent or that the language is right. Perhaps inevitably, the *EastEnders* products tend to emphasise the 'cosy community' aspects of the programme, rather than its focus on social problems or its attempts at grand melodrama. Negative characters – who admittedly tend to be short-lived – are thus excluded; and families which in the programme are riven with conflict are portrayed in the greetings cards and calendars as radiant with homely warmth. Compared with *Dynasty* merchandise, the products themselves are also largely inexpensive household commodities, rather than glamorous luxuries. As Judy Niner concluded: 'What you're seeing in the shops is very safe, middle-of-the-road, acceptable, good quality Albert-Square-type merchandising.'

The *EastEnders* records which have been released to date certainly reflect this conservative approach, yet they also draw upon experienced viewers' knowledge of the characters. Thus Anita Dobson's (Angie Watts) chart-topping single 'Anyone can fall in love', based on the programme's theme music, reflects obliquely on Angie's desperate marital situation. Nick Berry's (Simon Wicks) number one 'Every loser wins' was rechristened 'Every Lofty wins' by one cynical correspondent to the *Radio Times* on the basis of its rather obvious connection with Lofty's romantic misfortunes. 'Something out of nothing' by Paul Medford and Letitia Dean was also appropriately titled, and despite promotional 'plugs' in the programme made little impression on the charts.

The *EastEnders* novels, which have been serialised by a number of newspapers and magazines, are essentially 'prequels' for the serial, covering the lives of the characters in the years before the programme itself began. *Home Fires Burning*, for example, the first of the series, follows the parallel stories of Lou Beale and Harold Legg through the Second World War, while *Swings and Roundabouts*, the second, traces the Beales and the Fowlers through the 1960s. The novels thus provide historical explanations for the idiosyncrasies of the characters: in Book Three, *Good Intentions*, we learn that Debbie Wilkins' snobbery derives from her mother's influence, while in Book Four, *The Flower of Albert Square*, we learn that Ethel's absent-mindedness and her 'gift' of clairvoyance were caused by a knock on the head she received in her youth. In this way, the novels provide a history which can only be briefly referenced in the programme itself, so that when Lou Beale reminisces about her husband Albert, or Harold Legg refers to the tragic death of his young wife, viewers who are familiar with the novels are able to 'fill in' the missing details. At the same time, one's knowledge of the programme has a retroactive effect on one's reading of the novels, in that we know how the narrative will turn out. In *Swings and Roundabouts*, for example, we know that Pauline will eventually marry Arthur and Pete will eventually marry Kathy, and the novel itself plays with this knowledge by providing a number of 'false trails'.

One central theme, which recurs throughout the more historically distant of the novels, is that of working-class characters 'winning through' despite adversity. The publisher's blurbs epitomise this:

> HOME FIRES BURNING is a story of good times and bad times, of the indomitable spirit of the East End, a story rich with laughter and tragedy, and a story of the people of Albert Square winning through against the odds.
> THE FLOWER OF ALBERT SQUARE tells the moving story of Ethel Skinner – always managing to come up smiling against the knocks dealt her by life.

The latter book finds Harold Legg reflecting on 'the memory of loss that accompanied every sign of gain', and musing on 'the resilience of people'. Ethel herself, meanwhile, is discovered leafing through her photograph album, turning the pages sharply to quench 'the pain of memory' and 'to shut off hurtful recollection'. This sentimental view of working-class resilience is a fundamental aspect of the mythology of 'the Cockney' described in the previous chapter – a mythology which precisely excludes class politics. Bennie, a socialist with whom Ethel is briefly involved, is revealed to be more interested in studying than in sex, and is thus rejected in favour of what he terms her 'appetite for coarser pleasures'. In the novels themselves, broader social and political forces are registered merely to indicate the passing of time, as background to the human drama.

In general, then, the extensive marketing of *EastEnders* products serves to position audiences, not merely as viewers of the programme, but also as potential consumers of the commercial goods associated with it. In some cases, the connection between these two aspects has been quite direct: *EastEnders* records have been heavily 'plugged' in the programme itself, and have been effectively advertised in announcements directly following it.

At the same time, the products themselves have also served to define the 'image' of the programme and, by extension, of the BBC itself. Both by virtue of the ways in which they represent the programme, and by virtue of the kinds of products they are, they have emphasised its more consensual aspects, its embodiment of the solid, homely respectability of British family life, rather than the more subversive elements of working-class culture which are present in it. Ultimately, the success of this merchandising strategy depends upon the extent to which this emphasis coincides with the way in which viewers themselves read the programme. There is certainly evidence, both from the popular press and from my own audience research, to suggest that it does not.

Promotion

If marketing represents one way in which *EastEnders*' public image is defined, the BBC's own promotion of the programme is clearly another. Certain aspects of promotion remain 'in-house', for example in the form of on-screen trailers and features in the *Radio Times*. In the latter case, the programme was introduced by a series of profiles of the characters before it came on air – 'The EastEnders are coming!' – and then by a substantial feature article, including an annotated map of Albert Square, to coincide with the launch. Regular listings usually include a brief unattributed quote from each episode, encouraging viewers to speculate about who speaks the line in question, to whom, and in what context. In addition to further character profiles and interviews with the cast, there have also been a number of special features to coincide with major events in the serial, such as Den and Angie's second honeymoon in Venice and Michelle and Lofty's abortive wedding. *EastEnders*' anniversaries have also been celebrated by extensive coverage: a twelve-page feature on its first birthday, for example, looked back over 'a year of juicy gossip', and included a short story entitled 'A Right Royal Knees Up', which told of events in Albert Square on the day of the Royal Wedding in 1981. A full-page picture of 'Angie as you've never seen her before', 'going up West' to the Waldorf Hotel in a scarlet silk-satin 'glamour gown', together with a number of other pictures of the cast were available for sale as 10″ x 8″ colour prints; and the issue also included the first instalment of an *EastEnders* competition, whose prizes included a trip to 'Albert Square'.

Meanwhile, members of the cast have also been repeatedly featured as guests in other BBC programmes, most notably on chat shows such as *Wogan* and *Breakfast Time*, which interviewed Tom Watt (Lofty Holloway) on the morning after he had been left standing at the altar by his bride-to-be Michelle. Other appearances have included the game show *Blankety Blank*, and *The Royal Variety Performance*, in which most of the cast joined the singer Vera Lynn in a rendition of 'There'll always be an England'. *EastEnders* records have been promoted by appearances and videos on *Wogan* and *Top of the Pops*; and the programme has been the subject of a number of documentaries, both for Schools and general service television. Members of the cast have been used as presenters for programmes covering issues which relate to *EastEnders* storylines: Susan Tully (Michelle Fowler), for example, presented a documentary about teenage mothers entitled 'Too young to have a baby' for the Schools series *Scene*.

The BBC also operates an *EastEnders* phone line, in which Wendy Richard (Pauline Fowler) keeps viewers up to date on the latest developments in Albert Square – although experienced viewers might well ask how she appears to know so much. In its first year, between February and December 1985, over 400,000 calls had been received.

This in-house promotion tends to reinforce the definition of the programme's 'public image' which is present in the merchandising: the association with royalty, and with 'official' (and somewhat nostalgic) definitions of national identity ('There'll always be an England') provides an added dimension to the assertion of consensual values – an association which recurs throughout the press coverage.

Yet there also begins to emerge a rather more subversive play on the relationship between actors or actresses and the characters they portray. On the one hand, we are given details of the actors' private lives and their past careers, and they are asked to comment on the problems their characters face; while on the other hand, they are pulled, in restrained and sometimes ironical ways, towards identification with their characters. Thus, when Susan Tully appears in a documentary about teenage pregnancy, we know that in 'real life' she is an actress, but the main reason she is presenting the programme in the first place is because we have seen her playing a pregnant teenager in *EastEnders*. Likewise, when Tom Watt (Lofty Holloway) appears on BBC2's investigation of the effects of television, *Television on Trial*, he is referred to by the prosecuting counsel as 'Lofty' until he himself points out that this is not his real name. Another aspect of this phenomenon is the relationship between the mundane 'reality' of the characters and the glamour and celebrity associated with the actors: thus, we are treated to 'Angie goes up West', and to 'showbiz' gloss on *Wogan* and *The Royal Variety Performance*. Within the BBC's in-house publicity, this tension amounts to little more than a gentle 'knowing' irony – although in situations where the BBC is no longer in complete control, it tends to assume more exaggerated and bizarre dimensions.

This is certainly the case with personal appearances. According to a report in *Television Today* (15 May 1986), the 'soap star personal appearance trade' has been undergoing a boom, with *EastEnders* 'stars' largely taking the place of those from *Coronation Street* at the top of the pecking order, with fees as high as £1000 a time. Reports of the 'stars' being mobbed by semi-naked people in nightclubs or causing traffic chaos when opening shopping centres in Croydon have been widely featured in the press, while their less spectacular appearances for charity have often been ignored.

In undertaking such appearances, actors are engaged through their personal agents, rather than through the BBC; and there is a contractual obligation that their own names rather than their character names must be used in any publicity. However, in the event, they are likely to be introduced by their character names, and to speak 'in character' rather than as themselves. Certainly when such appearances are reported in the press, the distinction between actor and character tends to become blurred. The *Sunday Mirror* (25 May 1986) reported 'ANDYMONIUM!', an outbreak of '*EastEnders* fever' which occurred when Ross Davidson (Andy O'Brien) was mobbed during an appearance at the Pink Coconut club in Derby. Meanwhile, when Princess Anne presented Anita Dobson and Leslie Grantham with the Pye TV awards for the most outstanding personalities of 1986, the *Star* (20 May 1986) exclaimed with astonishment 'DIRTY WHO? Princess Anne met Dirty Den yesterday and confessed "I've never seen *East-Enders*" '.

This play on the relationship between reality and fiction is a central preoccupation of the popular press, and will be considered in greater detail below.

Press coverage
The volume and range of press coverage of *EastEnders* has been one of the most extraordinary aspects of the whole phenomenon: although other soap operas have in the past been subject to considerable press attention, it has rarely been as consistent and as extensive. To begin with, the BBC deliberately sought this publicity, yet it has inevitably been unable to retain control of the kind of information which has

been published. The popular press has defined the 'image' of the programme in rather different ways from the BBC's own in-house promotion and licenced merchandising; and this has in turn caused considerable problems for the Corporation, given its 'public service' responsibilities, and the widespread questioning of its role.

The scale of this phenomenon is reflected in the fact that *EastEnders* is the only programme in the history of BBC Television to have its own permanent Press Officer, Cheryl Ann Wilson. Her function is essentially to manage the programme's public image, both by seeking to promote it, and by responding to press interest. Thus, a wide range of publicity material is provided for use by journalists, including a large press pack which was produced for the launch of the programme, a weekly press information sheet giving advance details of the outline of the story, and 'TV Talk', specially written feature articles which, for example, profile members of the cast. Since stories are often published without consultation, press coverage is continuously monitored, both in order to ensure accuracy and to protect the 'reputation and integrity' of the programme.

Although most of the press coverage has been in national newspapers, and particularly the mass-circulation tabloids, *EastEnders* has also featured regularly in local newspapers and in specialist magazines. A brief survey of the latter amply illustrates the bewildering and often bizarre diversity of this material.

Women's magazines constitute one major outlet for *EastEnders* stories: for the more popular of these, such as *Woman*, *Woman's Own* and *Woman's World*, soap operas compete only with royalty as a means of attracting readers, and they have regularly run profiles of the cast, discussing the trials and tribulations of their real and fictional lives. Teenage magazines, such as *Just 17* and *Jackie*, have profiled the younger members of the cast, often with pin-ups using their character names, such as 'Wicksy' or 'Lovely Lofty'. More 'downmarket' weekly magazines such as *Titbits*, *Weekend* and *Weekly News* have offered 'The stars' lives revealed in intriguing, candid interviews', alongside the occasional '*EastEnders* knitting spectacular'.

Meanwhile, the range of smaller-circulation specialist magazines which have carried *EastEnders* stories is extremely broad. For example, *Gay Times* (March 1986) ran a cover story on David Dale, the drag artist who briefly appeared as 'Mr Fisher' in the Queen Vic; *Penthouse* (January 1986) published a photo-spread of 'The girl who wants to be Sharon Watts', a lookalike model posing nude in a pub; the *War Cry* (17 May 1986), a Salvation Army magazine, had a front page story 'Happy ever after' commenting on the positive outcome of Michelle and Lofty's romance; *Pub Leader* (21 February 1985), a trade paper for publicans, commented on the 'bad image' of the British pub provided by the Queen Vic; *Autocar* (21 May 1986) had 'DIRTY DEN

COMES CLEAN' in its 'Me and my car' column; while *Slimmer* (Autumn 1986) gave details of Letitia Dean's (Sharon Watts) 'slow but sure diet' and *Lean Living* (June 1986) asked 'Does Dirty Den's diet make him aggressive?'

In early 1986, the first of a series of glossy 'soap predictions' magazines was published, concentrating exclusively on *EastEnders* and bearing the legend 'TOTALLY UNOFFICIAL'. The cover promised 'sensational tales of lies, lust and illicit love', and the magazine itself included a number of predictions of future events in the serial, both accurate and wildly inaccurate, and mostly pertaining to the sex-lives of the characters. Letters to the characters from 'Paula Young' offered advice and help in handling their problems: 'Dear Kathy... Keep on with the therapy, love – it'll help you with *everything*. And tell that husband of yours he'd better shape up or ship out.' Other characters, particularly the men, received less sympathetic treatment: Den was castigated for his 'kinky sexual habits', while Pete was threatened with the exposure of his 'terrible secret', 'your threesome with Den and Angie'.

The magazine was lavishly illustrated with colour photographs of the cast – both what appear to be early publicity stills taken in 'Albert Square' and 'glamour' shots, for example of Susan Tully and Letitia Dean (Michelle Fowler and Sharon Watts), presumably obtained from agents. It was the photographs in particular which led the BBC to take legal action against the publishers for infringement of copyright, and to obtain an injunction to prevent the magazine being distributed. According to a report in *Television Today* (13 February 1986), 'The BBC says it felt that the magazine was not in keeping with the tone of the programme, and would damage both the reputation of the series and that of the BBC.' Despite the apparent success of the BBC's action, it was relatively easy to obtain copies of the magazine, at least in London newsagents, and the same people (albeit trading under a different name) went on to produce a monthly magazine entitled *Soaps*, which includes material on *EastEnders* alongside other British and American soaps.

Although soap opera magazines have been published in this country in the past, they have generally been one-offs, produced by the television companies themselves to coincide with major events or anniversaries in the serials. In the United States there are a number of magazines dealing with soap opera in general – most notably *Soap Opera Digest* – although *Soaps* represents the first British venture into the field. A typical issue contains a range of 'trivia' quizzes, competitions, star profiles, news and pin-ups (or 'Soap Dishes'). Comparisons between characters in different soaps are a further staple element: in *Soaps* issue one, for example, Den and Angie Watts were narrowly defeated by Sue Ellen and J. R. Ewing in the contest for 'The Lousiest

Marriage', while in issue two 'Dirty Den' got his own back by just beating J. R. as soap opera's 'Number One Rat'. Yet the major preoccupation of the magazine remains that of predicting future events in the serials, particularly those relating to the sexual exploits of the characters: issue two features 'agony aunt' Marje Proops' predictions for the impending marriages of Mike and Susan Baldwin and Lofty and Michelle Holloway, while 'Paula Young's Wicked Whispers' speculates about likely future partners for Bet Lynch and Angie Watts.

If the coverage of *EastEnders* in specialist magazines has been extensive, in the mass circulation tabloids it has often mounted to peaks of hysteria. Although their interest in soap opera is certainly nothing new, in the case of *EastEnders* it has been quite unprecedented in scale. This is at least partly a function of their continuing, and increasingly bitter, circulation war. Immediately prior to *EastEnders*, most of the big-selling newspapers were offering huge prizes in bingo competitions as a means of attracting readers, which have effectively been replaced by 'exclusive' *EastEnders* predictions, and revelations about the private lives of the cast – although the *News of the World* has managed to combine both techniques by using *EastEnders* to promote its own bingo competition. Clearly, *EastEnders* does sell newspapers, more effectively and less expensively than bingo. Yet at the same time, the coverage of the programme appears to serve as a focus for a number of moral debates, and raises questions about the shifting relationship between the public and the private in contemporary society.

In terms of the scale of press coverage, a survey of four newspapers in a relatively low-key month (November 1985) found that the *Daily Mirror* carried seventeen separate *EastEnders* stories, compared with the *Sun*'s nineteen and the *Daily Star*'s twenty-six (including five on one particular day); the *News of the World*, in its four editions that month, managed a total of ten. The range of stories was also extensive, including routine reviews and previews, readers' letters, predictions, news of the actors' private lives and of their public appearances, fashion features, profiles, pin-ups (predominantly of male actors), information about ratings, and merchandising offers. Meanwhile, as the *Daily Mirror* featured 'Dirty Den' choosing his 'Dishy Dozen' from the Miss World contestants, and the *News of the World* covered the appearance of the Queen Vic's male stripper 'Fabulous Frankie' as he was mobbed by 'frenzied female fans', the press also gave extensive coverage to Mary Whitehouse's criticisms of the programme, under headlines like 'EASTENDERS STRIP 'N WHIP RUMPUS' (*Mirror*, 4 November) and 'STRIPPING WHIPPING LYING' (*Star*, 4 November). The *Star* in particular displayed great inventiveness, featuring stories about a London car wash owner whose telephone number is almost identical to that of the *EastEnders* phone line, and who had been repeatedly bothered by callers wanting to catch up on the latest developments (1 November) and a 'copycat' story about a man who 'almost choked to death' after his friends had put a plastic fly in his drink 'hours after characters in BBC's *EastEnders* had been seen playing similar practical jokes in their local pub' (2 November).

In instances such as this, the *EastEnders* connection – and thus also the *EastEnders* headline – appears to merit the inclusion of material which might otherwise be deemed too trivial, even by the standards of what passes as 'human interest'. Thus we have reports about dogs who 'go bonkers' over the *EastEnders* theme tune (*Star*, 7 December 1985) or even pet baboons who 'go ape' over the programme (*Sun*, *Star*, *Mirror*, 27 March 1986). Meanwhile, if a copy shortage threatens, it is always possible to put together a soap opera quiz, a soap opera valentine guide (*Star*, 10 February 1986), a series of interviews with 'Den Watts' namesakes (*Sun*, 13 November 1985) or with 'lookalikes' of the cast (*Sun*, 16 October 1985), a feature about the presents and greetings soap opera characters might exchange at Christmas (*Star*, 23 December 1985), or a quiz which asks 'Is your fella a Dirty Den?' (*Sun*, 10 February 1986).

From this mass of material I have selected five major themes which recur throughout, and which in different ways inform the responses of viewers recorded in the following chapter. At least some of this material might broadly be described as providing a form of critical commentary on the programme, yet the majority of it can scarcely be described in this way. In many senses, it represents an extension of the fictional world of the soap opera beyond the television screen – yet it is an extension which is highly ambiguous. Although it remains a parasitical phenomenon, which is heavily dependent upon the programme itself, it also defines it in certain ways, and inevitably affects how viewers make sense of it. While most viewers are only likely to read a fraction of this material, they will also be influenced by it indirectly as it enters into everyday conversation. In this way, the popular press is at least partly responsible for setting an agenda, not merely for which aspects of television we discuss, but also for how we discuss them.

1. 'Soap Wars'

As far as the popular press was concerned, *EastEnders* was seen from the very start as an attempt to 'grab the ratings', and in particular as a challenge to *Coronation Street*. As early as June 1984, the *Daily Express* was predicting that the BBC's new serial would 'take on the Street' in 'the battle of the soaps', and by January 1985 it was describing the 'Soap Wars' in a 'Front Line Report from TV's Latest Battlefield', with 'commander' Julia Smith leading her 'troops' into battle.

This military metaphor was sustained throughout the first year of *EastEnders*' existence, which saw it 'retreating' after 'losing the battle' with *Emmerdale Farm* (*Express*, 15 March), and eventually 'walloping' the Street early in November (*Star*, 2 November). Meanwhile, those responsible for other soap operas were seen to be 'fighting back', both by questioning the way in which the viewing figures were calculated, and by criticising *EastEnders*' diet of 'sex and violence': the 'stars' of *Coronation Street* in particular aligned themselves with the Mary Whitehouse lobby, gaining headlines such as 'STREETS AHEAD! RIVALS LASH SEEDY EASTENDERS' (*News of the World*, 13 October) and 'CLEAN UP SOAP! Street Star Bill Lashes 'Steamy' EastEnders' (*Sun*, 22 October). Their response was not confined to 'lashing out' however; a report in the *Sun* (24 January 1986) headlined 'SOAPS FIGHT DIRTY IN RATINGS WAR' detailed recent developments in other soap operas which it saw as a response to *EastEnders*' success. According to this report, 'They have all gone fighting mad. Fist-flailing, head-butting, groin-grabbing are now the order of the day in homely shows where the most violent act used to be a knock at the door.' According to the *Sun*, not even *Emmerdale Farm* had remained unscathed since Matt Skilbeck had been transformed into a 'rural Rambo'.

The inevitable comparisons with *Coronation Street* functioned at a number of levels. Parallels were drawn, both between specific characters and between the overall formulae of the programmes: thus, the Queen Vic was compared with the Rover's Return (*Daily Express*, 2 June 1984), Angie Watts was 'the Beeb's Bet Lynch' (*Star*, 26 January 1985), while Lou Beale was its Ena Sharples and Ethel Skinner its Hilda Ogden (*Star*, 13 February). Once the serial was under way, however, attention shifted to the differences: according to the *Sun* (20 February 1985), Lou Beale 'makes Ena Sharples sound like Mother Teresa', while the *Sunday People* (31 March 1985) felt that Nick Cotton made Eddie Yates, 'the nearest thing the Street ever had to a villain', look like 'a choirboy'. In a more detailed comparison, the *Sun* (11 March 1985) gave its own assessment of the characters: Angie Watts beat Bet Lynch for her 'smouldering sexy looks', while 'sex bomb' Sharon Watts defeated the Clayton Sisters, and 'big hunk' Ali Osman ('No girl is safe from this cafe Casanova') won hands down against the Street's Brian Tilsley.

This comparison was also defined in terms of the North/South divide: indeed, the 'Soap Wars' were described in a number of newspapers as 'the great North versus South TV war' (*Sunday Mirror*, 17 February 1985). The 'tawdry glamour' of *EastEnders* was contrasted with the 'puritanism' of *Coronation Street*; the Southerners were typified as more 'brash and aggressive', with 'a touch more surface class and sophistication' in 'their fancy Marks and Spencers threads' (*Daily Mirror*, 15 May 1985). Great play was made of Cockney rhyming slang, and the stereotype of 'Cocky Cockneys with a lust for life' (*Daily*

Express, 4 October 1985), although elsewhere it was argued that the programme would 'banish forever the wearied myth of the lovable Cockney' (*Daily Express*, 1 March 1985).

In more general terms, however, the comparison hinged around two related issues – realism and morality – which are central to an overall understanding of the press coverage. *EastEnders* was generally described as more realistic and contemporary than *Coronation Street*, as 'gritty', 'raw' and 'uncompromising', whereas the Street was widely regarded as cosy and old-fashioned. According to the *Star* (19 September 1985), '*EastEnders* tackles social problems which the Street has shied away from – topical issues. In the Street, neighbours are pals, unemployment is not a problem, and drugs are only used in hospitals. Unfortunately, real life isn't as nice as that.' Jean Rook in the *Daily Express* (3 October 1986), a consistent advocate of *EastEnders*, drew attention to the strength of its black characters, compared with the 'scrubbed, white-washed' world of *Coronation Street*.

At the same time, concern was expressed at an early stage about *EastEnders'* use of 'bad language' and its emphasis on what the *Sun* (20 February 1985) called 'sex, spite and savagery', as compared with the more respectable approach of its rival. In the memorable words of *The Times* (22 February 1985), *EastEnders* made *Coronation Street* look like *Vegetarian Kitchen*.

These two issues of realism and morality were, at least for the popular press, intimately related. In a sense, they represent the positive and the negative sides of its critical coin. While positive judgments tended to focus on the programme's realism, negative judgments were almost exclusively concerned with its perceived morality. For a critic like Paul Donovan (*Star*, 25 October 1985), *EastEnders'* moral weaknesses derived directly from an *excess* of realism: while it dealt with 'social issues' with 'admirable honesty', he argued that 'its bleak realism seems to be squeezing out a sense of morality', leading it to concentrate on 'aggression, selfishness, indiscipline and crime' at the expense of 'happiness and hope'. While the newspapers were keen to praise *East-Enders'* explicit treatment of 'social problems', and while they made great play of elements which were seen as 'violent' and 'sexy', they were also more than ready to pass moral judgment when the climate of opinion appeared to be changing.

2. *Realism and 'Social Issues'*

One key aspect of the critical debate around *EastEnders*, therefore, has been this question of realism, and the related question of its representation of 'social issues'. Julia Smith's claims that the serial would reflect the reality of East End life and would not shy away from 'controversial' issues were widely reported; and although there were some early complaints about its abrasiveness, 'bad' language and violence, newspaper critics have generally been keen to praise what they regard as *East-Enders*' 'realistic' approach.

However, the kind of realism which *EastEnders* embodies has been defined using rather limited criteria, and in particular by seeking to compare its representation of East End life with the reality of the East End itself, at least as perceived by critics. For example, the *Daily Express* (20 August 1985) claimed that 'All the characters are firmly rooted in reality, the kind of street folk you can meet any day of the week in the streets of the East End'.

In an attempt to compare *EastEnders* with the perceptions of East Enders themselves, London's *Evening Standard* (20 February 1985) reported the responses of a group of East Enders gathered in a Stepney pub to watch the first episode: under the headline 'Leave it out! Cockney verdict on *EastEnders*', it detailed their complaints that the programme was 'corny', that the accents were 'phoney', and that *EastEnders* would 'give a false impression of us to the rest of the country'. Likewise, the *Sunday People* (24 February 1985) reported the comments of 'Cockney window cleaner Bill Cartwright', which themselves seem suspiciously 'phoney': 'Stroll on, guv. I've worked this manor for years. If anyone knows what life is like in these parts it's me. But this 'ere EastEnders fing is just twaddle, know what I mean?'

Later reports along these lines were rather more positive, however. The *Sun* (25 October 1985), in a feature headlined 'THE REAL EASTENDERS OF ALBERT SQUARE' gave an extended comparison between *EastEnders* and 'the genuine Albert Square in London E15', in which real people were invited to give verdicts on their fictional counterparts. The landlady of the Albert House pub, for example, claimed to be 'a lot like Angie' – 'I'm a terrible flirt at times' – and was invited to compare her husband with Den Watts. The comments of Carl Rampersaud, proprietor of the Square's corner shop, shed a bizarre light on this relationship between fiction and reality: 'Only the other day three coaches crammed with *EastEnders* fans popped in. They actually thought I was Saeed and my shop was the one used in the series.'

What emerges here, and in subsequent features on Den Watts namesakes and *EastEnders* lookalikes, is a fascination with the way in which people's perception of fiction comes to influence their perception of reality – not merely in the case of the 'fans' on the *EastEnders* coach tour, but also in the case of those fortunate (or unfortunate) enough to work in pubs in the East End, to be called Dennis Watts, or to look like Lofty Holloway.

However, the dominant view of *EastEnders* as 'realistic' has not been based merely on this kind of empirical comparison with 'the real world'. For some critics, its realism functions primarily on an *emotional* level, whereby the characters are seen to reflect the essential verities of human nature'. Nina Myskow, the *News of the World*'s 'Queen of the Box', wrote of the scene in which Den was revealed as the father of Michelle's baby (6 October 1985), 'They have shown us a soap situation that is real – no right, no wrong, just people being people. Life, really.' Scenes such as this, and the episode which featured the cot death of Ali and Sue Osman's baby Hassan, were widely praised by critics for their maturity and sensitivity in handling 'difficult' issues.

Such instances have occasionally been used by the press as pretexts for fairly serious investigations of 'social problems'. Both the *Daily Star* (8 October 1985) and the *Evening Standard* (17 October 1985), for example, followed up the story of Michelle's pregnancy, in the former case including advice from 'the experts' in Family Planning Clinics and giving details of local education authority provision for pregnant schoolgirls. The *Daily Mirror* (30 June 1985) followed up the cot death story with a feature giving information about advice and support services, and including the responses of a mother who had endured the cot death of her child – albeit alongside those of the mother of the child playing baby Hassan, whose 'death' was of course purely fictional.

At the same time, many other 'social issues' in the programme – and in particular the more explicitly political ones like unemployment and racism – have been largely ignored by the popular press. Although *EastEnders* has been widely praised for its commitment to representing controversial issues – particularly in comparison with *Coronation Street* – these issues have been defined in very limited ways. Consider, for example, the following report from the *Daily Express* (2 October 1985):

> *EastEnders*' hard sell is much boosted by the fact that *Coronation Street*, too complacent as Britain's best-known household soap, has gone soft. Always pale pink on controversial issues – no coloureds, no kinks, no aggro – it could now slip down the drain. Because *EastEnders* is raw carbolic. It peels the skin off sore social problems. It plunges up to its sweaty armpits in lust, racial violence, marital infidelity and teenage sexual tension.

What is particularly notable about such criticism is that 'social problems' are defined almost exclusively in terms of sex and violence, and in terms of 'personal' forms of moral deviance. The significance of this is not merely that the issues for debate are severely restricted: by implicitly connecting questions of realism and morality in this way, the press appears to have set the agenda, almost imperceptibly, for the 'moral panic' which subsequently ensued.

3. *Sex and Morality*

To accuse the popular press of hypocrisy on moral issues is scarcely original, yet the coverage of *EastEnders* provides such ample evidence in support of this view that it is difficult to avoid. What is perhaps most remarkable is the contradiction between the emphasis on sex and, to a lesser extent, violence which permeates the newspaper reports and the moral outrage which they have done much to articulate and encourage. These two conflicting elements often co-exist in the same stories. For example, the following report from the *Sun* (3 September 1985), under the headline 'TV SOAP "TOO SEXY FOR KIDS"', describes the claims of 'clean-up campaigners' that the programme 'could be a bad influence on children'. The report continues with a list of recent 'near the knuckle situations':

> Teenage temptress Sharon Watts – played by actress Letitia Dean – FLASHED her mini-skirted legs at pub customers and FONDLED a barman's bottom. Landlord Den Watts – busy conducting a torrid extra-marital AFFAIR – referred to a vibrator during a saucy pub raffle. And his dark-haired wife Angie – actress Anita Dobson – rubbed her CAMIKNICKERS over a pensioner's head during the same bawdy auction.
> Mrs Whitehouse said: 'The show should be x-rated. This kind of thing is just not on. It is an adults-only soap opera. I shudder to think of the embarrassing questions parents face from their children after Sunday afternoon viewings.'
> But a BBC spokesman said: 'It is not our policy to be sexually provocative. It just mirrors real life in the East End of London.'

This exchange illustrates many of the key issues in the moral debate around *EastEnders*. On the one hand, Whitehouse is particularly concerned about the programme's influence on children, whom she regards as innocent of sexual matters. It is parents, rather than broadcasters, whom she feels should have the power to control children's access to information, and to determine the ways in which such questions should be discussed. *EastEnders*, and indeed television generally, represents a clear threat to this power: it constitutes an invasion of the home which parents may find themselves powerless to resist. On the other hand, the 'BBC spokesman' provides the routine disclaimer: *EastEnders* simply 'mirrors real life', and as such the broadcasters have very little responsibility for what it contains.

Yet what is most indicative about the report quoted above is the salacious tone in which the programme itself is described: and in this respect it is typical of much of the press coverage. A future anthropologist seeking evidence of the sexual repression of late twentieth-century British society would need to look no further than its popular newspapers, and in particular their coverage of *EastEnders*. From the very beginning, the serial appeared to hold out the promise of explicit sexual material. Even before it came on the air, the press was describing it as 'meaty' and 'sexy', and appears to have been encouraged by the production team. The *Daily Mail* (11 October 1984) quoted Tony Holland's promise that 'It will be a very randy show because over-crowded and claustrophobic areas like our Albert Square are very sexy places'; while the *Star* (13 February 1985) quoted Shirley Cheriton (Debbie Wilkins), 'the sex symbol of the Square', as saying 'I've heard there are some hot scenes. I've seen the word "nookie" in the script.'

The press has particularly focused on the more explicitly *risqué* elements, notably the male stripper 'Fabulous Frankie', who appeared in the Queen Vic in November 1985, and the female stripper Sheena, who befriended Mary Smith and briefly led her astray. Both were featured as pin-ups in a number of newspapers, with the *News of the World* (3 November 1985) in particular offering its readers a 'teasing view of sex-pot Sheena' – 'This is just a taste of what *EastEnders* viewers might have seen'. 'Fabulous Frankie' – who in fact revealed far more, both in the programme and in the newspapers, than Sheena ever did – was the subject of an extensive follow-up story which played rather dangerously with the relationship between fiction and reality. The *News of the World* report 'STRIP KING'S SHOCK ROMP AS CAMERAS STOP' (10 November 1985) told how 'male stripper Fabulous Frankie's sensational *EastEnders* showstopper turned into a real-life frolic after the cameras stopped rolling': the actor Frank Jakeman was quoted describing how 'those cheeky East End girls seized me and covered me with baby oil ... [they] couldn't wait to get their hands on me.' Yet in a subsequent report in the *Sunday People*, 'SEX FREAKS PLAGUE THE EASTENDERS PARTY GIRLS' (17 November 1985), it emerged that his story had led to some of the cast being 'pestered by perverts'. 'Fabulous Frankie' himself, of course, claimed to have been 'misquoted like crazy'. Despite this, his moment of glory was far from short-lived: stories about both *EastEnders* strippers were still being featured in the press over a year after they had disappeared from the programme.

The press has seen fit to describe most of the characters in *East-Enders* at some point as being 'sexy', even characters for whom (to this viewer at least) the epithet seems singularly inappropriate, such as the Square's semi-resident villain Nick Cotton. Only the dogs seem to be exempt from the constant stream of sexual innuendo. Meanwhile, pin-ups of the cast in varying states of undress appear regularly in the more popular tabloids, with the male characters often displaying greater expanses of flesh – particularly 'the Stallion' Nejdet Salih (Ali Osman), 'sexy Saeed' (Andrew Johnson) and 'hunky heartthrob' Ross Davidson (Andy O'Brien). Female members of the cast have been significantly more modest, although the *Star* (February 1986) featured a series of colour spreads of 'Cockney Crackers' Letitia Dean (Sharon Watts) and Susan Tully (Michelle Fowler), whose 'glamour' poses were strikingly at odds with the more mundane roles they play in the serial. Personal appearances have also provided opportunities for photographs of the 'stars' signing parts of their fans' anatomies in night-clubs.

Alongside such reports, the press has given extensive space to the criticisms of Mary Whitehouse, and in certain instances – notably the *Daily Express* and the *Daily Mail* – has supported these in their editorial commentaries. Of course, Mary Whitehouse makes for good copy, and for more 'sexy' headlines: and indeed, in certain instances, journalists appear to make direct challenges to her to respond. Intriguingly, the *Evening Standard* carried a report on the day before the programme came on the air (18 February 1985) which suggested that Whitehouse had already made complaints about *EastEnders* being 'too violent'. At least in this case, it would seem that she was 'set up' by the popular press in order to generate controversy: although her criticisms were based on detailed (albeit partial) monitoring of the programme, there is a remarkable similarity between her account of it and that which emerges from the press coverage, in terms of what is emphasised and what is ignored.

The furore surrounding Angie Watts' attempted suicide in February 1986 provides a clear example of the ways in which the popular press and the Whitehouse lobby feed off each other. Whitehouse's criticisms – which, according to her, resulted in the Sunday repeat edition being cut just at the climax of the episode – were widely reported in the press, and provoked detailed responses from the BBC. Yet significantly, Whitehouse's letter of complaint to Alistair Milne, Director-General of the BBC, dated 26 March, included a copy of a story from the *Daily Express* (15 March) headlined 'TV FAN COPIED SOAP OPERA SUICIDE', which reported that a coroner in Maidenhead had blamed *EastEnders* for the suicide of a young man – and which, like most such stories, was based purely on speculation. The *Daily Express* in turn proudly reported that Whitehouse had used its article in her letter, under the headline, 'APOLOGISE, SAYS MARY IN EASTENDERS SUICIDE ROW' (1 April 1986).

These criticisms of *EastEnders* connected with broader criticisms of the BBC, which was regarded by some of the more high-minded critics as 'catering to the lowest common denominator' simply in order to feed the ratings. Heather Kirby (*Sunday Express*, 15 September 1985) declared that the BBC was serving up 'rakings from the trash can of society', and that she at least could do without such 'pornographic ... TV smut'. Likewise, Mary Kenny (*Daily Mail*, 16 November 1985) argued that the success of *EastEnders* marked 'the end of the BBC as public service broadcasting', and was symptomatic of its willingness 'to go to any length, or even descend to any depth, to get good ratings.'

Despite these strictures, the coverage of *EastEnders* both in the popular tabloids and in the more moralistic 'middlebrow' papers like the *Daily Mail* and the *Daily Express* has focused almost obsessively on the issues of sex and violence. *EastEnders* comes to be defined as a programme which is almost exclusively concerned with these areas – a definition which might perhaps account for at least part of its success, but which also places it at the centre of contemporary debates about personal morality. The questions which underly much of the press coverage, both of the programme itself and, more spectacularly, of the private lives of the cast, are those which are central to the contemporary backlash against moral 'permissiveness'. Yet while on the one hand the press is concerned to define and to police the boundaries of 'respectable' conduct, it is also fascinated with behaviour which in various ways is seen to violate them.

4. *Prediction*

The prediction of future events in the plot has been another significant element in the press coverage. The newspapers invite readers to participate in such speculation, by organising 'name the baby' competitions to 'help' Pauline Fowler (*Star*, 10 June 1985), or asking whether Den Watts will 'do the business' by giving his wife Angie 'what she craves – his body' (*Star*, 7 February 1986). 'Agony aunts' such as the *Daily Mirror*'s Marje Proops and the *Sun*'s 'Dear Deirdre' write to the characters, advising them on ways of solving their problems.

The newspapers also regularly publish 'exclusive' predictions, which they claim are derived from inside sources. As with the stories about the personal lives of the cast, much of this material is not verified before publication, and has often been inaccurate. Although the press has managed to foretell many of the major storylines in the period under consideration here, it has also published some quite bizarre and wildly inaccurate predictions. For example, the *News of the World* (3 November 1985) confidently predicted that Den Watts' lover would prove to be a man; while the *Sunday People* (19 January 1986) assured its readers that he was about to embark on an affair with 'Mr Fisher', the drag artist hired by his wife Angie for the Queen Vic. Meanwhile, the *News of the World* (13 October 1985) suggested that *EastEnders* was about to screen a lesbian affair; the *Sun* (14 October) 'revealed' that Kathy Beale was the mother of Den's adopted daughter Sharon and predicted that Mary Smith would drown her baby daughter in the canal (12 November). What is notable about these predictions, apart from their inaccuracy, is their focus on 'deviant' behaviour, whether of a sexual or a criminal nature, again suggesting a prurient fascination with such matters which is rather at odds with the repeated moral condemnation of the programme.

Inaccurate predictions have sometimes provided further grounds for criticism of the BBC. Following a *News of the World* report (27 October 1985) which predicted that Michelle Fowler was about to lose her baby, and speculated about whether she would be mugged, seriously injured in a car crash, or hurt in a fall on a patch of ice, The *Star* (30 October) attacked the BBC for betraying the educational function of Michelle's story: 'I'm not sure whether we can take any more grim realities. Not, anyway, when they are all thought up to justify the BBC's existence by making *EastEnders* super soap.' The BBC's denial of the rumour, which had been buried in paragraph nineteen of *The News of the World*'s story, was of course ignored.

This story, like most of the newspapers' predictions, claimed to be based on the testimony of a 'BBC insider'; and despite the many inaccuracies, it remains the case that 'insiders' do appear to have provided the press with a large amount of detailed information about future storylines, often in exchange for substantial amounts of cash. The *Sunday People* (24 November 1985) exposed one such source – 'the money-grabbing supergrass who has rocked TV's *EastEnders* with his spoilsport storyline leaks can be named by the *Sunday People* today' – although it rather undermined its public-spirited action by publishing another of his 'shock leaks' (which incidentally later proved inaccurate).

Nevertheless, the problem of leaks has yet to reach the proportions of US soaps. According to a report in *TV Guide* (26 November 1983), the theft of soap opera scripts is a growing problem, and cautious producers have taken to filming multiple versions of 'whodunit' endings. Apparently the scene in which *Dallas* revealed 'who shot J.R.' was filmed with each of the members of the cast (including Larry Hagman himself!) firing the gun. The BBC has yet to resort to such drastic measures, although it has been reported that members of the cast would have heart attacks written into their scripts if they were found to be responsible for leaks, and it was rumoured (by The *Sun*, 9 August 1986) that the BBC had filmed two versions of the cliffhanger ending of Michelle and Lofty's wedding.

5. *Private Lives in Public*

Although the press has generated a considerable amount of critical debate around *EastEnders* – and thereby partly defined the terms in which it will be discussed – by far the majority of press reports have been concerned with the private lives of the cast. This material also has a significant bearing on the issues of realism and morality, both because it plays upon the distinction between fiction and reality, and also because it focuses on behaviour which is seen to constitute a transgression of dominant moral codes.

In dealing with the private lives of soap opera 'stars', the press is often accused of attempting to blur the distinctions between actors and the characters they play. Although in many cases this is undoubtedly true, a good deal of such material in fact accentuates these distinctions. Information about the actors' past careers – 'Twenty things you never knew about soap star Wendy Richard' (*Sun*, 1 June 1985) – or 'trivia' about their personal eccentricities – 'Which EastEnder collects model frogs?' (*Star*, 3 February 1986) – serves to construct an identity for the actor which is distinct from the character. In some instances, an emphasis is placed on similarities between the actors and the characters: Peter Dean (Pete Beale), for example, is occasionally pictured working on the vegetable stall which he apparently runs in real life, just as he does in the programme. In the case of more unpopular characters, however, the differences are often emphasised: many of the newspapers made great play of the fact that John Altman, who plays the racist villain Nick Cotton, had an Asian girlfriend, whom he eventually married. The contrast between the mundane poverty of Albert Square and the glamour of the actors' private lives is a further common theme: pictures of the cast 'going up West' to expensive nightclubs or modelling high fashion clothes are featured both in the newspapers and in women's magazines. On such occasions, it is often the press itself which claims to have made the transformation: thus, *Woman's Own* (22 March 1986) featured a large photo spread of Gillian Taylforth (Kathy Beale) – 'We've taken her away from the humble fruit and veg stall she runs in TV's top soap, put her in a gorgeous Emanuel dress and the result, as you can see, is stunning.'

Actors are routinely invited to comment on their character, and on their own experience of playing their part, which also establishes a degree of distance between actor and character: thus, Anita Dobson is asked to speculate about why women identify with Angie Watts (*Western Mail*, 29 June 1985), and Susan Tully (Michelle Fowler) is invited to describe how it felt to play her 'big scene' with Leslie Grantham (Den Watts) (*Star*, 4 February 1986). Meanwhile, Grantham himself argues, with at least a hint of irony, that 'Den is a misunderstood person, a tragic hero' and that in playing the part he is 'only doing what the average man wants to do' (*Star*, 4 February 1986). Only in rare instances do the actors speak 'in character', and even then this is presented as a 'shared joke'.

The actors' comments about their characters can be quite negative. For example, Anna Wing (Lou Beale) argued that *Coronation Street*'s Ena Sharples had 'much more depth' than her own character (*Daily Express*, 4 October 1985); while Andrew Johnson, who played the Bangladeshi shopkeeper Saeed Jeffery, felt that there had been a lack of research into his character, and that much of his behaviour was inappropriate given that he was supposed to be a strict Muslim (*Sun*, 9 November 1985).

Other stories provide information about the way in which the series is produced, and about the actors' conditions of work, which similarly serve to accentuate this distinction. Thus, we are told that the pay of actors on *EastEnders* is significantly worse than their counterparts on

ITV soaps (*Daily Mail*, 19 February 1985), and that the cast is 'ganging up' to demand a rise (*Star*, 18 December 1985). Many of the newspapers have carried stories about the real babies who play parts in the serial: according to the *News of the World* (20 April 1986), Michelle's Vicky is in fact five different babies. Other reports tell of actors who want to leave the serial for fear of being typecast, or of rivalries between those who want to be seen as the 'stars' of the programme. One report in the *Sun* (25 May 1985) suggested that certain members of the cast were becoming unpopular with the wardrobe and make-up staff because of the amount of time they were spending 'dolling themselves up' before each scene.

At the same time, it is possible to find numerous instances where the distinction between actor and character is being deliberately blurred. Thus, a story headlined 'MY WIFE STILL LOVES ME SAYS DIRTY DEN' (*News of the World*, 6 October 1985) is in fact based on an interview with the actress Jane Laurie, the real wife of Leslie Grantham, who plays Den Watts. Similarly, 'EASTEND KATHY'S FALLEN FOR HER SON' (*Sun*, 30 November 1985) in fact concerns the (alleged) real-life romance between Gillian Taylforth (who plays Kathy Beale) and Nick Berry (who plays Simon Wicks). In stories such as these, the name in the headline is almost invariably that of the character, and in some cases, as with 'Dirty Den's Miss World Dozen' (*Daily Mirror*, 14 November 1985), a story may omit to mention the actor's name at all. To a certain extent, this is inevitable: unlike movie stars, who play different roles across a range of films, the actors in soap operas are known to the public primarily in one role. Clint Eastwood may temporarily 'become' Harry Callahan, but he remains Clint Eastwood; Leslie Grantham, on the other hand, 'is' Den Watts, at least as far as the viewing public is concerned.

In general, however, it is probably more accurate to describe these stories as *playing* with the distinction between reality and fiction, rather than seeking merely to obliterate it. On the one hand, they emphasise that 'in real life' the actors do a job of work, and in many cases are very different from the characters they play; yet on the other hand, they implicitly depend upon readers drawing parallels between the 'private' and the 'public' drama.

In many ways, press reports of the actors' private lives are very similar to soap opera narratives. They focus on the intimate detail of personal relationships, and allow the reader a privileged voyeuristic insight into events which are normally hidden from view. They are based upon hermeneutic enigmas, both about future events and about the revelations of hidden secrets from the past. In marketing terms, they 'hook' readers into an ongoing narrative, and thereby build a loyal paying audience.

Like the soap operas, the press reports are also concerned with exploring moral issues, and with testing the limits of morally acceptable behaviour. Both are preoccupied with investigating deviance of various kinds. The major difference is that in the case of the press, the forms of deviant behaviour which attract the headlines are often more spectacular, and more exclusively concerned with sex (and, to a lesser extent, violent crime) than those which are featured in the programme itself. Unlike the stars of Hollywood at its peak, whose distance from their fans enabled the studios to construct 'private' identities which were often wholly fictitious (Rock Hudson's 'girlfriends', for example), the stars of soap operas are far more accessible, and information about them far less easily controlled.

The actors' sex lives – or lack of them – are certainly a constant topic of interest and speculation. Romances between members of the cast achieve particular prominence, and are charted in considerable detail: thus, *Sun* readers have been able to trace the narrative of Tom Watt (Lofty Holloway) from 'EASTENDERS STARS IN LOVE AFFAIR: Lofty's passion for Angie' (21 September 1985) through 'LONESOME LOFTY' (13 February 1986) and, most recently, 'MICHELLE AND LOFTY IN LOVE FOR REAL' (5 July 1986) – a narrative which in fact had many parallels with that of the serial itself. Meanwhile, Gillian Taylforth (Kathy Beale) explains 'How *EastEnders* has ruined my love life' (*Woman's Own* 22 March 1986), and Wendy Richard (Pauline Fowler) complains 'I'm too knackered for nookie' (*Sunday People*, 9 June 1985). Revelations from the past also take their place here: the *Star* (February 1986) managed an entire week of 'WENDY RICHARD: MY SECRET TORMENT' – 'for years she has kept silent about the violence and horror in her life ... Until now. STARTLING. EXPLOSIVE. HEARTBREAKING.'

While the press has made great play of the actors' public indiscretions – printing photographs of 'public bust-ups' or drunken embraces in night clubs – it has also been more than ready to apply moral censure. Stories about the 'fuming Beeb chiefs' who have attempted to 'slap a ban on the top soap stars talking about their love lives' (*Sunday Mirror*, 9 February 1986), or 'told the stars to behave' after press reports of their misdemeanours (*Sun*, 18 October 1985) have often gained front page status, not least because they provide an opportunity to rehearse the details of the proscribed behaviour itself. The stories possess an uneasy mixture of voyeuristic fascination and moral condemnation: they bring areas of private experience into the public eye, allowing readers a vicarious glimpse of 'forbidden' behaviour, yet they also enable them to maintain a safe distance from which they can pass moral judgment.

Three major stories, which were widely covered by the popular press during the period under consideration here, amply illustrate these tensions, both around the relationship between fiction and reality and around public and private morality. The first of these concerns the affair between Shirley Cheriton (Debbie Wilkins) and Ross Davidson (Andy O'Brien), whose uneven relationship in the serial finally appeared to be leading towards marriage when Andy was killed off in a road accident in August 1986. Dubbed by the *Daily Express* (14 December 1985) 'the glamour couple of *EastEnders*', the development of their real-life relationship was charted in considerable detail by the newspapers, who seemed fascinated by the way in which their fictional relationship 'spilled over' into reality. The *News of the World* (24 November 1985), for example, talked about 'the hazards of their double life' and their 'on-screen chemistry': 'The screen sizzles when *EastEnders* love-birds Andy and Debbie go into action. Co-stars Shirley Cheriton and Ross Davidson say that some scenes are so intense that they are left trembling with emotion. "We have to remember that we're Ross and Shirley and not Andy and Debbie," says Ross.' Rumours of their real-life romance were fuelled by photographs of them 'smooching' at a London nightclub, which were published in a number of Sunday newspapers in June and July 1985; and the actors themselves gave interviews in which they revealed 'the sizzling secrets behind the top TV soap's great romantic cliffhanger' (*News of the World*, 23 March 1986).

When, in April 1986, the news broke that Ross Davidson was about to be written out of the serial, the press was quick to claim that this was a punishment for his indiscretions. Amid headlines like 'LOVE TALK EASTENDERS STAR FACES THE SACK' (*Sun*, 14 April), many of the newspapers ran confessions detailing the 'anguish' over the break-up of Shirley Cheriton's marriage, and the 'blossoming' of their romance in the BBC canteen. Subsequent stories portrayed Ross Davidson both as a 'heartbreaker' – 'CHEATING RAT ROSS TWO-TIMED SHIRLEY' (*News of the World*, 20 and 27 April) – and as a 'heartthrob'. A series of reports in the *Sun* in July speculated about whether he would be signed up for a part in *Dynasty*, and provided a number of large scantily-clad pin-up photographs of this 'top soap stud', while in November the *Star* ran a series entitled 'Randy Andy's A–X of Women', whose 'secrets of seduction' were apparently intended 'for red-blooded males (and suspicious females) only'. Ross Davidson's most recent – and, one suspects, not final – distinction was to be selected as a model for the *Sun*'s 'Page 7 Calendar' for 1987.

While there is a margin of ambiguity, at least in the visual images – the *Sun* in fact commented about the actor's substantial gay following – the overall definition of masculinity which emerges here is extremely one-dimensional: Ross Davidson/Randy Andy, like all 'red-blooded males' is celebrated for his rampant and even 'uncontrollable' libido. Female sexual desire, by contrast, is judged by rather different standards, as is apparent in the second major story, which concerns Anita

Dobson (Angie Watts). Her brief affair with Tom Watt (Lofty Hollo-way) was widely reported in the press, and gave way to a series of stories about 'Angie' and her 'toy boy lovers'. The *Star*'s 'exclusive' (5 February 1986) about 'the children's TV star who wooed the Queen of the Queen Vic – apparently 'he fell for her mind' – seems to have been the first of a series of 'confessions', which saw a succession of 'toy boys' coming forward to sell their stories. 'I WAS ANGIE LOVER BY TOY BOY, 19' (*Sun*, 3 June 1986) gave details of her 'torrid affair' with male model 'Jason', while, in a further permutation of this theme 'the man who broke the star's heart' confessed 'I DUMPED ANGIE FOR A SCHOOLGIRL' (*News of the World*, 11 May 1986).

Here again, part of the fascination of the story derives from the implicit parallels between reality (or what is claimed to be reality) and fiction: during this period in the serial, Angie's desperation about her husband's affair was driving her to 'get her own back' by seeking other lovers, and most of the men who came within reach (of whom Lofty was one) were significantly younger than her. The consistent use of the character name in the headlines indicates a degree of deliberate confu-sion: these are stories about Anita Dobson, but they are simultaneously about Angie Watts. Yet the stories also appear to be of interest precise-ly because they deal more explicitly with a form of moral transgression which the serial itself only hints at: Anita Dobson's sexuality is clearly defined by the press as deviant because, as the older woman, she is seen to be taking the active role.

Perhaps the most disturbing story in this connection was that run by the *Sun* (8 July 1986), alongside its page 3 topless model, under the headline 'I WANNA MAN! EastEnder Angie is open to offers from likely lads'. Quoting from an interview in *Woman's Own*, in which Anita Dobson had declared herself to be 'open to offers' from men, the story invited 'red-blooded suitors' to apply for its 'Date Anita' com-petition. The entry form asked for information, for example about when the applicant would wear a vest and how often he would expect sex, which would enable Anita to make her decision. In fact, the story was published without Anita Dobson's consent, and when on 30 July the *Sun* published details of the winners (with photographs of them in varying states of undress) it was unable to give details of her responses.

If stories such as this have been regarded by the broadcasters as overstepping the bounds of good taste, the press treatment of Leslie Grantham (Den Watts) has been in an altogether different league. The story of Grantham's conviction for the murder of a taxi-driver in 1966, when he was serving in the army in Germany, broke shortly after the series first went on the air (*Star*, 23 February 1985), and was widely reported at the time – most notably by a front page story in the *Sunday People* (24 February), headlines 'EASTENDER KILLER RUINED MY LIFE', in which the taxi-driver's widow spoke of her 'eighteen years of loneliness and hardship since the killing'. Although the story surfaced occasionally in the meanwhile, it was not until August 1986 that it took on the proportions of a full-blown moral panic. The *Daily Mirror* (11 August) appears to have started a flood of stories by printing the account of a fellow soldier, 'TORTURE DROVE DIRTY DEN TO KILL'. The challenge was taken up by the *News of the World* (17 August) in a story based on the confessions of a former cell-mate of Grantham, 'MY LIFE INSIDE JAIL WITH DIRTY DEN', which told how 'the hard-nut personality of *EastEnders* heart-throb Dirty Den was formed in the tough atmosphere of one of Britian's most notorious prisons'. The *Mirror* returned to the theme the following day with a front page story 'I BRANDED DIRTY DEN', based on the account of a former soldier who had once attacked Grantham with a steam iron.

However, it was the *Sun* which soon took the lead: its 'Dirty Den Murder File' was opened on 18 August with a large front page picture of what the newspaper claimed was the taxi-driver's skull, which had apparently been found in a military 'black museum' in Chichester. During the rest of the week, the *Sun* published 'DIRTY DEN'S CON-FESSION', which it had apparently unearthed from German police files; photographs of 'The Death Cab', complete with bloodstains, 'The Funeral', 'The Murder Weapon' and 'The Killer' being marched to the military court; an open letter from the taxi-driver's widow demanding £16,000 from Grantham to compensate for her 'torment'; and a story about how the taxi-driver's grave was about to be bulldozed. The week culminated with '*Sun* readers' passing sentence: 'DIRTY DEN SHOULD HAVE SWUNG FOR TAXI KILLING'. On each day, a brief statement was published, at the request of 'Dirty Den's Lawyers' (sic), to the effect that Leslie Grantham had not co-operated with the newspaper, and was not being paid for the articles.

Meanwhile, the other newspapers fought back, The *Star*'s Geoff Baker, claiming to be 'the actor's only true friend left in Fleet Street', pleaded with his colleagues to 'get off his back, you rats' and urged his readers: 'Now is the time to act. Now is the time for you to rally to him' (19 August). Mary Kenny in the *Daily Mail* (19 August) mounted a direct attack on the BBC, which she accused of leaking the story to the press: 'Is this the correct way to conduct a broadcasting policy? Should they benefit from the ghoulish publicity accruing to a grisly murder trial?' Kenny's criticisms drew a strong response on the following day from Michael Grade, who refuted the idea that the BBC had colluded with the newspapers: 'The ordinary canons of taste and decency are thrown to the winds in the scramble to squeeze the last ounce of competitive sensation out of the public's favourite television programme. This week's excesses are the latest in a long and ignoble line.' Meanwhile, ITV's satirical *Spitting Image* featured a sketch in which a rubber puppet 'Dirty Den' attempted unsuccessfully to hire a taxi to take him to the BBC.

Ultimately, it is difficult to regard this material as anything other than a campaign of persecution. While there have been occasional positive stories concerning Grantham – the women's magazines have often sought to define his allure for their readers, for example – the vast majority of press coverage has been overwhelmingly negative. In the weeks after the revived taxi-driver scandal, there was a small attempt to redress the balance by covering the birth of his child, but it was not long before the newspapers returned to the attack, this time describing Grantham's failure to visit his brother, who was in hospital dying of AIDS. Meanwhile, his criminal associations were reinforced by a front page story in the *Star* (8 November) featuring a picture of 'DIRTY DEN AND THE KRAYS' taken at a private party. Stories about the mounting pressure on Grantham – most notably one which featured a blurred photograph of him allegedly driving his car at a *Star* photographer (4 November) – became a regular feature in the press throughout November 1986, leading to rumours that he was about to leave the serial. It subsequently emerged that at least one of the 'DIRTY DEN WILL QUIT' stories had been planted by a veteran newspaper hoaxer (*Observer*, 7 December).

It is difficult to understand why Grantham has been singled out for such extraordinary public vilification. Despite having served his time for his offence, it is as if he remains unclean; and the newspapers, claiming to act as the agents of the law, must seek to eradicate him, at least from our television screens. The fictional sins of 'Dirty Den' (the nickname itself is an invention of the press) have been compounded by the real-life sins of Leslie Grantham, to the extent that he comes to be seen not merely as a 'tragic hero' or as 'misunderstood', but as a remorseless villain. The resulting composite of the two becomes a contemporary 'folk devil', who embodies everything that 'we' are not, and whose continued presence in our homes is an affront to the decent people whose values the newspapers claim to represent.[2] On one level, the detailed recounting of 'Dirty Den's' criminal past is simply another means of selling newspapers; yet he also acts as a convenient scapegoat on whom the newspapers can vent their moral outrage, detracting attention from more complex political issues, and enabling them to present themselves as the upholders of truth and decency.

The BBC's response

The press coverage of *EastEnders* has provided the BBC with problems which it has never faced before, at least on a long-term basis. While these problems are at least partly to do with protecting its employees, they are also centrally concerned with negotiating its relationship with its audience. The press treatement of Leslie Grantham, for example, clearly has distressing consequences for the actor himself, but it also reflects badly on the B B C, which is implicitly (and, at times, explicitly) blamed for employing him. Likewise, the newspapers' emphasis on the programme's treatment of sex and violence – and their tendency to ignore other aspects of it – sets an agenda for moral debate, in which the B B C can be accused of abandoning its public service responsibilities, particularly towards 'impressionable' younger viewers. Popular newspapers – in most cases owned by magnates who have much to gain from the deregulation of broadcasting – can thus feed off the success of the programme, while simultaneously representing it in such a way that it can be used as valuable ammunition in their attacks on the B B C. While *EastEnders* owes its existence at least partly to the B B C's attempt to 'popularize' its public image, the price of its success has been that others less sympathetic to public service broadcasting have been given the opportunity to define that image for their own purposes.

The broadcasters' response to the press coverage of the programme was therefore inevitably somewhat ambivalent. On the one hand, they felt that it could only help to increase the ratings, and were thus inclined to encourage it; yet on the other, they were obviously disturbed by the effects of certain stories, both on the programme-makers and on the public reputation of the B B C itself. Keith Samuel, Head of B B C Publicity, saw the role of his department as being to manage this difficult balancing act:

> You have the dividing line between what is acceptable press interest in a television show, and what is unacceptable. And that dividing line has been crossed with *EastEnders* on a number of occasions, quite spectacularly, and it's at that point that the B B C takes a dim view. You have a certain ambivalence here: having, if you like, seduced the press into taking an interest in *EastEnders*, you then have to live with the consequences ... But it's when that exploitation becomes injurious either to the reputation of the B B C, or, in a narrower focus, injurious to the atmosphere in which the programme is made, that we begin to worry. In other words, if artists have been pursued, if artists have been hounded to the extent where their standard of performance is perhaps threatened because they've had the *News of the World* sitting outside their front door all night, and they've got to come in and rehearse or do a recording the next day, that is a matter of deep concern, because it's actually threatening the quality of the show. And if that's the price of publicity, who wants it?[3]

At the same time, the sanctions available to the B B C in such cases remained limited: it was possible to make 'strenuous representation' to newspapers, and even threaten legal action, but they were most unlikely to retract allegations or to issue apologies.

Jonathan Powell similarly felt that with a popular programme like *EastEnders* the BBC was bound to have a 'symbiotic' relationship with the popular press; as such, he argued, it did not have a right to take a high moral tone, except perhaps on a few occasions where the newspapers were seen to have 'overstepped the mark'. On the question of storylines which had been 'leaked', he admitted:

> We may have been guilty at times of feeding inaccurate information. We may have been guilty of putting up smokescreens. But usually when we were trying to protect our audience, actually; usually when we were trying to keep our storylines secret, not because we're naturally secretive, but because it spoils it, it spoils the fun if everybody knows what's going to happen ... Lost in the middle of all that melée, there's a perfectly decent reason for secrecy or misinformation.

In general, then, while the broadcasters were dismayed by certain elements of the press coverage – by the leaks of storylines, and in particular by the intrusion into the private lives of the cast – they tended to regard it as the inevitable price of popularity. While they claimed to protect the cast and the audience as far as possible, they ultimately felt they had very little control of the relationship between the programme and its audience once it had entered into the broader public arena. In this sense, the BBC has been involved in a struggle to define the 'image' of its most popular programme, and, by extension, its own reputation – and despite its strenuous attempts to control this process, it is a struggle which it is inevitably bound to lose.

Mary Whitehouse: defending the audience?

It is precisely the issue of the broadcasters' relationship with their audience which has been at the forefront of Mary Whitehouse's attacks on *EastEnders*. As I have indicated, her criticisms have been widely reported by the popular press, not least because they provide it with valuable ammunition in its existing rivalry with the BBC. Yet if the relationship between the press and the broadcasters is at least ambivalent, Whitehouse's attacks on the BBC have been more straightforward. Purporting to speak *on behalf of* the audience, she directly challenges the power of the broadcasters and their claim to 'serve the public'.

Whitehouse's basic argument is that *EastEnders* represents a violation of 'family viewing time': it undermines the 'watershed' policy, which decrees that programmes shown before 9 p.m. should not be 'unsuitable for children'. Whitehouse's first major attack on the programme was contained in a letter to Stuart Young, Chair of the BBC Governors, dated 20 November 1985. She drew attention to the BBC's guidelines on 'The Portrayal of Violence in Television Programmes', which suggest that children may be particularly disturbed by scenes of domestic violence between family members, and which warn against 'setting examples which can easily be copied: such as the use of knives'. The letter went on to cite examples of scenes which (Whitehouse argued) had violated these codes: recent conflicts between Den and Angie Watts, whose relationship she perceived as one of 'undiluted and continuous bitterness, lying, deceit and verbal abuse', had contradicted the first of these guidelines; and the scene in which Pete Beale had taken a kitchen knife to threaten Nick Cotton had contradicted the second.

Whitehouse's letter continued with a direct attack on Michael Grade, whose reported responses to her earlier criticisms had merely added fuel to the fire:

> Quite how far Mr Grade's thinking is from the kind of responsibility which is surely laid upon him as controller of BBC1 was most vividly illustrated in his reported response (*Daily Mirror*, November 11 1985) to our criticism of the storyline about Mary the unmarried mother becoming a stripper and the assurance she received that she would get more money for 'whipping' – 'the whole point of Mary becoming a stripper is that it's a real solution for many unsupported mothers like her with no qualifications at all'. I am more than tempted to say that if that is the level of thinking within the BBC then heaven help us all – not least those young girls who might well get the message and find themselves involved in dangerous and demoralising situations.

Whitehouse was also critical of what she saw as the lack of response to her earlier complaints about 'bad language': despite assurances to the contrary, she argued,

> the bad language continues; for example (September 17) 'bleeding' this and that, 'bloody hell', 'bastard', 'kick in the crutch'. (November 12) 'Bastard', 'For Christ's sake', 'Jesus!'. (November 14) 'You daft pillock'.

The letter concluded with a further attack on Michael Grade, whom Whitehouse described as 'a law unto himself, whose prime concern is audience ratings irrespective of at what price they are won'; and with the assertion that the programme represented 'an onslaught on the BBC's own declared standards'.

EastEnders, then, has served as a focus for a number of Whitehouse's broader concerns about the potential influence of television, particularly on the young. She regards the programme as a fundamental assault on the family – which for her is synonymous with the nuclear family, and indeed with morality itself. Thus, she has been particularly troubled by *EastEnders*' representation of family life, and by what she sees as its emphasis on 'psychological and emotional violence' – on infidelity, 'verbal brutality' and deceit. The fact that marital conflicts, such as those between Den and Angie Watts, were left unresolved would lead to 'an insidious undermining of [children's] confidence, not only in the relationship between their own mother and father, but perhaps in the whole business of marriage'.[4]

The scheduling of *EastEnders* represents a second focus of Whitehouse's criticisms. One of the fundamental problems in relation to broadcasting, as she sees it, is that in the context of modern family life, parents are no longer able to control their children's viewing. The broadcasters' attempts to place responsibility on the parents are, according to Whitehouse, merely an excuse for denying their own. Children are fundamentally at risk from a medium which seeks to 'pressurise them into alien patterns of behaviour', and they must be defended.[5] The incursion of a programme like *EastEnders* into the heart of 'family viewing time' represents a 'watershed' as significant as *Till Death Us Do Part*, a programme which Whitehouse felt had done much to contribute to the decline in moral standards in broadcasting in the 1960s: if the BBC were to 'dispose of its obligations' in this instance, and if viewers simply became 'too weary of it all to complain', other programmes would be likely to follow its example.

Thirdly, she feels that the programme has provided dangerous models of behaviour, which young people might be led to imitate. The criminal activities of Nick Cotton, for example, were shown in considerable detail, allowing 'impressionable' viewers to copy his actions; and the recourse of Mary Smith to stripping might well have led young women in a similar position to do likewise. The attempted suicide of Angie Watts was a further case in point, which provoked Whitehouse to telephone Alistair Milne, then BBC Director-General, and Stuart Young. According to Whitehouse (and her account was confirmed by Jonathan Powell), it was at least partly due to her protests that the BBC screened an edited version of the scene on its Sunday repeat. Yet subsequent developments led to a further letter of complaint to Alistair Milne, in which Whitehouse enclosed copies of an article which had appeared in the *Daily Express* (15 March 1986) and a letter which had been published in the *Lancet* (22 March 1986). Both suggested that the episode had led to a series of 'copycat' suicides. According to Whitehouse, the episode was 'highly irresponsible, demonstrating as it did the Corporation's contempt for the widely held belief that television by its very nature has a unique power to influence human behaviour'.

Finally, the fact that *EastEnders* is produced by the BBC is also highly pertinent. Whitehouse's antagonism towards the Corporation has a long history: she regards it as a bastion of respectability whose moral deterioration has both reflected and encouraged the broader decline of British society into secular corruption.[6] As far as Whitehouse is concerned, *EastEnders* is fundamentally an attempt to grab the ratings, 'an unscrupulous exercise in competitiveness for viewers'. She particularly blames Michael Grade, whom she claims has brought an American 'mentality' to British television: he would 'stop at nothing', even 'putting youngsters at risk' in the battle for ratings: 'It would appear that the first thing is viewing figures, and only after that, and a very long way after that, is he concerned about the impact of what he's transmitting on the children who are viewing at that time.'

EastEnders' extraordinary popularity would not, according to Whitehouse, necessarily suggest that her own views were out of step with the majority: popularity was a consequence of controversy, rather than an indication of public approval.

Despite these criticisms, Whitehouse was able to find elements in the programme which she was prepared to praise: she described Michelle Fowler's decision not to have an abortion as 'a very positive storyline', and commented with approval on Sharon Watts' passing interest in religion, although she argued that these did not in any way justify the 'adverse effects' of the Angie and Den story which was the principal focus of her concern at the time. Whitehouse also felt that the programme had been 'cleaned up' as a result of her protests, and particularly in response to Winston Churchill MP's Private Member's Bill to extend the Obscene Publications Act to broadcasting, which her organisation, the National Viewers' and Listeners' Association, had drafted:

> From the day that Winston accepted our Bill, *EastEnders* was overnight cleaned up. The language went: there's hardly been any more bad language at all ... Everything became all sweetness and light. Christmas was lovely ... It's quite contemptible, in a way! For the mighty BBC! This sort of unscrupulous manipulating, although one's known it's been going on, when you think about the status of the BBC, it was really cynical.

However, according to Whitehouse, once Churchill's Bill had been defeated, the villain Nick Cotton 'came back with a big flourish' and *EastEnders* returned to its old ways – not quite as bad as it had been before, but nevertheless 'it certainly has had its moments'.

While one might justifiably accuse Whitehouse of overestimating her own influence – the production schedule of *EastEnders* would have made it impossible for the broadcasters to respond as quickly as she suggests here, even had they wished to do so – it remains the case that her criticisms have to be taken extremely seriously by the BBC.

In a detailed response to Whitehouse's first letter of complaint, dated 19 December 1985, Stuart Young admitted that 'misjudgments' had occurred in the case of the 'stripper' story in *EastEnders*, and that the BBC was 'giving serious thought to the question of language in the early evening'. Nevertheless, Young also argued that Whitehouse was wrong to discuss particular scenes and incidents in isolation from their context in the storyline, and that the programme had very 'healthy' moral effects:

> If you were to view the programme [as a continuing serial] – as its regular adherents do – I think you would find it took a positive and compassionate approach to the problems with which it deals, and *re-inforced the value of the family unit*. Beneath all the tensions and preoccupations of those who live in Albert Square, lies a strong sense of community, a healthy neighbourliness and a wholesome acceptance of the multi-racial nature of society today' (my emphasis).

Young's letter continued by arguing that the programme merely reflected 'real life', and that it was therefore bound to contain incidents such as those Whitehouse had condemned:

> As the guidelines to which you refer indicate, a broadcasting service has an obligation, whether in news, documentary or fiction programmes, to the truthful reflection of life. In real life, regrettably, people's feelings sometimes express themselves in physical or verbal violence, and if that fact was not occasionally acknowledged in *EastEnders* the programme would soon be regarded as presenting a sanitised and artificial view of human behaviour. This does not mean that the idea of the watershed has been abandoned or that the programme 'amounts to an onslaught on the BBC's own declared standards'.

In a subsequent response to Whitehouse's complaints about the attempted suicide of Angie Watts, dated 23 April 1986, Young also questioned what he implied were her 'simplistic assumptions about copy-cat effects'. While acknowledging that television was 'a major part of the experience of many people', and was 'an influential medium' he argued that 'it must reflect the complexities of life in a sophisticated and responsible way if it is to continue to command attention and respect'.

In retrospect, Michael Grade argued that Whitehouse had simply made an error of judgment in her attacks on *EastEnders*:

Mary Whitehouse helped us a lot in the early days ... But she finally realised she'd made a terrible mistake with *EastEnders*. She thought she'd had a big effect on it, and that she'd got us to clean up the show: that's the way she rationalised the fact that she'd made a terrible mistake. She misjudged the programme entirely.

Grade and others refuted the suggestion that the programme had in any way been 'cleaned up' in response to Whitehouse's criticisms. As Jonathan Powell argued, the BBC had to be careful not to dismiss her arguments out of hand, but at the same time it had to avoid becoming involved in a 'privileged discussion' with the Whitehouse lobby. Particularly in the context of the Churchill legislation, it was important to distinguish between genuine criticisms and instances where people were simply 'scoring political points'.

Nevertheless, Whitehouse has since returned to the attack, and has again reached the headlines. Her 1987 address to the Annual Convention of the National Viewers' and Listeners' Association reiterated many of her former complaints, and particularly focused on the presence of prostitution and homosexuality in the serial. Significantly, this co-incided with a further attempt to apply stricter censorship laws to broadcasting, this time in the form of a Private Member's Bill proposed by Gerald Howarth MP – a Bill which proposed to outlaw as obscene anything which 'a reasonable person' would find offensive. In a sense, it is the very popularity of *EastEnders* which makes it such a visible – and hence extremely useful – focus for the criticisms of those who seek a return to Victorian morality.

Mary Whitehouse's denunciations of *EastEnders*, then, are a further symptom of the changing moral climate of British society in the late 1980s. In many ways, *EastEnders*' approach to moral issues derives from the secular, liberal consensus of the 1960s, which has increasingly come under attack. As Julia Smith argued, the essential difference between herself and Mary Whitehouse was not so much a matter of morality, as of their approach to moral education:

> Mary Whitehouse and I have had a love-hate relationship for a great many years. She's a very moral person, and so am I. We're not actually all that dissimilar in terms of age, although we may be mentally. I don't disagree with a lot of things she says. The only thing we disagree about is the way we do it. I think the world is better if things are discussed and everyone is aware of them. She is of the school that would sweep things under the carpet. That is the only difference.

In this sense, the debate about morality is essentially a debate about the control of information. What is particularly interesting about

Whitehouse's role is that she raises very clear questions about broadcasters' accountability to their audience. The problem, of course, is that these questions tend to be discussed in very limited terms. Indeed, the arguments advanced by both sides appear highly disingenuous. Whether or not one agrees with Whitehouse's moral position, one might certainly dispute her claim to represent 'public opinion'; and her arguments about the effects of television are clearly based on inadequate evidence. Yet the broadcasters' claims that television is simply 'a truthful reflection of life' are no less questionable. In response to Whitehouse's attacks, the broadcasters simply retreat into their own 'professionalism', insisting that they are, on the contrary, highly 'moral' and 'responsible' people, with a firm belief in the value of family life. Yet ultimately, such responses fail to address the fact that it is the broadcasters who retain a significant degree of control of information, and that they remain largely unaccountable to the public they claim to serve.

Conclusion

In this chapter, I have considered a number of factors which intervene in the relationship between *EastEnders* and its audience. These factors represent and mediate the programme in a variety of ways, and must therefore inevitably influence the processes by which viewers make sense of it. At the same time, the sheer amount and diversity of this material, and the fact that different viewers will have access to different aspects of it, means that the nature of this influence is likely to be variable and, in certain cases, contradictory. Far from generating uniformity, it may well produce a greater variety and flexibility in the ways in which audiences respond to the programme.

Thus, certain elements of the press coverage may reinforce viewers' belief in the 'reality' of what they watch, while others may undermine it. When 'agony aunt' Marje Proops writes letters of advice to the characters, she is addressing them as real people: yet when we read profiles of the actors, their characters are clearly seen as fictional. Revelations about the actors' private lives may reinforce our perception of their fictional characters – and vice-versa – yet they also remind us that the actors have identities which are independent from the parts they play. Much of the pleasure of such material derives from the way in which it plays on the distinction between fiction and reality: yet even where that distinction seems in danger of being blurred, it is never entirely obliterated.

The material itself is therefore highly ambiguous; and readers' responses may be equally ambiguous. Predictions about future developments in the plot, for example, may remove the suspense from certain scenes; but the fact that they are often inaccurate may introduce it into others – viewers may wait in vain for revelations that never come. Yet if predictions have proven ill-founded in the past, viewers may regard them sceptically in the future, and seek to test them against the evidence provided by the programme itself. Similarly, although the popular press has attempted to establish the terms for critical debate – for example in its discussion of the 'realism' and 'morality' of the programme – viewers compare these with their own judgments and may define these terms in very different ways.

Thus, while viewers may at least partially take on the agenda provided by the popular press, they do so critically and selectively. As will be seen from the responses recorded in the following chapter, audiences retain a considerable degree of autonomy in defining their relationship with television. The commonsense view of the 'power' of television, particularly over 'impressionable' younger viewers – a view which is paradoxically shared by Mary Whitehouse and by the broadcasters themselves – is one which I shall argue is certainly open to question.

4

POPULAR TELEVISION
AND ITS AUDIENCE

In the preceding chapters I have looked at a number of different ways in which the relationship between *EastEnders* and its audience has been established and defined – by its producers and by the institution within which they work, by the specific characteristics and strategies of the programme itself, and by factors which mediate between the programme and its audience, such as marketing and the popular press. In describing these elements I have sought to identify the diverse – and sometimes contradictory – ways in which viewers are invited to make sense of what they watch.

In this chapter, I shall examine how the audience itself – or at least one segment of it – responded to these invitations. I shall argue that viewers actively seek to construct their relationship with the programme on their own terms – terms which are often very different from those which appear to be on offer. The meaning of *EastEnders* is not something which is wholly contained within the text, and which is there to be discovered by viewers. On the contrary, it is determined through a process of negotiation between the text and the viewer, in which viewers retain a considerable degree of autonomy to construct their own meanings and pleasures.

This view of the relationship between television and its audience is hardly new in Media Studies, although it is one which flies in the face of many commonsense understandings of the 'power' of television. This is particularly the case with the segment of the audience I have chosen to study here – namely, young people.

In contrast to more established British soap operas, *EastEnders* has particularly sought to attract a younger audience, and appears to have been extremely successful in doing so. During the school year 1985–86, in which this part of the research took place, *EastEnders* acquired what could fairly be termed a cult status among young people. It was this extraordinary popularity which led many teachers to use the programme in their schools, both as an object of study, within formal

Media Studies courses, and as a teaching aid, for example as a means of introducing the discussion of various 'social issues' within Social Studies or English lessons. The fact that the programme was being used in schools was noted with a certain cynical amusement by the popular press, and with something approaching horror by Mary Whitehouse in a debate on BBC2's *Did You See?* in November 1985. *EastEnders* featured (and continues to feature) regularly on in-service training courses for teachers; and the Inner London Education Authority, which has long had an interest in Media Education, funded a two-term secondment of a teacher to produce teaching materials about the serial, beginning in April 1986. This interest on the part of teachers was initially received by the producers with some surprise, and not a little suspicion:

> JULIA SMITH   People are destroying our audience before they even watch it, because they're taking away the 'let's believe it'. Because people want to appear to educate, they are saying 'These aren't really real people, this is the way it's done'. Why not just let kids watch it and enjoy it?

In concentrating on young people's responses to the programme, it is at least partly my aim to inform and develop this educational work. In particular, I hope that the account provided in this chapter will go some way towards questioning some of the commonsense assumptions about children's experience of television which continue to influence Media Education. As I have argued elsewhere, the dominant view of Media Education as a form of 'inoculation' against the presumed effects of the media is based on a rather limited understanding of what children *already* know, and the critical faculties they already possess.[1] Children are generally seen as passive and uncritical consumers of television, helpless victims of a predominantly negative influence, which has an extraordinary power to mould their attitudes and determine their behaviour.

This view is not one confined to the likes of Mary Whitehouse, but is shared by many critics of television right across the political spectrum. On the one hand, there is a long history of 'moral panics' about the effects of televised sex and violence. Although researchers have experienced considerable difficulty in establishing causal connections between television violence and violent behaviour, the belief that children – and particularly those who are 'disturbed' or 'emotionally deprived' – are likely to imitate the anti-social acts they see on television remains part of commonsense wisdom.[2] Another focus of public debate has been the effects of television on children's thought processes. Watching television, it is argued, encourages mental laziness, retards the development of the brain and destroys the imagination: it is an 'insidious narcotic' which turns children into 'TV zombies', and thereby undermines family life.[3] Critics on the Left have been more concerned with the potential influence of television on children's attitudes, and in particular on racial and sexual stereotyping.[4] Analyses of television content – often simple statistical analyses which, for example, quantify the numbers of men and women appearing in particular occupational roles – have been used as evidence to support broad rhetorical assertions about the power of television to form stereotyped beliefs. As Ian Connell has noted, the Left has often adopted a view of audiences as the innocent victims of an all-powerful 'propaganda machine'.[5]

Although there are clearly differences between these approaches, there are also significant similarities. Each of them conceives of watching television as an act of passive consumption. Children, in particular, are seen as innocent and vulnerable targets for manipulation, largely incapable of resisting the seductive and yet dangerous messages with which they are daily 'bombarded'. This vulnerability is even more acute in the case of children whose family background is regarded as providing them with inadequate protection – and here, of course, such writers are particularly referring to working-class families. There is little sense here that children may compare their experience of television with their experience of the social world, or that they may question, or distance themselves from the representations it provides. Children are typified as indiscriminate and uncritical viewers, who are often unable to distinguish between fiction and reality. The reasons why children choose to watch television in the first place can only be explained in terms of their pathological weaknesses, or as a consequence of parental irresponsibility. The pleasure they experience from television is predominantly regarded as a means of detracting attention from its insidious effects, and hence as something to be suspected.

In rejecting this view, I do not wish to suggest that, on the contrary, television has very little influence on young people: on the crucial issue of *long-term* effects, as opposed to short-term changes in attitudes or behaviour, the research evidence is very limited.[6] Rather, I would argue that notions of influence (literally, a one-way flow) and cause-and-effect are inadequate ways of defining the nature of children's experience of the medium.

Recent research into children and television has begun to indicate an alternative approach to these questions.[7] Using models derived from semiotics and cognitive psychology, researchers have increasingly emphasised, and sought to explain, the role of children as *active producers of meaning* from television. Children are seen here as far more critical and sophisticated viewers than the commonsense wisdom outlined above invariably assumes. In making sense of television, children employ a wide range of abilities in processing, interpreting and evaluating information: there is a complex interaction between the meanings which children bring to television (the kinds of 'prior knowledge' identified in Chapter Three) and the meanings they construct from it. Recent accounts of the social context of television viewing also indicate that the view of children as 'TV zombies', 'glued to the box' for twenty-five hours a week, is highly inaccurate.[8] Both within the domestic viewing context, and beyond it, in peer-group discussion, the production of meaning from television is also an interpersonal activity.

There are certainly some dangers in this position. Cedric Cullingford, for example, argues that children regard television primarily as a source of relaxation and entertainment, for which they make very little mental effort – a suggestion which could lend support to the view that television is fundamentally rather trivial, and certainly not something worth taking seriously.[9] Yet while children may indeed approach television in a relatively casual, and even irreverent, manner, their extremely detailed recall of events, and their often passionate debates about the moral rights and wrongs of particular characters, suggest that at least in the case of *EastEnders* they had a good deal 'invested' in their relationship with the programme.

Perhaps more seriously, this view of children as active, critical viewers might be seen to support the idea that there is an infinite plurality of meanings which may be produced from a given text, which the text itself has little power to determine or restrict. Again, the responses to *EastEnders* recorded here suggest that this is not necessarily the case. On the one hand, there is a considerable degree of diversity in the young people's judgments of the characters and their behaviour; yet there are also significant continuities across the major divisions of race, age and gender in terms of *how* they make sense of the programme and relate to it. The fact that readings are to a certain extent shared is inevitable, given that the meanings – or, more accurately, the tools and strategies for producing meaning – which viewers bring to the programme are themselves also likely to be shared. To characterise the process in these terms is implicitly to ascribe a degree of 'power' to television – yet it is also to suggest that this power derives from the active involvement of viewers in producing meaning, rather than from the ability of texts merely to impose it.

There is a growing body of research which supports the account of children's experience of television which I have briefly outlined here. However, much of this research investigates children's viewing practices in fairly general terms, and tends not to pay close attention to the variations in responses to different types of television. Although my research here is more limited in scope, and therefore does not seek to *prove* any more general assertions about children and television, it does seek to extend this particular line of enquiry by means of a detailed case study.

Methodology

The account which follows is based on a series of small group discussions with a total of sixty young people aged between seven and eighteen, held in the London area in the Spring and Summer of 1986. In all, twelve groups were interviewed, with an average of five participants in each. The discussions lasted a minimum of one hour, and a maximum of two, with an average length of around one hour twenty-five minutes. Most took place in schools, during the normal school day, although four took place in youth clubs or youth centres.

My intention was to make these discussions as open-ended as possible, and to avoid directing them towards particular issues. I began each session by asking some fairly basic questions about viewing habits: when and why had they started to watch the programme, how many times a week did they see it, did other members of their family watch it, and so on. I would then ask each member of the group to identify their favourite, and their least favourite, characters, and to give reasons for their choices. This question was normally sufficient to guarantee animated discussion for the remainder of the time available; my only subsequent questions were to clarify points of confusion, and occasionally to draw out more reticent members of the group. Sometimes, generally towards the end of the discussion, I would draw the group's attention to characters or stories which they had failed to mention, at least partly to discover if there were reasons for this. Finally, usually for about the last twenty minutes of the session, I would screen a videotape of the last few scenes from the latest episode of *EastEnders*, occasionally pausing the tape to invite comments from the group.

By adopting this relatively self-effacing role, I was attempting to allow the group to define its own agenda for discussion. What the groups chose to talk about, and what they chose to ignore, were in themselves significant. Furthermore, by intervening as little as possible, and encouraging the group members to interact directly with each other, rather than through a 'mediator', I was aiming to identify more accurately *how* they would discuss the programme in their everyday conversation.

Ultimately, of course, it is impossible to render oneself invisible. The very fact that these discussions took place in schools, or in other institutional contexts, and that they were artificially convened by an adult of somewhat 'teacherly' appearance, clearly must have influenced what was said, albeit in ways which I would find difficult to define. I certainly did not feel that the children were telling me what they thought I wanted to hear: in fact, it would be difficult to imagine how they would have been able to guess what I wanted to hear, given that I had very little idea of this myself. It was not as if I were asking them about their political beliefs, for example – a subject on which they might well have attempted to guess my own position.

In fact, I was initially rather bored and depressed by the tendency, particularly of the younger children, to recount the plot of past episodes at considerable length. This was not, I felt, the stuff from which significant research is made. It was only on subsequently transcribing the tapes that I became interested in which parts of the plot they chose to recount, and the ways in which they did so – observations which led to some broader insights into their relationship with the programme.

In general, the groups had no difficulty in sustaining discussion for the time available, which – at least for the younger children – was in itself remarkable. If anything, the most significant problem (and it became highly significant in transcribing the tapes!) was preventing the group members from all talking at once. At least to some extent, their enthusiasm for the subject overcame any inhibitions which might have arisen from my presence. It is perhaps worth noting in this respect that the groups were largely 'friendship groups', rather than random collections of individuals: as such they were likely to be very used to talking to each other – and, not least, to talking about *EastEnders* itself. In this sense, what was being asked of them was simply to continue their everyday social conversation with an outsider present, and their interest and pleasure in each other's contributions was certainly greater than any desire they may have had to please me.

I should also say a little about the *social* constitution of the groups. In general, I made no systematic attempt to segregate the participants according to race, class or gender. In the event, nearly all the children interviewed might broadly be termed 'working class'; certain groups were almost exclusively black; and while the majority were mixed, three were single-sex (two all-girls and one all-boys). Although I was concerned to investigate differences between the responses of these different social groups, I remain somewhat uneasy about making generalisations about these on the basis of a fairly small sample. One of my reservations about previous research on media audiences is that it has all too often led to rather simplistic causal connections between the readings produced by certain groups and their social position: thus groups are seen to respond in particular ways *because* they are black, or female, or working-class.[10] Furthermore, such classifications typically ignore individuals' own perceptions of their social position. While it is comparatively easy for researchers to classify their subjects according to observable physical or biological characteristics, or according to their parents' occupations, this may tell us very little about the meanings which the subjects themselves ascribe to their own social position. To define somebody as *male* is unproblematic, although the way in which that person chooses to define his own *masculinity* can clearly vary. Towards the end of this chapter, I shall indicate some significant differences between the readings produced by different social groups and also some differences *within* them.

159

Viewing patterns

It would probably be fair to describe all the young people I interviewed as 'fans' of *EastEnders*. Those I asked were quite willing to accept this description of themselves; and in volunteering to join the discussion in the first place, they were clearly indicating a positive enthusiasm for the programme. This is not to say that they were uncritical of it – indeed, as the following account reveals, there were certain respects in which they were extremely critical, and elements which they found merely inept or ridiculous. It is important to emphasise at this stage that this critical distance was not incompatible with their overall enjoyment of the programme, and indeed made certain forms of enjoyment possible – albeit ones which the programme itself may not have sanctioned or invited. Critical distance is not the sole prerogative of those intellectuals influenced by what Ien Ang terms 'the ideology of mass culture'.[11] Laughing *at* television and questioning its representation of the world is one of the everyday pleasures of viewing, even – or perhaps particularly – for children.

Although most of the young people interviewed were familiar with other British soap operas, they were generally not particularly fond of them. *EastEnders* was described as 'the best British soap that's been out so far', and one which its rivals were increasingly being forced to imitate:

> DIONNE (17)* I think all the soaps are trying to get back into *EastEnders* style now.
> JACKIE Like *Crossroads*. That was never like that before. Now *Crossroads* is doing rape and leaving husband and all that. It was never like that.
> KAREN What about that other soap opera that's trying to be like *EastEnders*, *Albion Market*?
> DIONNE But the thing about it, you know, they just can't come against it!

In fact, a particular contempt was reserved for *Albion Market*, which was widely regarded as a poor copy – or, in the words of one boy, a 'parrot' – of *EastEnders*.

> CLAIRE (11) They've tried to copy the *EastEnders* people. That man and that woman that ran away, it was like Angie and Den.
> STEVEN It's rubbish.
> ELAINE It's boring... It's got no *thing* to it.
> DB What do you mean, it's got no thing?
> ELAINE You know, got no story to it... all different bits.

---

* In all cases, the age indicated in brackets after the name of the first speaker is that of all members of the group.

160

Although some of the children were also viewers of *Coronation Street*, many appeared to have switched their allegiance to *EastEnders*: the former was seen by the majority as 'old fashioned', 'full of old grannies', and generally 'boring'. One group defined the problem with *Coronation Street* as follows:

RUTH (15) They try to make it too lifelike. They make things worse than they are.
TAMMY They always seem much harder up for money. They make it seem as though everyone that's on the dole goes around in really trampish clothes. But I've seen people on the dole, and they don't go around looking like that.
RUTH *EastEnders* is quite depressing, but it's still happy, they look as if they have a good time.

Although *EastEnders* was typically described as 'realistic', its realism was not seen as incompatible with a degree of glamour and excitement, or even a fair amount of 'thing': in the words of one eleven-year-old, 'it's not just boring everyday life'.

In this respect, it is interesting that American soaps like *Dallas* and *Dynasty* were generally preferred to the home-grown variety, despite (or rather perhaps because of) their acknowledged lack of realism. In the vivid words of one nine-year-old boy, Preston: '*Dynasty*'s really good. Fridays, I just watch it. I say I want to get my eyes *stuck* into this telly, I don't want to move my eyes.'

A number of children made direct comparisons between the American soaps and *EastEnders*: Den Watts was described by many as 'the J.R. of *EastEnders*' and one girl (perhaps with some irony) described Sharon as its Joan Collins. To a certain extent, then, it may well be those elements of *EastEnders* which are more characteristic of American than of British soap opera which account for its unique popularity with a younger audience.

Most of these young people regularly tuned in to the Tuesday and Thursday editions, and many also watched the repeat transmission on Sundays. Some even recorded episodes for further repeated viewing of selected 'highlights'. This phenomenon of repeat viewing – which was a major source of controversy in the 'ratings war' between *EastEnders* and its rival soaps – is perhaps a consequence of the fast pace of the programme. As one fourteen-year-old boy said, watching the programme again provided a chance to catch up on parts he might have missed 'daydreaming' first time around. For older children, who tend to watch less television than other age groups, *EastEnders* remained popular despite the attractions of activities outside the home:

DARREN (14) I usually miss the episodes during the week 'cause I'm out most of the time. And when I get home on Sunday, as soon as I get my dinner it comes on the telly, so I might as well watch it when I'm eating my dinner... See what's been happening in the week, see what everyone's been talking about.

This desire to 'see what everyone's been talking about' reveals a degree of *social pressure* to watch the programme, a pressure derived at least partly from the publicity 'hype' which preceded the launch, and from the extensive press coverage. As Sandra (17) said, 'It had such a good write-up: everyone was talking about it before it even started'. However, it was particularly experienced as a form of *peer group* pressure: many of the children said that they had started watching in order to avoid feeling left out of conversations:

MARK (15) I started watching it 'cause everyone else was watching it.
TAMMY You look a bit stupid if everyone else is talking about it and you've got nothing to say.

Even worse than feeling left out was being discovered when *pretending* to have watched the programme:

MAXINE (10) But if we don't watch it, right, everyone talks about it in our class: 'Did you see *EastEnders?*' 'What about when Ethel got mugged?'
SAMANTHA And if you don't know about it, you're saying 'yeah, yeah' and you never even seen it! [Laughter]
BRIAN Like Lianne. I was saying all these things, and she goes 'yeah' and I goes 'what happened then, at the end?' and she goes 'I don't know!'

This peer group pressure could even extend to preferences for particular characters: one group of eleven-year-olds all chose Kathy Beale as their favourite character – a choice which in terms of the overall pattern was fairly idiosyncratic – largely because of the almost single-minded obsession of the most dominant member of the group (of whom more shortly).

These conversations about the programme were thus part of a broader process of social interaction, through which friendships and enmities were constructed and reconstructed. They typically took place on the margins of 'official' school life, and at times in resistance to the demands of teachers:

FIONA (12) That's what we talk about every day in class.
LEE It gets on Miss's nerves!

162

For most of these children, however, their actual viewing of *East-Enders* obviously took place in the home, in the company of family rather than friends: as Jamie (14) said, 'That's the quiet time in my house'. The programme was sometimes the focus of disputes over control of the television set – disputes which fathers usually won, and mothers and children lost.[12] In certain cases, the children were banished upstairs to watch the programme on the black and white set, while in others it was recorded so that dad could watch the Channel Four News. Although in certain cases with the exception of the men in the house, *EastEnders* was generally a programme which the whole family watched together. One seventeen-year-old felt that it had an almost therapeutic function in that it enabled him to talk to his parents about problems like drugs:

> PAUL The other thing that it does, is that you sit there, and normally you're with your parents, and you're sitting down watching it, and you just talk... The conversation arises from that, and so you're talking to your parents about it, and so it probably makes you feel a bit comfortable, like if you need the backing from your parents, and the security there.

However, to infer from this that most everyday conversation about *EastEnders*, whether in the family or in the peer group, or indeed in any of the discussions reported here, is focused explicitly on 'problems' or 'issues' would be misleading. Just as Tony Holland and Julia Smith were keen to disclaim any self-conscious attention to 'social issues' (see Chapter One), so in my experience it was rare for any of the groups directly to address particular themes of this nature. Although, as I argued in Chapter Two, the programme does at certain points adopt a more didactic approach, it would be fair to say that this passes almost unnoticed, particularly by younger children. It would, I think, have been extremely difficult for any of these groups to answer a question like 'What do you think *EastEnders* is saying about racism?', and when, on one or two occasions, I did attempt to raise such issues explicitly in the discussion, the response was either confused or minimal. This is not, I would argue, because they were not aware of these issues, or lacking in a vocabulary to discuss them – as some of the quotations below will illustrate. Nor is it the case that this awareness did not enter into the discussion. On the contrary, it did so, not on the level of abstract argument, but through the collective discussion of the characters' moral dilemmas, through the rehearsing of past incidents and the prediction of future developments.

Telling secrets

A significant part of the pleasure of everyday conversation about television derives from the re-living of its narratives, and in particular

163

from the rehearsal of concealed or confidential information which narratives reveal. This re-telling of the 'secrets' which television invites us to share is often referred to, somewhat pejoratively, as 'gossip'. For younger children, this often has a particular fascination, akin to voyeurism. Television may provide them with representations of aspects of adult behaviour which are usually hidden from them, although they may well be aware of their existence. Discussing television may thus provide a relatively 'safe' way of acknowledging things which they are normally forbidden to talk about; as well as allowing us to look without being seen, television also allows us to pass comment without fear of reprisals. In many instances, these 'secrets' were discussed in tones of whispered confidentiality and barely suppressed excitement:

DELROY (7) A long time ago in the programme, Kathy got raped when she was fourteen, when she was coming home from work. This man wanted to go to Marley Street and Kath went in the car. They wanted to check up in the A to Z. They was miles away. And then he raped her in the back. Then after, Nick Cotton breaked into Dr Legg's surgery, and he took the files, and he knew she had a baby, right. Then after, she didn't want to tell Pete...

As this example shows, the children's recall of past events in the programme (often events which had taken place many months previously) was extremely detailed. It was also a collective process: the children would interrupt each other to dispute particular points of detail, or to provide additional information, often searching for the accurate wording of a particular line of dialogue. When I was able to screen a videotape of the previous night's episode, the children would talk along with the characters, often anticipating particularly comic or dramatic pieces of dialogue.

Lisa, the eleven-year-old whose fixation on the character of Kathy Beale was briefly mentioned above, was perhaps the most extreme example of this. At the beginning of our discussion, she produced a bulging scrapbook containing an assortment of press cuttings about the programme and a number of detailed accounts of past events within it which she had written. She proceeded to read her own version of Kathy Beale's 'confession' to her husband Pete, in which she told of how she had been raped, and of the subsequent birth and adoption of her child. What was remarkable about this account was not merely its detailed accuracy – Lisa assured me that she had not transcribed the scene from a videotape, but had recalled it from her viewing of the episode – but also the mixture of sincerity and hilarity with which it was both read and received by other members of the group. If the sheer detail of Lisa's 'obsession' suggested a strong degree of identification with the character, the melodramatic and satirical way in which she imitated her pretending to break down in tears indicated an equally strong degree of distancing. Her other remarks about Kathy suggested that it was precisely her *ordinariness* as a character which Lisa valued: Kathy was described as 'just local', and as being 'sensible' in ways that other characters were not. Her husband Pete was particularly singled out for criticism:

> LISA   Pete's a bit of a chauvinist. Know what I mean, a sexist pig.
> ALISON   Pete's been cheating...
> LISA   They don't spend too much time together. They just don't talk to each other. When it comes time when Pete wants her, and she's trying to explain to him, he doesn't want to listen. He just wants her for himself, really.
> ALISON   As his body lover, know what I mean?

Yet at the same time, Lisa was clearly aware that 'Kathy Beale' was a fictional character, played by an actress called Gillian Taylforth: 'You know Gillian Taylforth? She had an ache in her left breast. And she mentioned the word "breast" in the papers *fourteen times*!' This shifting between an intense involvement in the fiction and a critical (often satirical) distancing from it was characteristic of many of these discussions.

This example illustrates something of the tone in which the 'secrets' of *EastEnders* were related, and is also representative of the *kinds* of secrets which were considered most fascinating. As well as sexual activity – particularly 'taboo' activities such as homosexuality or adultery – crime and violence were also major topics of discussion. Scenes such as that in which Pete Beale beat up Nick Cotton, or Nick threatened his mother with a kitchen knife, were retold with considerable relish, particularly by the boys. Nevertheless, such descriptions were not without a degree of ironic distance, which suggests that these elements of the programme were not taken entirely seriously either:

> VICKY (9)   And you know when Nick Cotton's mum was out, he nicked some cheques. What he done, he wrote on them and gave them away, what he owes people. And his mum has to pay for it. That's what the robbers do when they get in your house. They get some of your cheques, they write it out [miming the actions], write another one out, write another one out, tear it out, give it to people they owe to. Like they say, 'Can I borrow a thousand pounds, and here's a cheque.' And they put it in their pocket and scram. And then they go to another one and say [American accent] 'Can I borrow six hundred grand?'
> MARK   I don't think Dot's got that much!

VICKY   And they give the cheque... And he might go to them [American accent] 'Can I borrow a thousand hundred million grand?' And he puts it in his pocket and he gives them a cheque. And his mum, she has to pay for it. And she ain't got that kind of money, see.

The pleasure Vicky takes in imitating and exaggerating the characters' behaviour was one shared by many of the children. The more obviously comic characters, such as Dot Cotton and Ethel, were a particular focus for ridicule. Ethel's malapropisms and her concern about 'her Willy' were a cause of considerable hilarity. Instances where more 'serious' or self-important characters were 'shown up' or 'put down' were also retold with great amusement: what one boy described as Den and Angie's mutual 'sarcasticness', and Den's trade in abusive repartee, were much admired.

This ironic tone extended even to the description of scenes which were perceived as high drama, such as Den's discovery of Angie's suicide attempt:

SAMANTHA (10)   [miming] She was like a dummy!
MAXINE   And he said 'Speak to me! Speak to me!'
[Laughter]
MARTIN   He was really crying.
RANI   You felt really sorry for him.

Here again, the ability to be moved by the fiction was not necessarily incompatible with a desire to ridicule it.

Although it is clear that *what* is revealed by the programme is in itself a source of great fascination, it is the *process of revelation*, both within the narrative and in its subsequent reconstruction in discussion, which constitutes much of the pleasure. This emerged particularly from the children's discussion of two of the major hermeneutic 'teasers' of recent episodes: the identity of the father of Michelle Fowler's baby, and that of Debbie Wilkins' dirty phone caller:

ELAINE (12)   I do like that bit when Michelle... Where it's all suspicious, like Den goes in his car, Ali goes in his car... I really do like that bit.
NICOLA   Like when Debbie got those funny phone calls and they was all at the phone. And she didn't know...
MILO   She thought it was Ali.
NICOLA   And Andy was just about to yank hold of him and start beating him and the phone rang... And then Sue started throwing tantrums.

At least part of the pleasure identified here derives from the knowledge that one is being manipulated, that information is being deliberately withheld; and of course this is most obviously the case with the 'cliffhanger' at the end of an episode.

MAXINE (9)   I remember that bit when you see Michelle walking on the bridge and that...
SAMANTHA   Near the canal. And Den came...
MAXINE   You see, everybody came out and they went in their car. And me and my mum, we didn't know who it was!
SAMANTHA   Yeah, nor did I. And they always stop it when it's so exciting!
DB   Why do you think they do that?
BRIAN   They've got to save the next bit for the next episode.

The children's predictions of future developments were sometimes concluded with a collective rendering of the final theme tune, suggesting that these moments of revelation, and their promise of further excitement, were a crucial element in their pleasure. In other words, they were expressing a strong desire to be 'shocked', to partake of secrets normally hidden in the course of daily life, and which occasionally burst through its calm surface with unforeseen consequences; as Darren (11) said, summarising his reasons for liking *EastEnders*: 'It's not just boring everyday life. Something interesting happens every day. The thing about *EastEnders*, it interests me because every time they've got something that's shocking people – like Mary doing stripping.'

As many of the children exclaimed, *EastEnders* was 'wicked' – a slang word which indicates a considerable degree of approval, and particularly implies an ability to say things in a way nobody else can.

Prediction

This desire for the revelation of hidden secrets also emerged strongly from the children's predictions of future developments in the narrative. For example, many felt that if the identity of the father of Michelle's baby were to be revealed to other characters in the programme, exciting developments would ensue:

DANIEL (11)   If Angie finds out that he made Michelle pregnant, then she might leave him.
ALISON   The baby could resemble Den, right. And they might suspect.

This was also seen as one of a number of potential obstacles to the impending marriage of Lofty and Michelle:

NATALIE (9) Lofty's going to find out. He don't know. And he's going to be Michelle's husband.

PRESTON Guess what? He got a ring off Den. And when she finds out, she might get divorced.

VICKY I reckon that Michelle's not going to turn up, or something like that. Give him the elbow.

Alternatively, Den himself might intervene:

MAXINE (9) I think if Lofty marries Michelle, I don't know what would happen with Den. His jealousy would creep in, boy. You'll see him get really jealous.

SAMANTHA He'll try and mess up their marriage.

MAXINE Try and divorce them, boy.

Only very rarely did anybody express a desire that characters might live 'happily ever after'. The occasional wish that Angie and Den might 'get back together' counted for little compared with the fervent belief, particularly on the part of the girls, that she should 'get her own back', and get it good. This occasionally amounted to an almost sadistic desire to witness others' suffering – particularly characters like Den Watts and Debbie Wilkins, who for different reasons were widely disliked. Yet it is perhaps more appropriate to regard this as arising primarily from the desire for the narrative to continue, and the recognition that in soap operas it is often suffering which is the most powerful motor of narrative.

Another 'secret' which many looked forward to being revealed was the identity of Kathy Beale's daughter – a secret which most felt they already knew, despite the fact that they had not learnt it from the programme. Only with the older groups was any doubt cast on an idea which all the younger children accepted as fact:

MAGDLIN (17) I reckon they should reveal some things, 'cause it's getting really boring nowadays. They should reveal a bit more. Like Kathy getting to know Sharon's her daughter.

HEBA She's not!

MARIAN How come Nick didn't find out about it when he took her records? If Sharon is her child, why didn't it come out then?

DONNA He could have blackmailed her again.

MAGDLIN They could make it up, because it is a good story, that she finds out that Sharon is her daughter. Now she's going out with Ian, it would be more interesting, because a sister going out with a brother, that is really interesting.

HEBA No!

DONNA Pete and Kath must know something, that's why they

want to stop Ian going out with Sharon.

SHARON Yes, that's why they're trying to stop him.

HEBA No! They don't know anything about that anyway!

In this fairly heated debate, there is an interesting series of shifts occurring. On the one hand, there is an acceptance of the reality of the fictional world, or diegesis, for example in Donna's second remark; while on the other, there is a critical distance from it, for example in Magdlin's ideas about what would make 'a good story'. Yet many of the speakers fluctuate between these two positions: Heba, for example, protests – at least partly out of moral outrage – at the idea that the programme should feature incest (thus from a position outside the diegesis), yet in her final remark she shifts her position to one within the diegesis, arguing that although Sharon is Kath's daughter, Pete and Kath herself do not know this fact, and therefore any incestuous relationship which might be occurring is doing so without anybody's knowledge – except the viewer's that is. This process of shifting into and out of the fictional world of the programme was very frequent in these discussions.

Perhaps the greatest irony here is that Sharon is in fact *not* Kath's daughter, and the idea that she is comes not from *EastEnders*, but from the 'misinformation' circulated by the popular press. Most of the children claimed to read press coverage of the programme regularly, and it was this material which informed many of their predictions. For example, many were convinced that Michelle would lose her baby in a motorcycle accident; that Den's lover would be a man; that Nick Cotton would be pushed off a tower block; and that Sharon would try to seduce her father in order to take revenge for him making Michelle pregnant. All these predictions subsequently proved to be false. In other cases, predictions which turned out to be correct only served to fuel further speculation. For example, the news that Michelle's baby would be called Vicky led to suggestions that she had been named after Michelle's night of passion with Den in the Queen Vic, and that her parents would 'put two and two together'. The news that Andy was about to leave the programme led to considerable speculation about the precise way in which he would be written out – possibly as a result of Den discovering him in bed with Angie and giving him 'two black eyes'.

For the younger children, the press coverage offered a further source of voyeuristic fascination, both in terms of its revelations about *EastEnders* and also in its insights into the private lives of the stars:

VICKY (9) [confidentially] You know Debs and Andy? In real life, they're in love and they're going to get married. And d'you know Matthew Kelly, who used to be on *Game for a Laugh*? I think it's

Matthew Kelly... You know Ange, she's going out with him. And you know Harry, she's in love with him. 'Cause I seen in this newspaper, there's a big square with his face in it, and she's going all lovey-dovey.

However, while the younger children were slightly more inclined to accept what they read as the truth, they rarely confused characters with actors: even in the case of Angie's attempted affair with Lofty (described by one girl as a clear case of 'going too far'), a line was drawn between events in the programme and the fact that 'in real life she's going out with him'. If anything, information about the actors' private lives, and their comments on their roles in the programme, had the opposite effect, of undermining any belief in the reality of the fictional world.

Although they enjoyed this process of speculation, many of the children were sceptical about what they read, particularly in the light of past predictions which had failed to come true:

ELAINE (12)   Most things that they say in the paper, what's going to happen, like, some of them don't come true. Some of them are just lies.
CLAIRE   Like Michelle's going to lose her baby.
NICOLA   Or that she's pregnant in real life.

Some of the older children had applied considerable tests of logic:

RODNEY (17)   I want to know if Ian's going to find out that Sharon's his sister.
SHEILA   She couldn't be.
DONNA   There's no way that could happen, because they're the same age, aren't they?
CALISTA   It's impossible, because she met Pete afterwards.
SANDRA   She's still going to be his step sister.
DONNA   But Sharon's not older than Ian, Ian's older than Sharon.
CALISTA   D'you get it? It couldn't have happened, it's not possible.
DONNA   'Cause we read everywhere, in the *Sun*, that Sharon was meant to be Kath's daughter, who Den and Angie adopted, but it's not possible.
SHEILA   We worked it out, didn't we?

While any faith they may have had in the accuracy of the newspaper reports was thus potentially undermined, this did not affect their willingness to play along with the collective game of predicting future events, and debating the likelihood of these predictions. What this final example reveals is how viewers constantly test their own and others' predictions against the evidence provided by the programme in their attempts to get it right.

Inside and outside the text

While the desire to be entertained by shocking and scandalous revelations was an important reason why these children watched *EastEnders*, it would be far from true to suggest that it was necessarily the only one. For all of them, discussing the programme was also an opportunity to engage in a moral debate, which in the case of the older children was often extremely sophisticated. The following transcript provides an extended example of such debate, which illustrates a number of crucial findings. The speakers are all seventeen-year-old girls; there was only one boy present, whose contribution was confined to the final comment below.

CALISTA Michelle, in a way, is not the perfect teenager, is she? She's got all her family around her. Not everybody's like that.

SANDRA She's very selfish anyway.

CALISTA I think that's why she's using Lofty.

SHEILA She won't listen to anybody's advice. Her mum and her nan and her dad tried to sit down, tried to go to the clinic with her, and she just didn't want to know. She just wanted to keep herself to herself, and now she wants Lofty to take the burden off her. [...]

CALISTA When she first found out she was pregnant, it was 'Oh, gran, I'm pregnant, Oh gran, help!' or whatever, and then all of a sudden it was '*my* baby, *my* life, I'm going to do what I want to'. [...]

SHEILA Her mum's got a lot of burden, right. She's just not taking her mum into consideration. Her mum has to go through a lot. Now supposing something happens to that baby, or if it dies or whatever, who's going to have to look after Michelle, to try and get her out of it? Her mum. Now, when she wants to go out to parties, who's going to look after that child? Her mum. Everything falls on the mum, I reckon. Even though it's her baby, she's got her mum, she's got her gran, she's got her dad, she's got people round her to help her. Other people haven't got that, they're just there by themselves, they usually get chucked out or something.

CALISTA She's got to take the other people around her into consideration. I mean, it is her baby, it is her body, it is her life, but these other people, she's living with them, and they're the ones who've got to bear the brunt of whatever is happening. She's going to have this baby, and she's too young to have a baby, anyway.

DONNA She's under age now, isn't she? She's still under parent guard. [...]

SHEILA   I think it was wrong that she didn't tell her parents who the father is. Any parent is going to find out. Any parent is going to drag it out of them. I mean, your parents know you better than anybody does. I think that the father should have the right to know. I mean, it would bring out more in *EastEnders*, wouldn't it?

CALISTA   I suppose they're saving it really, to use later on. And if their ratings go down, then they're going to use that to pick up their ratings.

SANDRA   I read somewhere that they're going to name the baby Victoria and then everyone's going to start saying 'Aha! Victoria! It must be Den!' [Laughter]

DONNA   That's what it said, it's going to get some tongues wagging. [...]

SANDRA   But all the time, she keeps dropping hints. Like when she heard about Jan coming down to the pub, she sat down and started crying. I mean, things like that, you would pick up these little pieces and start putting it all together. And I reckon Lofty should know who the father is. He should demand to know.

CALISTA   Think about it though: why did Den give him that engagement ring? All these things! If it was me, I'd start thinking 'Why is he giving me this ring?'

RODNEY   But Lofty's stupid in the first place! [Laughter]

What is particularly interesting about this discussion is the way in which the speakers constantly shift back and forth between two positions – at certain points, they appear to be judging the programme and the characters from *outside* the fictional world, while at others they seem to accept the reality of that world, and make their judgments, as it were, from *inside* it. In each case, they also use different types of *evidence* to support their arguments.

Furthermore, within each perspective there are a range of different, but related, concerns. From the more distanced 'outside' perspective, there is firstly a concern about *representation*, in this instance about the ways in which teenagers (that is, they themselves) are typically represented. Elsewhere in their discussion, this group had been critical of the 'problem teenager' stereotype which they detected both in *East-Enders* and in more recent episodes of *Coronation Street*. Thus, they argue that Michelle is 'not the perfect teenager' – unlike other pregnant teenagers, who would 'get chucked out', Michelle has 'got all her family around her', and is therefore in a position which the girls consider untypical. Secondly, they are clearly aware that the programme is a *constructed artefact*, and that decisions about how particular stories develop may be determined at least partly with a view to ratings. They use evidence from their reading of the popular press to predict how in future the programme may seek to involve, if not manipulate, its audience: naming the baby Victoria will 'get some tongues wagging' both inside *EastEnders* and outside it, in everyday conversation.

From an 'inside' perspective, the group is concerned to debate the *moral* validity of Michelle's behaviour. Two points are particularly notable here. Firstly, the girls are extremely critical of what they regard as Michelle's selfishness, which is surprising given that they are very close to her in terms of age, gender and class background. This would suggest that the notion that viewers will automatically 'identify' with characters who are like themselves is perhaps an oversimplification. Secondly, particularly in Sheila's long speech early in the discussion, it is clear that this criticism derives from a specific class and gender perspective, in this case from the experience of women's roles in a working-class extended family. It is this experience which, I would argue, leads them to question Michelle's attempt to 'keep herself to herself', and to take on the mother's perspective.

Cutting across this inside/outside movement is the group's concern for *plausibility*. On one hand, for example, they argue that the other characters would have picked up the 'hints' in Michelle's behaviour and would 'start putting it all together'. Their failure to do so is clearly regarded as implausible – although it is, by implication, something which they regard as necessary if the plot is to keep the audience guessing, and keep its tongues wagging. On the other hand, however, this failure is seen to be a result of the characters' stupidity – particularly that of Lofty, who, as Rodney indicates, any regular viewer will know to be 'stupid in the first place'. Sheila's speech which begins 'It was wrong that she didn't tell the parents...' exemplifies the dual nature of this concern for plausibility. On one level, she sees it as 'wrong' on moral grounds: 'her father should have the right to know'. Yet it is also 'wrong' because it is implausible: 'any parent is going to drag it out of them'. And it may also be 'wrong' in terms of the development of the narrative, the need to reveal or 'bring out more' in the programme.

Finally, it is worth emphasising that this discussion is itself extremely pleasurable for the participants. As Dorothy Hobson observes:

> It is actually fun to talk about the characters in a soap opera, and yet the game that viewers play with one another is interpreted as some form of psychological disorder, when for the most part they are well aware that the game is going on.[13]

I have chosen to discuss this extract at length because it serves to introduce many of the major issues to be considered in more detail in the remainder of this chapter – in particular, the role of moral and ideological judgment, questions of realism and plausibility and, finally, of identification and representation. Although it provides a fairly condensed and complex example of these processes, it is also representative of the ways in which even much younger children interacted with the programme.

Moral and ideological judgment
As I argued in Chapter Two, *EastEnders* directly *invites* its viewers to make moral and ideological judgments. By virtue of its characteristic modes of address and uses of narrative, it invokes specific moral and ideological discourses, through which viewers are encouraged to make sense of the characters' behaviour. However, as the above discussion shows, it is not necessarily easy to predict *which* discourses or perspectives will be brought into play at the point of reception.

This is partly a function of the complexity of the text itself. While it is characteristic of the narratives of soap operas to provide a constantly shifting series of perspectives, and while the text may encourage viewers to arrange these in hierarchies, and to reject some as wholly deviant, it would be false to suggest that it seeks to impose a *single* moral or ideological position on its viewers. The rare didactic moments in *EastEnders* are noticeable precisely because they attempt to do this in a manner which is uncharacteristic of the genre. Furthermore, given the lack of narrative closure, viewers may well have trouble *locating* a moral or ideological norm among the characters, given that these norms – happy families or faithful couples, for example – are rarely left undisturbed for long. For experienced viewers, a norm may come to seem rather like a state of grace to which all aspire, yet which none are able permanently to achieve.

These norms may also be perceived by audiences as unattractive or uninteresting: the Devil may have all the best lines. This was certainly the case with responses to *EastEnders*, both in the popular press and among the children interviewed. The stormy, often vicious relationship of Angie and Den Watts – which was admittedly very prominent in the serial at the time – was seen as infinitely more fascinating than the cosy stability of the Beales or the Fowlers, whose moments of crisis were yet to come. The latter in particular were seen as the embodiment of 'boring everyday life', and were rarely deemed worthy of discussion.

However, this process of judgment is not wholly open or arbitrary. As I have suggested, the serial encourages viewers to organise its moral and ideological universe in certain ways, and only makes available a *limited* range of perspectives. Furthermore, the kinds of judgments which are invited are more frequently moral rather than ideological ones – that is, judgments which relate to the rights and wrongs of *individual* behaviour, rather than to broader social forces.

Nevertheless, in criticising and discussing the characters, viewers may well be using television as a vehicle for working out their own ideological perspectives, or for giving voice to their own needs or desires. Their judgments may often extend beyond questions of morality to address broader ideological or political issues, even where these are not made explicit within the programme itself. For example, gender differences were a crucial factor in the debates about Den and Angie. Den was widely seen – particularly by the girls – to possess double standards:

> SAMANTHA (9) Den expects Angie not to go out with nobody, but Den can. That's what he said, and they had an argument when she came back.
> RANI They had this drink, and he said that he could go out with any girl, and she can't.
> MAXINE But that ain't the way they should put it though. If he could go out with anyone he wants to, then she can.

Many wanted Angie to 'get her own back' on Den by having an affair with another man:

> CLAIRE (12) She should have all the rights to go with a man, specially if her husband's going with another woman.

Yet Angie was regarded by many as fundamentally weak, even implausibly so:

> NATASHA (12) Angie's too soft, though. She always says [whining voice] 'I'm sorry, Den'.
> JOHN If he was doing that, you wouldn't go out with him. He goes out with Jan, right, and you wouldn't stick up with it. I would either leave him, or...
> FIONA I wouldn't give him a second chance.
> NATASHA She should smack him in the face, or boot him one.
> LEE I know what my mum would do. She'd get a frying pan and knock him over the head with it.
> FIONA And if I was Angie, I would have got Jan and booted her one.

In one instance, with an all-girls group, this criticism again moved *outside* the fictional world of the programme, and became a debate, not merely about the rights and wrongs of Angie's behaviour, but also about *EastEnders*' representation of women more generally.

> MAGDLIN (17) I think she's dull and boring. She goes on about the same point all the time. About Den going with that woman. That's the only thing she ever cares about.
> HEBA I don't think so. I think she makes it more interesting.

MAGDLIN   All she talks about and cares about is men. She said it: her life is useless because of men.
DB   So you think that's a problem?
MAGDLIN   I think it degrades women a bit actually.
HEBA   I don't think so. Most women are like that really, if you come to think of it.

Although this group felt that Angie should 'kick Den out', 'kill him' or at the very least 'cut off his good bits', they agreed that this would be an unlikely development: the end of Den, they argued, would be the end of *EastEnders*. Vengeance against Jan, his mistress, was seen as a more likely alternative:

DEANNA   I think she should do something to Jan though.
MAGDLIN   She should, yeah. She should have at the time. She acted like she was going to hit her, but she didn't. If it was my mum, right, she would have ripped the woman apart! But I suppose they can't show that on telly. It seemed so unreal, the way she goes on... She's sort of passive in a way. I don't think that's real enough. A lot of women would not sit back and let their husband go sleep with another woman. Stupid!

It is significant here that the debate about morality shifts into a debate about plausibility, and, in certain of Magdlin's remarks, about representation. As in many of these discussions, these different ways of perceiving the programme influence each other to the extent that it is often difficult to disentangle them. Judgments about plausibility in particular may often be based, not so much on a comparison with 'what life is really like' as with aspirations about what life should be like. The disagreement between Magdlin and Heba is not so much a result of their different life experiences (they are in fact sisters) as of different ideological positions – perhaps fuelled by a degree of sibling rivalry.

These differences were certainly more apparent across the gender division. Boys were far more inclined to approve of Den, although they were often reluctant to offer detailed moral justifications for his behaviour. Rodney was unwise enough to attempt this:

RODNEY (17)   Michelle's a little hussy anyway.
SANDRA   No! It's not her fault. It's Den's fault.
RODNEY   What do you mean?! She's going after all the men.
SANDRA   Yes, but Den shouldn't have taken advantage of her. A big man like Den, he's old enough to be her father. He should have known better, shouldn't he?

DONNA   'Cause he's got a bit on the side, and then he went and had Michelle.

RODNEY   She should have picked someone her own age, not a big man like that.

SANDRA   She was looking for someone to give her advice, right, and she was down at the time, and Den just took advantage, that's all.

CALISTA   But Den is like that anyway, isn't he?

RODNEY   That's what I like about him. He's a bit of a bastard.

Rodney's approval of Den's behaviour, and his condemnation of Michelle, can only be maintained temporarily in the face of the evidence the girls provide. As his last remark suggests, the boys' admiration for Den was based on an implicit acknowledgment of his amorality: Den was a manipulator, a 'schemer', 'the J.R. of *East-Enders*' – somebody we might sometimes wish to be, but whose 'dirty tricks' we could not ultimately be seen to approve.

In most cases, then, the children responded enthusiastically to the programme's invitation to sit in judgment on the characters. Their comments were clearly informed by their social position, and in the case of some of the older children, by fairly consciously-held ideological positions as well. Magdlin, for example, was led to question the ideological terms of reference which she perceived in the programme, and thus also to question its plausibility. In other cases, such as the boys' approval of Den, they were clearly enticed by the fatal allure of positions which they knew to be 'wrong'. Yet in general, the children appeared to be able to apply their own moral and ideological frameworks to the programme without feeling that it was encouraging them to adopt different ones. Few of the children felt that the programme had 'designs' on them – and in cases where they did feel that a particular lesson was being put across, there was considerable dispute about precisely what the lesson was:

SHARON (17)   I like Michelle, because she solves teenage problems. Like, she had it off with Den, and now she's pregnant. Loads of teenagers today get these kinds of problems. And I like her because she solves them, or *tries* to solve them.

MAGDLIN   I don't think she solves teenagers' problems in any way. By getting pregnant she encourages more teenagers to go and get pregnant.

HEBA   That's not true.

MAGDLIN   No, it's true, because the way her mother treats her, it's as if she hasn't done anything, she didn't mind her getting pregnant. If I did that, my mum would kill me.

HEBA   I don't agree. I think it would stop it.

Here again, the different ways in which Magdlin and Heba read the programme and its potential influence derive from their opposed ideological positions. Heba's view is that Michelle's decision is ultimately 'up to her', but that her story might serve as a warning to other teenagers. Magdlin, on the contrary, feels that Michelle's decision to have the child is fundamentally wrong: she regards her parents' support for her as implausible, and as tantamount to encouraging teenage pregnancy.

Magdlin's concern about the possibility of viewers imitating the characters' behaviour was shared by a number of the other children. Although most were keen to refute the Mary Whitehouse position – she was described by one girl as 'an interfering old woman', and by others in even more abusive terms – at least some of them appeared to share her fears about the dangerous effects of television. Yet, as Cedric Cullingford observes, while children may often mimic the moralistic arguments of adults, for both groups it is always *other people* who are seen to be most at risk:[14]

CLAIRE (12) I don't think Angie should have done that, though [attempted suicide], because of children ... It encourages other people, little kids.

One group of nine-year-olds engaged in an extended debate about the dangers of 'bad language' in the programme.

PRESTON You know Angie called Den a b—— [sic]. I reckon she went over the top then. I reckon that spoilt the show when she said that. I know that was good to say, she deserves to say that ... But I was really angry with her, you know. I was going to stop watching *EastEnders* then. I thought the programme was going to start being swearing and all that.

Vicky, however, was keen to acquit Angie herself from blame:

VICKY Angie don't tell them what she's going to say, they tell her what she's got to say.
DB Who are 'they'?
MARK Scriptwriter.
VICKY The description writer, or whatever it was. He comes, he gives them the description, they've got to read it, and they read it over and over till they learn it ... She has to say what the description man gives her. She can't say what she wants.
PRESTON Well the description man shouldn't have said it like that, innit?

This distinction between the characters (or actors) themselves and the 'description men' was one which many of the children felt was essential to preserve. The latter were often blamed for being unfair to particular characters, or for making viewers dislike them:

> VICKY   I like Ange, I like all the people really, I just don't like the 'scription writer, 'cause he makes them be horrible. He made Nick Cotton horrible, but I really like him in real life.
> PRESTON   Yeah, like when he called Kelvin a jungle bunny.
> MARK   They're trying to make it real life.

As Mark's last comment suggests, however, the prerogatives of realism were sometimes perceived as being in conflict with the desire for likeable characters. Certainly for the older children, it was the programme's realism which was the most significant aspect of its educational role:

> NORMA (17)   Not everybody knows what it really is like. Some of us ain't been picked on by coppers. We don't know what it's like. But if you watch it on *EastEnders* you get an idea of what it's like, and you're more sympathetic to the people. It puts over a more realistic view of what's going on ...

The programme was thus seen by many to reveal areas of experience usually hidden from view, not least by other television programmes: and while this may allow a degree of voyeurism, it could also perform a more therapeutic or educational function.

> SHEILA (17)   I think it's aired quite a lot of good things. Like the cot death, I think that was really good, the way they handled that. Things like that should be brought out into the open, 'cause people do experience them, and they sort of hide away, and shut themselves out.
> CALISTA   Seeing it happen to somebody else on television that they know, it's really good.

In these instances, the belief in the reality of the fictional world – the notion, for example, that characters on television are people that we know – is often paramount:

> PAUL (18)   It shows that there is a problem, and there are people that are actually on drugs. I don't think there's any other programme that shows up that sort of thing.
> DIONNE   It puts the wind up you. Like, I know a lot of kids that are on drugs, cocaine, the whole lot. Like, when they say 'Oh, I had

so many lines' and the rest of it, you think they're bullshitting you. But if you watch it on television, then you sort of think, they might not be mucking about, they might be taking it ... There's always this thing, it's always enticing, they're saying 'Go on, try a bit, it's not going to hurt you first time, it's not going to do you in or nothing' ... I've been tempted, but I ain't never done it. But watching *EastEnders*, and seeing all the drugs problems and all the rest of it, you don't want to do it.

Significantly, Dionne uses her belief in the plausibility of the programme – her conviction that it reveals 'problems' which actually do exist in the real world – to question the truth of her friends' claims. Yet a belief in the *realism* of television, in its ability to 'tell the truth' about aspects of the social world which are often hidden or misrepresented, does not necessarily entail a belief in the *reality* of its fictional world. Indeed, the extent to which the children were prepared to accept the reality of *EastEnders'* fictional world was strictly limited.

Realism
Many of the young people in these discussions described *EastEnders* as 'realistic'. Yet, as Aimee Dorr suggests, what children might mean by this term may vary: as they mature, they become increasingly aware that at least some of what they watch is fabricated, and their criteria for assessing the 'reality' of television content become significantly more stringent.[15] The extent to which the children I interviewed were prepared to question the plausibility of events in the programme was quite remarkable. Yet this questioning was informed, not merely by comparisons with their own experience, but also by an understanding of the *production process* of television. Although they clearly enjoyed playing the game of make-believe, they were also, as Dorothy Hobson argues, well aware that it was only a game. Yet the pleasures gained through this willing suspension of disbelief were, if anything, enriched by the pleasures gained from questioning and, in many instances, ridiculing the artifice. What was perhaps most remarkable was the children's flexibility of response, their ability to shift between these two perspectives with little sense of contradiction.

For many of the children, the particular 'realism' of *EastEnders* lay some way between the 'boring everyday life' of *Coronation Street* and the glamorous excess of *Dallas* and *Dynasty*. Yet while the former was generally dismissed, the blatant absurdity and implausibility of the latter were often described with great relish:

DONNA (17)   I just had to laugh when they brought the old Miss Ellie back.
SANDRA   It was silly, 'cause they didn't even say 'Oh, you've got a

180

nice new hairstyle' or something like that ...
DONNA   Or plastic surgery ...
SANDRA   ... to break the ice in that way. They just went on as if
nothing had happened.

By comparison, *EastEnders* was seen as less artificial, and its narratives less improbable; yet many of the children criticised it in very
similar ways to those in which they criticised the US soaps. It is crucial
to emphasise, however, that this awareness of the programme's artifice
was not incompatible with the pleasures of believing in it:

SANDRA   If you compare *EastEnders* to another soap opera, say
for instance *Dallas* or *Dynasty*, then it's very realistic. But if you
take it on its own, then there are parts that aren't.
CALISTA   But I watch it saying 'This is not real, they've tried to
make it real'. In my mind, I know it's not real, so I always watch it
criticising it. [...] I get into the characters, I watch it twice a week,
I've watched it from the beginning, but I know it's not real.

Despite the fact that Michelle's pregnancy was a cause of considerable debate, for example, it was also ridiculed by many of the children:
as many exclaimed, 'you can see all the wrinkles in her pillow!' What
many perceived as the baby's uneven rate of growth was also questioned:

ABBY (15)   One minute she had no belly, and the next minute, she
was out here, man!

Some also questioned the length of the pregnancy itself, arguing
(against the evidence) that it had continued well beyond nine months.
This questioning of the authenticity of the pregnancy was particularly
informed by their reading of the popular press:

ELAINE (12)   Michelle gives it away, because she says in the paper,
she's fed up of having all stuffed pillows underneath her belly and
everything.
MARTIN (9)   She said it seemed like she was having a real baby.
MAXINE   And when she was having it, she said it doesn't seem like
a baby, it seems like an elephant!

While Simone (7) confidently predicted that the baby itself would be 'a
dolly', others had more authoritative information:

NATALIE (9)   She had a choice out of five babies really, in real life.
It's playing a girl in it, but really it's a boy.

Angie's suicide attempt was also ridiculed in this way: Preston (9) asserted that 'it was water and Smarties', while Raymond (15) exclaimed 'I don't know why she took a carton full of Tic-Tacs'. Marian (17) regarded the speed of her recovery as 'a bit of a joke'. Meanwhile, Sheila (17) questioned Michelle's rather limited wardrobe – 'Everytime you saw her she had that green thing on!' – and the contents of Angie's kitchen cupboards:

> SHEILA   Have you noticed, when Angie opens her cupboards, there's nothing in those packets? No, seriously. When they fell, they didn't make no sound. It was just, like, empty boxes.

The considerable hilarity which accompanied these observations also extended to comments on, and in many cases imitations of, instances of 'bad acting'. The actress playing Cassie Carpenter came in for particular criticism: Darren (11) argued that 'she can't help looking at the camera', while according to Samantha (9), 'she always wants to get your [the viewer's] attention'. Jamie (14) asserted 'I bet they've wasted two miles of film on her!' Instances of high drama, such as Lofty's declaration of affection for Michelle in front of the assembled patrons of the Queen Vic, or Angie's confrontation with Jan across the ironing board, were re-enacted as farce by certain groups.

At the same time, there was also praise for what was seen as 'wicked acting', particularly that of Angie, described by Raymond (15) as 'the top lady'.

> VICKY (9)   I like Angie. She plays it really good, with her problem. She can make out she's drunk. She can make out all those eyes things [mimes flashing eyes]. She can make out she's really upset because Den goes with Jan.

It is perhaps worth emphasising that the children's comments on the quality of *acting* in *EastEnders* were quite spontaneous, and were often volunteered in response to my question about their favourite *character*. In certain instances, they even responded by giving the actor's name, rather than that of the character he or she played. In some cases, their judgments of acting quality were clearly linked with their assessment of the character – although they were rather more likely to be positive in the case of characters who were generally liked, than negative in the case of characters who were disliked. Nevertheless, the assessment of acting quality and of character were generally kept separate, suggesting that the children made clear distinctions between the two.

These distinctions were encouraged by the fact that at least some of the actors were familiar to the children from previous roles. At times, this familiarity was regarded as a distraction: Wendy Richard (Pauline

Fowler), for example, 'used to be a lot younger' in *Are You Being Served ?*, while the previous incarnation of Susan Tully (Michelle Fowler) in *Grange Hill* was also a source of confusion:

> DANNY (14) I keep thinking of her in *Grange Hill*. I think, a couple of years ago she was at school, and now she's in *EastEnders*!
> JAMIE Once you've watched *Grange Hill* and then you go to *EastEnders*, you think she's fourteen and she's having a baby.

In general, however, the familiarity of some of the actors from other roles served to accentuate the distinction between actor and character.

The children's more distanced perspective was informed by their understanding of the production process, in this case by their knowledge of actors' conditions of employment, gleaned largely from newspapers.

> MARK (15) I was reading in the paper the other day, they said that Lofty, the actor that plays Lofty, he's got the hump with his character, he doesn't like it. He wants a more sort of silky image in the programme.
> TAMMY He said that he wanted to change because people are going to associate him with that person too much, and he won't be able to get other parts.

In this group, there was considerable discussion of the departure of Patrick Duffy (Bobby Ewing) from *Dallas*, and the attempts to encourage him to renegotiate his contract. Mark at least saw acting very much in terms of alienated wage labour:

> MARK I don't think any of the actors are really worried about what they have to say, as long as they get their wage packet at the end of the month. They get their script or whatever, and they do it, and they don't care.

In other instances, the children had read of disputes among the cast:

> LISA (11) D'you know that Fabulous Frankie? [A character who appeared briefly as a male stripper in the Queen Vic] He said that he wouldn't mind playing Dirty Den's sex lover.
> ALISON I heard in the papers that they ain't going to let him do it.

As in the case of Angie and the 'description man', 'they' were typically seen as being to blame for misfortunes which befell the characters:

RANI (9)   In the papers it said that Angie and Pauline had a little argument because Angie said that Pauline was trying to be head of the show, and Pauline said that Angie was trying to be head of the show. But none of them are.

BRIAN   It's the writers' fault, like what happened with Lofty. Lofty was going to leave because he don't get the time to talk and everything.

MAXINE   He should be brighter, not so shy. They should give him a break, man. Let him talk a bit more.

The belief, fervently expressed by this group, that 'it should be equal for all of them' and that 'they should all have a turn to talk' suggests that the utopian fantasy of the happy community is sought, not so much in the fictional world of the programme, as in the audience's understanding of its production context. Interestingly, it also coincides with Julia Smith's view of the cast as a 'repertory company', without individual stars.

These criticisms of the writers of *EastEnders* also extended to more general comments on the overall shape of the narrative. A number of groups felt that the programme was in danger of running out of material.

BRIAN (9)   I think it's going a bit off Angie and Den.

SAMANTHA   Yeah. There ain't as much as there was before.

DB   Why do you think that is?

BRIAN   'Cause they've done everything. They've said everything in one go.

MAXINE   They can't say a little bit and then save a bit for the next episode. [...] The people who write it, they should have thought about it twice before they start rushing everything. 'Cause if they rush everything they won't have anything else to say.

Another group felt that the writers were becoming increasingly desperate in their search for interesting material:

MARIAN (17)   I think because they got famous too quickly, they've used up all the good ideas. Now they try and push anything in. They just get any story and stick it in.

Some of the older children also noted what they felt were inconsistencies between consecutive episodes, or major gaps in the narrative. For example, the climax of one episode was a confrontation between Lofty and his prospective father-in-law Arthur:

SANDRA (17)   It was stupid … I was waiting for Tuesday, waiting for Tuesday, and it started off with them all living perfectly together.

SHEILA   After that, Arthur accepted him. I suppose another father would just not speak or keep himself to himself for a couple of days. But Arthur didn't. He just sort of accepted it the next morning, which I don't think a father would.

SANDRA   I think there was a scene missing, where Pauline sat Arthur down and talked to him, you know. We should have seen that, but we didn't see it. It wasn't real.

CALISTA   But they do that quite often. To the viewers it looks as though you're missing out on a bit.

SANDRA   You've got to figure it out in your own mind.

Although the group implicitly accepted the idea that the characters pursue what Christine Geraghty calls an 'unrecorded existence' between episodes, they felt that events should not go unrecorded if they are significant in terms of our understanding of future behaviour.[16] The resulting lack of psychological plausibility thus led them to imagine a scene which would explain Arthur's change of heart.

Although the rapid pace of *EastEnders*' narrative was generally admired, therefore, it was sometimes regarded as excessive:

DONNA (17)   They seem to have stopped the darts team. You don't hear anything about that any more.

CALISTA   I don't like the way they cut off some subjects just like that. They shouldn't do it. They should explain it somehow. You've got to explain it for yourself.

DB   So why do you think they do it?

CALISTA   I think they haven't got time to finish everything. They just bring up too many issues. Before they've finished, they bring in another big issue. They haven't got time to finish things off properly.

Yet even the younger children were aware that the pace of narrative developments in soap opera was determined at least partly by external pressures:

NATALIE (9)   Because too many people are watching *EastEnders*, and they think it's really good, they're trying to make *Albion Market* gooder and gooder, so people will stop *EastEnders* and start liking that. But we don't like it.

MARK   *Coronation Street*'s trying to run out *EastEnders*, getting people watching that. That's why they burned down the Rover's Return, isn't it?

As these comments show, it is not simply that the children were aware that *EastEnders* is a fabrication, but that they were also able to judge the quality of its fabrication compared with that of other programmes, and compared with its own standards. In this sense, their description of the programme as 'realistic' may be seen to be as much an *aesthetic* judgment as an assessment of the *accuracy* of its representation of reality. In other words, by describing it as realistic, they were not merely judging it to be a relatively truthful depiction of the world – particularly insofar as it showed aspects which were often kept hidden from view; they were also, I would argue, identifying it as a generally good example of the category 'realism'. Here, as in many other areas of their discussion, their comments indicate a quite sophisticated grasp of the critical concepts which many adults (and teachers) assume they do not possess.

Identification and character
As the above discussion of Arthur's dispute with Lofty reveals, psychological consistency was regarded as indispensible if the programme's authenticity was to be maintained. Indeed, a central feature of the children's discussion of the characters was their attempt to infer motivation, and thereby to construct consistency.

> SAMANTHA (9)   I don't think Michelle's going to marry Lofty.
> MAXINE   She doesn't look all that happy about that, you know.
> RANI   Den's jealous! 'Cause when they were talking about Michelle's baby, he went 'I'll just see if Sharon's upstairs'.
> MAXINE   Oh yeah? What about when Michelle was talking to Den then? Sharon was jealous, I think. She said, 'Oh, you don't even care about your daughter'.

In attempting to fill 'gaps' in the text, the children were largely accepting the 'invitations' described in Chapter Two; and in other respects, the ways in which they understood and related to the characters bear out the general arguments made there. Thus, for example, most of the children distinguished between complex characters, with whom they were more likely to identify, and simpler characters, whom they were more likely to ignore, or in many cases, to ridicule. Den and Angie were clear favourites in the former category:

> NICOLA (11)   With Sue, right, she's on about babies and everything. With Ali, he's always betting. The Fowlers, they're always on about Michelle's baby and everything. But with Den and Angie, they're on about all sorts of different things.

At the other end of the spectrum, Ethel and Dot were typically regarded as objects of ridicule, although at least in Ethel's case, many children felt some warmth for her: as Tony (12) said, 'She's a funny old lady ... but a bit mad!' Judgments of Dot were rather more spiteful – many found her 'moaning' merely irritating – although some of the older children were prepared to take seriously her difficulties with her errant son Nick. Lofty was another character who was widely ridiculed, albeit affectionately: Heba (17), for example, described him as 'sort of like a village idiot'.

The children also categorised characters in terms of their degree of authority. Thus, Lou Beale and Dr Legg were typically described as 'wise', although the fact that Dot and Ethel were discounted in this respect shows that age itself was not regarded as sufficient qualification for such deference. Physical attributes were also important, particularly for the boys: Tony Carpenter, for example, was described as 'the hardest' and 'the bad [i.e. tough] geezer of the square', while Den and Pete Beale also earned the positive epithets 'hard' and 'wicked'.

The character of Detective Sergeant Quick, who, as a police officer, might in another context have been taken as a figure of respect, was almost universally disliked, not merely for his unwelcome attentions to Debbie, but also for his attempts to establish his own authority. Elaine (12), for example, was particularly critical of his efforts to ingratiate himself with the community by 'turning a blind eye':

ELAINE He thinks he can just go round the East End and tell people what to do all the time. He isn't very good ... He says he don't see people when he does. I think he should say when he sees things. When Nick Cotton got slung out of the pub, he said he didn't see him, he didn't want to know anything about it. But when Debbie got mugged, he wanted to do everything about it that he could.

Elaine's comments, like those of many of the other children, were certainly informed by a more general distrust of the police, but they also suggest that, as Magdlin (17) observed, 'he's certainly put across as a character people should dislike'.

On balance, however, although characters like Sergeant Quick, not to mention more obvious 'villains' like Nick Cotton, were much disliked, they were seen as necessary, both in order to guarantee continued narrative interest and in order to ensure realism:

TAMMY (15) I suppose it makes it more realistic ...
RUTH Even though we don't like those characters, if they didn't have them, it wouldn't be as good.
ABBY It'd be too one-sided.

RUTH It gets you into it, if you've got characters you really hate, 'cause they get on your nerves.

This is not to suggest, however, that the particular balance of characters provided by *EastEnders* went unquestioned, or that it was regarded as an unproblematic representation of the social world. While the children clearly accepted many of the 'invitations' provided by the text, they were also disposed to question them in ways which will be described in the following section.

Character and representation

The issues of morality and authenticity considered in the previous sections were both significant factors in the children's discussions of their character preferences. It was here that the differences between the readings produced by different groups and individuals were made apparent and, in many cases, debated. It was here also that the relationship between the programme and its audience assumed a more directly ideological dimension and, particularly with the older children, provoked some explicitly ideological criticism of it.

The extended discussion of the character of Michelle quoted above illustrates the way in which moral judgments about the behaviour of characters blend into a discussion of the plausibility of the narrative, a discussion which is clearly informed by an understanding of the constructed nature of the programme as a whole. These considerations in turn feed into a broader critique of the *representation* which is provided.

If (as I have argued in Chapter Two) the text 'implies' its readers, the readers also infer an author, or a collective author, for the text. Furthermore, they also assign *motives* to this author – not merely the more general motive of seeking to entertain, and thereby to keep us watching, but also, in certain cases, more specific ideological motives. Although few of the children discerned any directly 'educational' intentions on the part of *EastEnders*, they were in some cases critical of what they perceived as the partiality and lack of authenticity of its representation of the social world.

When discussing Michelle, for example, the girls implicitly regarded her character as a *misrepresentation* by the writers of *EastEnders* of the problems facing teenage girls – a misrepresentation which they also detected in other television programmes. As we have seen, Magdlin (17) argued that Michelle represented 'a negative image of teenagers' which could accentuate these problems, by encouraging others to follow her example. This criticism suggests, not merely a questioning of the authenticity of the programme, but also a rejection of its claim to speak on behalf of its audience – in this instance, its teenage audience. While few of the children voiced this kind of direct rejection, the type of questioning which informs it was a feature of many of these discussions.

Magdlin's use of the term 'negative image' is, I would argue, an explicitly *ideological* judgment. Although the children's awareness of representation was often expressed as a judgment of the programme's lack of *accuracy*, it was in many cases simultaneously a judgment of its *ideology*. To explain this more fully, I would like to consider an example where the issue of *EastEnders'* authenticity was discussed at some length, yet from a rather different ideological perspective.

Although a number of the schools I visited were in or near London's East End, it was in one in particular that the programme's representation of the area was discussed in detail. Perhaps contrary to expectations, the group of fourteen-year-old boys whom I interviewed felt that in many respects *EastEnders* did provide an authentic representation of the area in which they lived:

DANNY (14) I like Den because he does all these funny things on the side. He's like an East Ender. He talks like one and he acts like one.

JAMIE Lou Beale, she seems like an East Ender. I've got a nan like her, a great nan, really acts like her. She seems as if she knows everything.

DANNY That's what I like about *EastEnders*. When you watch it properly, it shows you people that you know, that's what they're acting like.

DARREN It's like real life. What happens round here.

At the same time, the group did identify a number of aspects which they regarded as implausible. As with other groups, these particularly concerned the representation of young people, and their relationships with their parents. They questioned Kathy Beale's attitude to her son 'bunking off' [truanting] from school: 'If I got caught bunking off, my dad see me, he'd have a right go at me, and so would the school'. Likewise, they argued that Cassie Carpenter 'should have got suspended' from school for bullying another child, and thought it implausible that Michelle's parents would have allowed her to ride a motorbike during her pregnancy. Like a number of other groups, they felt that the social world of *EastEnders*, and particularly that of its younger characters, was rather limited.

ANAND But in *EastEnders*, you don't really hear much about the school.

JAMIE You don't even know if there's a school that exists. You never see it.

ANAND They just talk about their own area and their own problems.

189

DANNY That's it. The only places I've ever seen in my life in *EastEnders* is in the square and down the park when Den goes and meets that bird. There's no school, no going down the West End or nothing when you go out.

Although these criticisms were shared by other groups, what distinguishes the comments of this group is that their judgments of the programme's lack of authenticity were informed by two specific, and related, ideological concerns – firstly by their notions of masculinity, and secondly by a rather different East End mythology from that provided by *EastEnders*. Thus, Den was nominated by nearly all the boys as their favourite character, largely because of his involvement in 'dirty tricks':

DANNY He gets illegal booze in and that.
DARREN He's sort of like the Mafia.
DANNY The Godfather!

Ian, on the other hand, was rejected for being a 'softy':

DANNY It's too far fetched. 'Cause if he lived round here, right, there ain't really a soft person that can't stick up for themselves.
JAMIE That's one of the examples of when it's not like East Enders. There's not people round here like that. They all stick up for themselves round here.
DARREN All he can do is cooking. That's all he thinks about.
JAMIE That's all he's got: cooking. That sounds like a right softy to me.

Clearly, the boys rejected Ian because he failed to conform to their definition of acceptable masculinity. Yet, significantly, this also led them to question the *plausibility* of his behaviour. In the case of Lofty, however, their knowledge of the actor's life outside the programme enabled them to salvage him:

ANAND I like Lofty. Because he stands for Den having a go at him and all this, but in real life he's a martial arts expert. He's a karate expert, judo, all this. All he has to do is give Den one kick in the throat and he's dead.

The boys' comments on the plausibility of the characters were thus directly related to their own investment in a particular notion of masculinity. They regarded Ian as 'too far fetched', I would suggest, because he does not behave in a way the boys themselves would like to be seen to behave. This definition of masculinity was reinforced by the

190

boys' enthusiastic identification with the mythology of the East End underworld:

> DANNY The thing I don't like about *EastEnders* is, like, round here you've had all sorts of villains. Like the Kray twins only lived half a mile away down Vallance Road. All the characters that have been round here! This is the East End, it's all up Commercial Road and that, it's all villains, well-known people, isn't there? On *East-Enders* you don't hear nothing about people in real life.

The group was keen to relate stories from their own experience which exemplified this view of the 'real' East End – stories of local murders, and of their own confrontations with the police. The Euston Films series *Prospects* and Thames' *The Bill* were both praised by the boys as more accurate representations of these aspects of East End life. This authenticity was seen to derive at least partly from their use of location filming, and partly from the fact that the actors were believed to be 'real East Enders' themselves – unlike the actors in *EastEnders*, whose 'posh' accents had been revealed by their appearance on chat shows.

It is not my intention here to suggest that the boys were merely seeking refuge in fantasy, and that their criticisms of certain elements of *EastEnders* as 'unrealistic' derived simply from its failure to provide the type of fantasy they required. On the contrary, the boys' perception and understanding of their *own* experience, and hence their judgments of what was and was not realistic, were dependent upon their own social position as young working-class men, and their attempts to define that position in positive terms. The ideology which informed these perceptions and understandings was therefore bound up with their sense of their own identity. Their investment in an ideology of masculinity, then, was a significant aspect of their sense of identity as young men, and their attempts to find a degree of security within it. In the same way, what I have called the 'mythology' of the East End underworld was an influential part of the way in which they made sense of their own experience of living in that particular working-class neighbourhood, and attempted to construct it as 'glamorous'; and in this respect it would be mistaken to regard it merely as a romantic falsehood perpetuated by outsiders. As in the debate between Magdlin and Heba about Angie's 'passivity' (quoted on pp. 175–6), judgments about what is realistic are *inevitably* ideological.

Although I would support Ien Ang's critique of what she terms the 'empiricist' definition of realism – the notion that texts can be judged 'realistic' by means of a straightforward comparison with the outside world – it is precisely these judgments as they are made in everyday conversation about television which indicate the *ideological* dimension

191

of viewers' responses.[17] While it would be naive to define the ideology of *EastEnders* merely by comparing it with what it seeks to represent, the fact that viewers themselves do this should not be swept aside quite as hastily. In the remainder of this section, therefore, I propose to consider four major aspects of this dimension: class, race, gender and age.

a. Class

One of the most consistent features of these discussions was the almost universal loathing and contempt with which the children regarded the middle-class characters in *EastEnders*. Many, for example, expressed considerable pleasure at the mugging of Debbie Wilkins, tempered only by their disappointment that she had not been more badly hurt. In certain cases, this attitude was clearly a form of *moral* judgment. Thus Debbie, for example, was accused of 'using' her fiance Andy, and of 'wanting her own way all the time'. Hannah Carpenter was also described as a 'user' and as a 'bad mother'. However, in both cases these criticisms also revealed an explicit class dimension: both characters were repeatedly described as 'posh' and 'stuck up', and Debbie was often called 'bossy' and 'a busybody'. Dionne, for example, who described Debbie as a 'stuck up bitch', defined her objections as follows: 'People who are upper-class think they're better than lower-class. They look down their noses, sort of thing, snub them, know what I mean?' Neither, it was argued, were 'real East Enders': as Deanna (17) observed, 'Debbie's too upper-class for that sort of area. She doesn't fit in.'

The authenticity of these characters was also questioned: Sandra (17), for example, felt that Debbie was not a '*real* middle-class person':

SANDRA She hasn't got any history behind her. There's no family. There's lots of characters like that, but she just puts herself over as so rich and posh and everything. I'd love to see her mum, or her sister, or somebody else. Maybe to make the character a bit fuller, because she's not real.

Of the more middle-class characters, only Dr Legg was described at all positively: by comparison with Debbie, Sandra described him as '... a *real* middle-class character. He doesn't live around the square, he has his surgery there. You know he's a doctor, a professional man. He fits in all right.' Others, however, questioned even his authenticity, and, in this instance, his authority as well:

RUTH (15) He doesn't fit into it, does he?
PERRY But they've got to have a local doctor on the scene.
MARK He's more like a policeman and a doctor all in one. He's

too busy for my liking. A doctor's supposed to be a doctor. If you're unwell, you go to the doctor, but he doesn't know what you do at home. He seems too much like the sheriff of *EastEnders*, know what I mean?

By contrast, the working-class characters were widely regarded as far more authentic – although, as noted above, the actors' appearances on chat shows had caused some to question this. For Elaine (12), our discussion of *EastEnders* provided the pretext for an extended monologue on the significance of being a 'Cockney'. She defined Cockney as primarily a matter of accent and 'manners', although it was clearly for her a question of class identity, in which the elements of language, culture and power were intimately related. Elaine's self-image as a Cockney was thus a significant part of her generally antagonistic attitude towards authority:

> ELAINE I was in a detention once with my teacher. You know teachers try to make the kids well spoken for. He said something to me, and I said 'watcha say?' And he started shouting at me: 'Who do you think you are, telling me about "watcha say". Say pardon.' So I tell him, 'I won't say fuck all to you, you old cunt!' On my life. I nearly got suspended ... I told my nan. She said, 'You can't tell 'em what to do.' She's born and bred a Cockney. Something like that. I am a Cockney. All of us here are Cockneys, really.

The fact that *EastEnders* engaged with these more oppositional elements of Elaine's class experience, and indeed her class consciousness, perhaps explained her preoccupation with the question of its Cockney authenticity:

> ELAINE They say, right, that Ethel's a right grass, a right snob. Some people put their Cockney accent on ... The proper Cockneys of all of them, I reckon is Kathy, Den, Pete and Angie.

In general, however, this kind of questioning was rare. Insofar as 'class' featured explicitly or implicitly as an issue in these discussions, it did so not in relation to the working-class characters, but to the small minority of middle-class ones. The children were less interested in questioning the authenticity of *EastEnders'* representation of working-class people than in using it as a vehicle for expression their dislike of 'snobs', and other figures of authority.

b. Race

Although the attempt to provide a positive representation of a multi-ethnic community was a significant element in the initial conception of

EastEnders, this theme was conspicuous by its absence from these discussions. When I did attempt to introduce it, the children soon directed the conversation onto other topics, manifesting not so much reluctance as indifference.

The judgments of the black characters noted above were largely shared by both black and white children. While few appeared interested in discussing Tony Carpenter, comments on his wife Hannah were almost universally negative:

> DARREN (14) When she was with Neville, right, she didn't want to know Tony, but now Neville's left her, she wants to get round Tony. She doesn't really want to get back with him, she just wants to grovel round him until things get better, until she moves out and just dumps him. She's not really a mother.

Although Darren himself is black, the fact that Hannah is also black did not enter into his account: his criticism of her was made exclusively in terms of her failure to be a good wife and mother. Likewise, the comments on Cassie Carpenter's 'selfishness' and her alleged lack of acting ability were made by both black and white children. Few were interested in discussing her brother Kelvin, however, although some expressed disappointment at his involvement with his 'political' friend Harry:

> RUTH (15) He used to be all right, but now he's getting a right drip with his friend Harry – the revolution of the working class and all that.

Similarly, the characters of Naima and Saeed Jeffery, the Bangladeshi couple, were not generally considered worthy of attention.

The racist attitudes of some of the white characters were more of a focus for discussion, however: Pete Beale's disapproval of Wicksy's relationship with Naima, for example, and Nick Cotton's abuse of Ali and Kelvin were condemned by many as 'racist'. For some of the white children, this element was clearly something which made them uneasy:

> STEPHEN (12) I'll tell you a bit I didn't like, when all them men was beating up all the Asians. You know, they was taking money off them, the blacks and the Turks. It was all racist ... It was horrible, I couldn't watch it.
> LEE That's what *should* be banned, is racism.
> STEPHEN Yeah.
> NATASHA But in a way, that's life, so it's got to be there.
> STEPHEN Yeah, but it's a bit bad, isn't it?

This uneasiness was not confined to white children, however: Preston (9) also expressed concern at Nick Cotton's racist insults, although, like the children quoted above, he was prepared to accept that it was part of the programme's attempt 'to make it real life'.

Some of the children did discern the programme's 'multiculturalist' intentions, however. Elaine (12: white) and Dionne (17: black) both commented favourably on its 'mixture of races':

> DIONNE   One thing about *EastEnders* you can say, right, they put every race in there. Black, Indian, white, Turkish. They've got every one, and that's good, because not a lot of the soaps have got them in there. Usually you see black and white, that's the furthest they go, or else it's pure whites.

Magdlin (17: black) felt that Tony Carpenter in particular offered a positive image of black people:

> MAGDLIN   He's so wise and goody-goody. Everyone's always asking his advice. And I think that's quite good, because most blacks, when you get them in movies or series or whatever, they've always got a negative side to them. But he's shown as a wise man.

Donna (17: also black) felt that Kelvin's romance with Michelle had also been valuable in this respect:

> DONNA   They're showing that does happen, white and black people go out together. That was a good way of putting that over.

However, some of the older children were rather more suspicious of the programme's didactic intentions, and accused it of tokenism:

> SHEILA (17)   If you think about it, you've got this East End street, you only ever see one little black face over here, one little black face over there. They're better than *Coronation Street*, you don't see any black faces there. But in *EastEnders* you only see one black family, the Carpenters.
> CALISTA   You go through the market, and you see them on the stalls or something like that, but you hardly ever see them talking with their friends, or in the pub.
> SHEILA   *EastEnders* has gone where no other soap opera has gone, as far as I'm concerned, but it still doesn't do it well. [...]
> SANDRA   I think they don't want to upset the old people about the East End.
> SHEILA   Maybe they're portraying the East End how they think it is, not how it really is – all Cockneys and that.

Nevertheless, this kind of criticism was exceptional. What was far more typical was the general lack of interest in this aspect of the programme. On one level, this seems surprising, particularly on the part of the black children: as with the long discussion of Michelle quoted above, the children sometimes failed to identify with characters who were 'like them', and whose perspective one would therefore expect them to share. In the case of the younger characters, this appears to have resulted from the fact that they were generally seen as inauthentic. Yet the *authenticity* of *EastEnders'* black characters was rarely questioned. This might be regarded as an endorsement of the programme's accuracy: yet what was notable was precisely the *lack of explicit reference* to ethnicity in the children's discussions of these characters. Their responses might be seen as a consequence of the programme's tendency to *suppress* ethnic difference in its attempts to provide a positive representation of a 'multicultural' community. One is reminded of Julia Smith's remark about including 'a couple of nice Bengali characters', and her hope that nobody would realise they were Bengali.

c. Gender

Gender difference, on the other hand, was a far more significant factor in the children's responses, as we have seen. On the level of character preferences, the girls were far more likely to favour female characters whom they regarded as 'strong', such as Lou Beale:

> SHARON (17) She's funny. The way she treats Arthur, it's just a joke, the way she carries on. She's got no respect for him. She tells him what to do. She was telling him how to spend his money a couple of weeks back, 'cause he just lost his job. She gave him a list of things to do, 'cause he's unemployed. She wants him to fix her shoes. She takes liberties. That's what makes me laugh.

Debbie, on the other hand, was regarded as somewhat hypocritical:

> ABBY (15) She's really feeble. She goes round making out she's really independent, she wants to stand on her own two feet, women's liberation and all that. But then Sergeant Quick comes over and she goes 'Would you like some tea, darling?'

Above all, however, the girls' clear favourite was Angie, and although many were clearly exasperated by her 'weakness' and her failure to 'get her own back' on Den, there was little doubt whose side they were on. While some risked describing Den as 'gorgeous', they were often attacked for such treacherous remarks. Heba's claim that 'Den's the reason why most women watch *EastEnders'* was vigorously disputed by the other girls, and Maxine (9) also dismissed the idea of him as a 'sex symbol':

RANI (9)   Samantha Fox fancied him. We read about it in the paper.
MAXINE   She ain't got no taste, man. Who would fancy him?

Den's double standards were strongly condemned, and he was identified by some at least as 'a male chauvinist pig' and 'a sexist'.

For the boys, however, Den was a clear favourite, although few were in any doubt as to his moral failings – notwithstanding Rodney's rather heroic attempt to blame Michelle (quoted above). Stephen (10) even went so far as to nominate Nick Cotton as his favourite character, on the basis of his being 'an 'ard nut' and 'good at stealing money'. Lee and John (12) argued that Nick Cotton 'livens it up', but according to Fiona (12): 'All he does is make trouble. That's boring. Just nicks things, does people over ... He's boring.' The boys accordingly fought back:

JOHN   It's getting a bit boring now everyone's pregnant. It's getting a bit silly now.

Nevertheless, it would be false to conclude from these exchanges that the boys merely valued action and violence, while the girls favoured more emotional and domestic storylines. The issues which the children were prepared to discuss inevitably depended on how they wished to appear to each other; and particularly in the case of the boys, I would argue that this acted as a strong constraint on their contributions. In nearly all the discussions, and especially those with older groups, the boys were markedly more reticent – indeed, untypically so. The following extract suggests a possible reason for this:

FIONA (12)   Men don't really like soap operas.
STEPHEN   My dad watches it, but he pretends he don't like it. He goes 'Oh that's a load of rubbish, they can't even act'. So why does he watch it then?
DB   Why do you think he pretends?
NATASHA   So he can be more macho! [...]
STEPHEN   Like *Dynasty*. My mum loves *Dynasty*, and my brother. I call him a pouff.
FIONA   *Dynasty* is good!
NATASHA   I wouldn't call nobody a pouff ...
DB   But you watch it as well.
STEPHEN   Yeah, but I pretend I don't like it. That's what me and my dad do, when it comes on we start whistling and singing the tune.

DB   So what is it about *Dynasty* that boys and men aren't supposed to like?
STEPHEN   In *Dynasty*, it's all kissing everywhere, isn't it?

While Stephen at least was willing to admit that men's professed dislike
of soap opera is partly a pretence, his honesty was fairly unique. Most
of the boys were far more rigid in their responses, and were keen to
mock characters like Ian who represented an affront to their notion of
masculinity. Lofty came in for a good deal of criticism in this respect,
although some of the girls tried to argue on his behalf:

RAYMOND (15)   I think he's silly. He's an idiot. I don't like his
glasses.
ABBY   He's sweet!
RAYMOND   He's a pouff!
RUTH [ironically]: He's shy and sensitive.

The word 'silly', used by Raymond here and by John above, is characteristic of the boys' contempt for qualities which were seen as too
'feminine'.

Thus while *EastEnders* contained a number of elements which the
boys claimed to enjoy, these were fairly limited in scope. Yet, as
Stephen's observations suggest, there may well be significant differences between what boys actually enjoy, and what they are prepared to
admit to enjoying.

d. Age
As I have already noted, the children did not generally display much
interest in the younger characters in *EastEnders*. Even when I drew
attention to this, many of their comments were quite perfunctory. Ian
was widely regarded as 'boring', and although opinions of Kelvin
were slightly more positive, both were generally considered unworthy
of further discussion. For one group of boys, Sharon appeared to represent something of an enigma:

DANNY (14)   You don't know what she's doing. She's one of them
people you don't always see. She's in this sort of phase. It really gets
on my nerves watching her, 'cause I don't like her.
DARREN   One minute she's with Kelvin, the next she's with Ian.
One week you're watching it, and you think she's with Kelvin at
last. And then the next week she's with Ian. You don't know who
she's with.

If Sharon's failure to be paired off was perhaps slightly threatening for
the boys, some of the girls were more interested in what they saw as her

198

weight problem. Nevertheless, few were particularly concerned about her either. Of all the young characters, only Michelle was discussed in any detail, albeit in fairly negative terms.

To a certain extent, this lack of interest reflects what some children regarded as the relative insignificance of these characters in the programme as a whole. Indeed, this was itself a cause of some complaint:

SANDRA (17)   They don't show them every week. Sometimes you can go for ages without seeing Sharon or Ian, and you're just concentrating on the elders.
SHEILA   Like this week, we haven't seen Sharon once, yet she's meant to be with them. We're meant to believe she's there all the time, upstairs or at school.
SANDRA   They just slip her in once in a while to say something to her mum, and that's it, she's gone again.

Nevertheless, perhaps the main reason for their indifference was that the younger characters were widely regarded as inauthentic. Many of the children argued that the social world of these characters was rather limited: as Danny (14) observed 'You don't ever see them mucking about. They're always sitting about at home, or they're at school'. Sheila, at least, was able to provide a likely explanation for this:

SHEILA (17)   You don't ever see any of their friends. I would have thought they would have brought their friends home, but they don't seem to. Like they talk about them, but you never see them.
DB   Why do you think that is?
SHEILA   It's the money, I suppose. They'd have to pay them.

However, it was not just this restriction which caused the children to regard them as implausible.

TAMMY (15)   The young people, they're all angelic. They don't smoke, don't drink ... If you go round to your friend's house and there's a bottle of drink, you're not going to say [as Sharon had done in a recent episode] 'No! I've seen what it does to my mother!'
RUTH   If you get the chance to try something, you try it.
ABBY   If they were real East Enders they would.
RUTH   If Kelvin was seventeen, I don't think he'd be as naive as they're trying to make out. [...]
TAMMY   I don't know many young people like Ian or Kelvin.
MARK   I don't know anyone like that.
DB   So how are they different from people you know?
ABBY   They're too straight.
RAYMOND [mocking]   'Let's go to my house and listen to some tapes!'

199

RUTH   There's not many trendy people there either, are there?
TAMMY   If it was more realistic, there would be more casuals or trendies, different styles.

For this group, the younger characters in *EastEnders* were lacking in plausibility not only because of their apparent innocence, but also because of their lack of *specificity*: they are seen as 'straight', all-purpose young people, without the diversity and detail of specific 'youth cultures' ('casuals or trendies'). As with *EastEnders'* black characters, it is the authentic distinguishing marks of *difference* which are missing – and it may be this absence which resulted in them being ignored.

These children's enthusiasm for *EastEnders*, then, was not primarily based on their identification with its younger characters – although this was at least partly the producers' intention in including them. On the contrary, much of their fascination – and particularly that of the younger children – arose from its inclusion of aspects of *adult* life from which they were normally 'protected'.

Conclusion

In many ways, these responses point to the inadequacies of the simplistic views of children and television outlined at the start of this chapter. These young viewers were clearly not 'dupes' of television, passively absorbing its influence. They were aware that *EastEnders* is constructed, and did not confuse its representation of the world with reality. Although they were prepared to grant a degree of credibility to this representation, they were also highly critical of what they regarded as its partiality and implausibility. The accuracy of their observations is in this sense neither here nor there: what is important is the considerable degree of critical distance they displayed.

Nevertheless, this critical distance was not incompatible with their general enjoyment of the programme. Contrary to many writers on soap opera,[18] I would argue that this critical distance did not undermine their pleasure, but in fact made certain forms of pleasure possible. While the pleasure of passing moral judgment on the characters is to some extent premissed on a belief in the psychological coherence and plausibility of their actions and motivations, the pleasure of questioning and even ridiculing the artificiality of the programme is clearly based on an awareness that it is, precisely, a fiction. The children's comments thus reveal a complex and shifting combination of different responses. They were by turns moved, deeply involved, amused, bored, mocking and irreverent. The essentially playful way in which they were able to move between these different positions suggests that they had a considerable degree of autonomy in defining their relationship with television.

Did they then accept the claim of popular television to speak to their interests and aspirations – to speak, as it were, on their behalf? In certain respects, I would say that they did. For example, by perceiving *EastEnders'* middle-class characters as unsympathetic, they were able to give voice to their own frustrations and their own class-consciousness. The group of East End boys were able to use their pleasurable identification with the character of Den Watts to support a positive interpretation of their own experience as male, working-class Londoners.

In other respects, however, many of the children rejected this claim. They argued that the programme did not represent young people in ways which related to their own experience, and implicitly found this inadequate and patronising. Some of the girls felt that its female characters were often presented as unrealistically passive, and were frustrated by the characters' failure to assert themselves in the way they would have wished to do in their own lives. In some respects the children simply failed to recognise that the programme was seeking to address them at all, and largely ignored aspects of it which they might have been expected to seize upon as relevant to them. While this was partly the case with the younger characters, it was most notable in the way in which the black children I interviewed effectively ignored the presence of black characters in the programme.

Most of these processes were apparent in the comments both of the older children and of the younger ones. The main difference, I would argue, was that the older children were generally more articulate and self-reflexive about their own viewing experience. While many of the younger ones clearly possessed a grasp of some of the categories and concepts which might explain that experience, they lacked a more 'theoretical' vocabulary with which to describe it.

The argument that popular television exerts a reactionary or merely soporific effect on its audiences, and that young people are particularly vulnerable targets for its manipulation, is thus highly questionable. As Terry Lovell has observed:

> ... the oppositional valences of popular culture are not treasure buried in the depth of the text, and recoverable only with the aid of the right kinds of readings which are the exclusive preserve of a highly educated elite. They are very much more on the surface of the text, part of the staple pleasures which popular culture affords its audience.[19]

The responses recorded in this chapter would suggest that these pleasures may involve, not merely the recognition of 'oppositional' elements, but also the questioning of elements which viewers regard as failing to adequately represent their own interests and experience.

CONCLUSION

Debates about television are inevitably a focus for broader moral and political concerns – whether they are conducted in people's homes or workplaces, in newspapers or academic journals, in classrooms or in parliament. Television can function as a convenient 'bad object' onto which a whole series of other anxieties and tensions can be displaced. As Ian Connell has argued, blaming television may deflect attention away from genuine difficulties and complexities, and thereby make it easier for us to live with uncomfortable facts.[1]

The major problem with such debates is that they tend to regard the relationship between television and its audience in isolation from the broader pattern of social relationships of which it is merely a part. This leads in turn to a very limited agenda of questions, which are primarily concerned with the 'effects' or 'influence' of television on people's attitudes or behaviour. Communication is seen here as a one-way process, in which meaning is simply delivered to viewers, rather than constructed by them.

Yet the ways in which viewers makes sense of television are dependent, not merely upon texts, but also on the knowledge which they bring to them.

Indeed, in the case of *EastEnders*, it is almost impossible to isolate the text at all, not merely because it remains unfinished, but also because of the complex variety of ways in which it has become embedded in everyday social interaction. To suggest that the programme merely imposes meaning on viewers is to oversimplify the process, and to accord it a degree of power which it does not possess.

As has been shown, the relationship between *EastEnders* and its audience is marked at each stage by diversity and contradiction. The programme-makers' conceptions of their audience, for example, are ambiguous and largely impressionistic. The success of the programme has led to an uneasy compromise between the ethos of public service broadcasting and the need to cater to what are seen as popular tastes.

Yet in order to retain its audience, the programme itself cannot afford to be too prescriptive: rather than offering a single position from which it may be understood, it has to encourage a diversity of readings. The ways in which the programme is mediated, for example by marketing and by the popular press, are also likely to prevent a single, uniform interpretation. Finally, viewers themselves are actively engaged in negotiating meaning: while certain meanings which are perceived in the text may be refused, others may be seized upon for reasons which are quite different from those which its producers intended.

The relationship between the programme and its audience therefore cannot be seen as one of simple cause-and-effect: to do so would be to ignore the contradictions on which it is founded, and in particular to deny the very real power of audiences. This is why the ideological 'effects' of television cannot be identified solely through an analysis of its conditions of production, or through the analysis of texts in isolation. A programme cannot be judged 'progressive' or 'reactionary' merely on the basis of a comparison between the text and the world it claims to represent, or indeed on the basis of its form.

Perhaps the most significant problem with such an approach is the assumptions about *audiences* which typically underlie it. As Robert Allen has observed, much of the criticism of soap operas implicitly presumes that they are to be judged, not as fictional, but as exclusively mimetic in nature.[2] Soaps tend to be regarded as a form of documentary, whose primary intention is to provide an accurate representation of the real world. More crucially, it is also assumed that this is the way in which viewers interpret them. Yet the view that soap operas are essentially based on the illusion of realism – that they attempt to 'pass off' a representation as reality – implies that audiences are somehow the victims of an aesthetic con-trick. However, viewers are clearly aware that fictional texts work according to certain conventions; and simply in order to make sense of them, are bound to compare the representations they provide with their own social experience. Furthermore, it may well be inaccurate simply to consign soap opera to the category of 'realism': in the case of *EastEnders*, there are significant elements of comedy and melodrama which disrupt its predominantly naturalistic approach, and draw attention to the artifice by which it is produced.

Ultimately, then, the text does not 'contain' a meaning which can simply be extracted and defined. Yet if we cannot say what the text *means*, we can at least begin to describe how it *works* – that is, *how it enables viewers to produce meaning*. In doing so, we will need to restrain the rush towards instant moral and political judgment which characterises so much debate about television.

If popular television cannot be seen merely as an exercise in mass-deception, it would be equally false to regard it as an unproblematic expression of popular experiences and desires. The fact that a television programme attracts twenty or thirty million viewers does not necessarily mean that it is imposing a monolithic 'dominant ideology', or that it merely reflects shared values. Both positions assume that such a consensus exists, or that it can easily be achieved; both fail to acknowledge the unresolvable conflicts which characterise the social order, and which television itself is bound to address. Indeed, as Jane Feuer has argued in relation to US television, the emergence of soap opera as the dominant form of the 1980s may represent a response to the increasing cultural contradictions of the period.[3] While other genres such as police series or situation comedies tend to rely more heavily on shared values and beliefs, the relative openness of the soap opera allows it to be read and enjoyed in a wider variety of ways, and thus to appeal to a more fragmented and diverse audience.

Perhaps the most appropriate metaphor for soap opera is to regard it as a form of collective game, in which viewers themselves are the major participants. The programme itself provides a basis for the game, but viewers are constantly extending and redefining it. Far from being simply manipulated, they know they are playing a game, and derive considerable pleasure from crossing the boundaries between fiction and reality. Yet although the rules of the game are flexible, they are ultimately determined by the programme-makers: while viewers may seek to play by their own rules, they must inevitably acknowledge those which are set for them.

Critics of popular television have typically refused to participate in this game, condemning it as mere delusion. Yet their assumption that the ordinary viewer is somehow being deceived is one which cannot be sustained. If we want to understand the experience of popular television, and even to change the rules of the game, we can no longer afford to stand outside it.

Notes

Introduction

1. See Muriel Cantor and Suzanne Pingree, *The Soap Opera* (Beverly Hills: Sage, 1983), and Robert Allen, *Speaking of Soap Opera* (Chapel Hill: University of North Carolina Press, 1985). ا ۷۷ .
2. Herta Herzog, 'What do we really know about daytime serial listeners?', in Paul F. Lazarsfeld and Frank N. Stanton (eds.), *Radio Research 1942–43* (New York: Arno Press, reprinted 1979).
3. Dorothy Hobson, *Crossroads: The Drama of a Soap Opera* (London: Methuen, 1982).
4. See Robert Allen, *Speaking of Soap Opera*, p. 26.
5. Muriel Cantor and Suzanne Pingree, *The Soap Opera*, p. 133.
6. See, for example, Bob Hodge and David Tripp, *Children and Television* (Cambridge: Polity Press, 1986), Chapter Four; Aimee Dorr, 'No shortcuts to judging reality' in Jennings Bryant and Daniel R. Anderson, *Children's Understanding of Television* (New York: Academic Press, 1983).
7. For example, Dorothy Hobson, *Crossroads*, and Ien Ang, *Watching Dallas: Soap Opera and the Melodramatic Imagination* (London: Methuen, 1985).

1   Creating the Audience

1. All quotations from Michael Grade are taken from an interview with the author.
2. B B C Broadcasting Research Special Report, *Bi-Weekly Serial: The Appeal of Different Regional and Social Class Concepts*, February 1984.
3. All quotations from Julia Smith and Tony Holland are taken from an interview with the author, unless otherwise indicated.
4. Laurie Taylor and Bob Mullan, *Uninvited Guests: the Intimate Secrets of Television and Radio* (London: Chatto & Windus, 1986).
5. All quotations from Jonathan Powell are taken from an interview with the author.
6. See note 2 above.
7. Julia Smith, 'How to get started: creating a soap opera from scratch', *EBU Review*, vol. 36, no. 6, November 1985, p. 48.
8. Ibid., p. 47.
9. *Daily Mirror*, 21 May 1985.
10. *Broadcast*, 26 October 1984.
11. B B C Broadcasting Research Special Report, *Bi-weekly Serial II*, June 1984.
12. All quotations from Vivien Marles are taken from an interview with the author.
13. Vivien Marles and Nadine Nohr, *EastEnders: The role of research in the launch of a new brand into a difficult market*, paper delivered to the Market Research Society Conference, 1986.
14. Philip Elliott, *The Making of a Television Series: A Case Study in the Sociology of Culture* (London: Constable, 1972), Chapter 8.
15. See Tom Burns, *The BBC: Public Institution and Private World* (London: MacMillan, 1977).
16. For a useful account of contemporary developments, see Michael Leapman *The Last Days of the Beeb* (London: Allen and Unwin, 1986).

2 The Audience in the Text

1. Useful brief introductions to each of these areas may be found in Terry Eagleton, *Literary Theory* (Oxford: Blackwell, 1983), and Janet Wolff, *The Social Production of Art* (London: Macmillan, 1981). On reception theory in particular, see Robert Holub, *Reception Theory: A Critical Introduction* (London: Methuen, 1984).
2. For examples of this criticism, see David Morley, *The Nationwide Audience* (London: British Film Institute, 1980), Chapter Seven, and Paul Willemen, 'Notes on subjectivity' (*Screen* vol. 19 no. 1, Spring 1978).
3. See Stanley Fish, *Is there a Text in this Class? The Authority of Interpretive Communities* (Cambridge, Mass.: Harvard University Press, 1980); Fish's notion of 'interpretive communities', however, enables him to evade the charge of relativism.
4. This notion derives from the work of Umberto Eco: *The Role of the Reader: Explorations in the Semiotics of Texts* (London: Hutchinson, 1979). For a valuable discussion of this theory in relation to American daytime soap opera, see Robert Allen, *Speaking of Soap Operas* (Chapel Hill, University of North Carolina Press, 1985), Chapter Four.
5. Dorothy Hobson, *Crossroads: The Drama of a Soap Opera* (London: Methuen, 1982), p. 136.
6. The terms 'protension' and 'retension' derive from reception theory: see Wolfgang Iser, *The Act of Reading: A Theory of Aesthetic Response* (London: Routledge and Kegan Paul, 1978), Chapter Five.
7. This term derives from the work of Roland Barthes, *S/Z* (New York: Hill and Wang, 1974).
8. See Shlomith Rimmon-Kenan, *Narrative Fiction: Contemporary Poetics* (London: Methuen, 1983), Chapter Three.
9. Wolfgang Iser, *The Act of Reading*, Chapter Five.
10. See Hans-Robert Jauss, *Aesthetic Experience and Literary Hermeneutics* (Minneapolis: University of Minnesota Press, 1982), Section B.
11. Christine Geraghty, '*Brookside*: No Common Ground' (*Screen* vol. 24 no. 4/5, March 1983).
12. Roland Barthes, op. cit., pp. 209–10.
13. Marion Jordan, 'Realism and Convention', in Richard Dyer et al., *Coronation Street*, tv Monograph 13 (London: British Film Institute, 1981).
14. Jane Feuer, 'Melodrama, Serial Form and Television Today', *Screen* vol. 25 no. 1, January/February 1984.
15. For a detailed discussion of this area, see Richard Dyer, *Stars* (London: British Film Institute, 1979).
16. This term derives from the work of Roman Ingarden, and is employed by Wolfgang Iser in his work, *The Act of Reading*.
17. Iser, *The Act of Reading*, p. 100.
18. For a useful typology of 'modalities of identification', see Hans-Robert Jauss, *Aesthetic Experience*, pp. 159–88.
19. Charlotte Brunsdon, '*Crossroads*: Notes on Soap Opera', *Screen* vol. 22 no. 4, 1981.

20. For a parallel analysis of *Dallas*, see Gillian Swanson, ' "*Dallas*" Part One', *Framework* no. 14, Spring 1981; 'Part Two', *Framework* nos. 15/16/17, Summer 1981.
21. Peter Willmott and Michael Young, *Family and Kinship in East London* (London: Routledge and Kegan Paul, 1957). For more recent accounts, see Peter Willmott, *Whatever's Happening to London* (London: London Council of Social Service, 1975) and Andrew Friend and Andy Metcalf, *Slump City: The Politics of Mass Unemployment* (London: Pluto Press, 1981).
22. Christine Geraghty, 'The continuing serial: a definition', in Richard Dyer et al., *Coronation Street*, p. 15.
23. See, for example, Julian Franklyn, *The Cockney: A Survey of London Life and Language* (London: Andre Deutsch, 1953); V.S. Pritchett, *London Perceived* (London: Chatto and Windus, 1974); Peter Wright, *Cockney Dialect and Slang* (London: Batsford, 1981).
24. Gavin Weightman and Steve Humphries, *The Making of Modern London* (London: Sidgwick and Jackson, 1983).
25. Michael Chanan, *The Dream That Kicks* (London: Routledge and Kegan Paul, 1980).
26. For a very incisive consideration of this issue, see T.E. Perkins, 'Rethinking stereotypes', in Michèle Barrett et al., *Ideology and Cultural Production* (London: Croom Helm, 1979).
27. For a fuller definition, and a critique, of this approach, see Hazel Carby, 'Multiculture', *Screen Education* no. 34, Spring 1980.
28. *The Times*, 19 February 1985.
29. Terry Lovell, 'Ideology and *Coronation Street*', in Richard Dyer et al., *Coronation Street*, pp. 50–52.
30. See, for example, Raymond Williams, *Television: Technology and Cultural Form* (Glasgow: Fontana, 1974) and John Hartley, 'Encouraging signs: the power of dirt, speech and scandalous categories', in W.D. Rowland and B. Watkins (eds.), *Interpreting Television: Current Research Perspectives* (Beverly Hills: Sage, 1984).

3 Between the Text and the Audience

1. All quotations from Judy Niner are taken from an interview with the author.
2. This term derives from Stan Cohen, *Folk Devils and Moral Panics* (London: McGibbon and Kee, 1972).
3. All quotations from Keith Samuel are taken from an interview with the author.
4. All quotations from Mary Whitehouse are taken from an interview with the author, unless otherwise indicated.
5. Mary Whitehouse, quoted by Roy Wallis, 'Moral Indignation and the Media: An Analysis of the NVALA', *Sociology*, vol. 10, May 1976, p. 278.
6. See Michael Tracey and David Morrison, *Whitehouse* (London: Macmillan, 1979).

1. David Buckingham, 'Teaching about the media', in David Lusted (ed.), *The Media Studies Book: A Guide for Teachers* (London: Comedia, 1987).

2. For a recent example, see Geoffrey Barlow and Alison Hill (eds.), *Video Violence and Children* (London: Hodder and Stoughton, 1985); Martin Barker (ed.), *The Video Nasties* (London: Pluto Press, 1985).

3. For example, Marie Winn, *The Plug-In Drug* (Harmondsworth: Penguin, revised edition, 1985); Martin Large, *Who's Bringing Them Up?* (Gloucester: Martin Large for the TV Action Group, 1980).

4. For example Maureen Lalor, 'The hidden curriculum', in Rick Rogers (ed.), *Television and the Family* (UK Association for the International Year of the Child/ University of London Department of Extra-Mural Studies, 1980). Kevin Durkin, *Television, Sex Roles and Children* (Milton Keynes: Open University Press, 1985) summarises several such studies and provides a useful counter-argument.

5. Ian Connell, 'Fabulous powers: blaming the media', in Len Masterman (ed.), *Television Mythologies* (London: Comedia/MK Media Press, 1985).

6. See, for example, Joseph Klapper, *The Effects of Mass Communication* (New York: Glencoe Press, 1960), and Shearon Lowery and Melvin L. DeFleur, *Milestones in Mass Communications Research: Media Effects* (London: Longman, 1983).

7. For example, Cedric Cullingford, *Children and Television* (Aldershot: Gower, 1984); Aimee Dorr, *Television and Children* (Beverly Hills: Sage, 1986); Kevin Durkin, *Television, Sex Roles and Children*; Jennings Bryant and Daniel R. Anderson (eds.), *Children's Understanding of Television* (New York: Academic Press, 1983); Bob Hodge and David Tripp, *Children and Television: A Semiotic Approach* (Cambridge: Polity Press, 1986).

8. For example, David Morley, *Family Television: Cultural Power and Domestic Leisure* (London: Comedia, 1986); Patricia Palmer, *The Lively Audience* (Sydney: Allen and Unwin, 1986).

9. Cedric Cullingford, *Children and Television*. For a similar approach, see Laurie Taylor and Bob Mullan, *Uninvited Guests: The Intimate Secrets of Television and Radio* (London: Chatto and Windus, 1986).

10. See David Morley, *The Nationwide Audience* (London: British Film Institute, 1980), and 'The Nationwide Audience: a critical postscript', in *Screen Education* no. 39, Summer 1981, pp. 3–14.

11. Ien Ang, *Watching Dallas: Soap Opera and the Melodramatic Imagination* (London: Methuen, 1985), Chapter Three.

12. See David Morley, *Family Television*.

13. Dorothy Hobson, *Crossroads*, p. 125.

14. Cedric Cullingford, *Children and Television*, p. 139.

15. Aimee Dorr, 'No shortcuts to judging reality', in Jennings Bryant and Daniel R. Anderson (eds.), *Children's Understanding of Television*.

16. Christine Geraghty, 'The continuing serial: a definition', in Richard Dyer et al., *Coronation Street* (London: British Film Institute, 1981), p. 10.

17. Ien Ang, *Watching Dallas*, pp. 36–38.
18. Most notably Ien Ang and Dorothy Hobson.
19. Terry Lovell, 'Ideology and *Coronation Street*', in Richard Dyer et al., *Coronation Street*, p. 52.

Conclusion

1. Ian Connell, 'Fabulous powers: blaming the media', in Len Masterman (ed.), *Television Mythologies* (London: Comedia/MK Media Press, 1985).
2. Robert Allen, *Speaking of Soap Opera* (Chapel Hill: University of North Carolina Press, 1985), Chapter Two.
3. Jane Feuer, 'Melodrama, serial form and television today', *Screen* vol. 25 no.1, January-February 1984; see also Jane Feuer, 'Narrative form in American network television', in Colin MacCabe (ed.), *High Theory/Low Culture* (Manchester: Manchester University Press, 1986).

Other Books on Television from BFI Publishing

Framing Science: The Making of a BBC Documentary

Roger Silverstone

Scientific developments affect all our lives, and television is one of the principal means by which we understand the resulting benefits and possible dangers. Yet science documentaries are first and foremost television programmes, not scientific reports. To what extent are programme-makers influenced by the demands of television and the need to tell a dramatic story which will appeal to a wide non-specialist audience, rather than purely scientific considerations? To answer such questions, Roger Silverstone followed, from initial research to final broadcast, the making of a BBC *Horizon* programme on the social and economic impact on the Third World of genetically developed varieties of staple crops. He has produced a book of exceptional interest which explains how science programmes on television come to be the way they are.

Television in Transition

Edited by Phillip Drummond and Richard Paterson

The first International Television Studies Conference was held in London in 1984 and brought together over seventy distinguished speakers to deliver papers on all aspects of contemporary television. This book is a selection of the most challenging and innovative contributions. The range of topics covered is wide and includes papers on television history, television news, audience behaviour, popular programming (including the ubiquitous *Dallas* and music videos), television's relation to education and mass culture, and the increasing threats to public service broadcasting and national identity from new kinds of media imperialism and information technology. *Television in Transition* opens up a perspective on the wealth of research being carried out at this critical time in the development of world television.

MTM: 'Quality Television'

Edited by Jane Feuer, Paul Kerr and Tise Vahimagi

MTM can lay claim to being the most innovative company in American television. Its initial success was based on the long-running sitcom, *The Mary Tyler Moore Show*, from the star of which the company draws its name. This show led to successful spin-offs such as *Phyllis* and *Rhoda*, before MTM branched out into the production of award-winning drama series such as *Lou Grant* and *Hill Street Blues*. This book contains a detailed history of the company to date and a collection of essays on the most important MTM shows, together with full credit lists.

Made For Television: Euston Films Limited

Manuel Alvarado and John Stewart

As a name, Euston Films may be better known within the film and television industries than to the general public. But its programmes are among the most popular on television. *The Sweeney*, *Out*, *Fox*, *Widows* and *Minder* are only some of the highly successful TV series which the company has produced in the last few years. This book about Euston is based on extensive research, including in-depth interviews with the company's leading personnel. The authors' account of how and why Euston was formed, and what is so distinctive about its production methods, offers unique insights into how popular television is created. The book also includes critical assessments of Euston programmes and full credits of all the company's programmes.

Powerplays:
Trevor Griffiths in Television

Mike Poole and John Wyver

Trevor Griffiths is widely recognised as one of the most important and influential of contemporary dramatists and his stage plays *Occupations* and *Comedians* are landmarks in recent political theatre. Yet his strongest commitment has been to television, for which he has written single plays, adaptations of Chekhov and D. H. Lawrence and the remarkable series *Bill Brand*, about the stormy private and political career of a Labour MP. This critical introduction to Griffiths examines all of his consistently radical and challenging work, including his involvement with the multi-million dollar Hollywood epic, *Reds*, but concentrates on the dynamics of his frequently controversial relationship with television.

Popular Television and Film

Edited by Tony Bennett et al.

Although designed as a Reader for the Open University's course *Popular Culture* (U203), this collection of important and innovative essays on film and television is an excellent introduction for all students to current debates in media studies. The essays represent new trends in programme analysis and concentrate on the forms and meanings of films and television programmes produced for mass consumption rather than the structures or economics of broadcasting.

Popular Television and Film is divided into four parts, each with its own introduction. Part One assesses the importance of the study of genre. Part Two discusses the presentation of current affairs, sport and science programmes on television. Part Three turns to the cinema and an analysis of *Jaws* to consider theories of pleasure and popular film. Part Four examines television's treatment of history, politics and the classical narrative, focusing in particular on the much celebrated series, *Days of Hope*.

Monty Python: Complete and Utter Theory of the Grotesque

Edited by John O. Thompson

When Monty Python's Flying Circus erupted on to the small screen in 1969 it was indeed Something Completely Different – at least as far as television was concerned. But the forms of humour and grotesque which the Pythons introduced to television have a long and varied history in literature and art.

John O. Thompson has assembled an extraordinary variety of historical and contemporary texts dealing with the grotesque and its Pythonic variants. Mingling quotations from interviews with the Pythons and press responses to Python films and programmes with a broad spectrum of critical and historical material, Thompson offers a remarkable set of insights into the development of humorous and grotesque art forms. For scholars there is a complete Pythonography.

Television Monograph 1
Structures of Television

Nicholas Garnham

An analysis of the organisational structures of British television particularly in relation to the effects on them of social and ideological factors. With some proposals for structural change, revised to take account of the Annan Report.

Television Monograph 8
Television and History

Colin McArthur

The past is a recurrent source of subject matter for television programme-makers but its presentation tends to be governed more by the needs of television than by the requirements of historical knowledge. Even when such programmes are informed by a conception of history, it is usually one which is uncongenial to social change.

Television Monograph 10
Everyday Television:
'Nationwide'

Charlotte Brunsdon and David Morley

A detailed analysis of BBC's *Nationwide* which tries to uncover exactly what image of the 'nation' the programme was working with. This is an important study of the ideology of popular television.

Television Monograph 12
WDR and the Arbeiterfilm:
Fassbinder, Ziewer and Others

Richard Collins and Vincent Porter

The Arbeiterfilm, 'worker film', developed by the Cologne television station, WDR, is of two-fold interest. Firstly it has revitalised realist aesthetics, long the mainstay of British television production but increasingly under attack from media theorists. Secondly, WDR has employed a different interpretation of 'balance' in producing programmes which take up definite positions within the political spectrum.

Television Monograph 13
Coronation Street

Richard Dyer et al.

Coronation Street, first broadcast in 1960, is still one of the most popular serials on television. The essays in this monograph suggest ways of understanding the programme in terms of its production context, its use of narrative and convention, the construction of characters and, in particular, the concern for a realist image of a northern industrial setting. The book includes some background material, potted biographies and a close look at two episodes. It is aimed at a general interest readership as well as students of the media.